Praise for other books by Kyriacos C. Markides

THE MAGUS OF STROVOLOS:
The Extraordinary World of a Spiritual Healer

"This work is a real contribution and exemplifies the best aspects of participant observation."
—Michael Harner
Author, *Way of the Shaman*

". . . a marvelous book . . . I certainly think it is one of the most extraordinary accounts of a 'magical' personality since Oupensky's account of Gurdjieff."
—Colin Wilson
Author, *Beyond the Occult*

HOMAGE TO THE SUN:
The Wisdom of the Magus of Strovolos

"A haunting book—not only for what it is, a remarkable study of a modern Christian mystic—but for what it implies: a vast source of spiritual knowledge, understanding, and practice, that is largely unknown to us."
—Dr. Jacob Needleman, San Francisco State University
Author, *Lost Christianity*

". . . a profound and exciting work of major importance . . . it may be that Professor Markides and others like him who have the courage to explore are on the brink of remarkable discoveries about the nature of man."
—Raymond Moody, M.D.
Author, *The Light Beyond*

"We need to make more room for human possibilities and Kyriacos C. Markides succeeds where Carlos Castaneda came up short."
—Antonio T. de Nicolas
Professor of Philosophy, SUNY Stonybrook

FIRE
IN THE
HEART

FIRE IN THE HEART

HEALERS, SAGES, AND MYSTICS

Kyriacos C. Markides

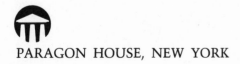

PARAGON HOUSE, NEW YORK

First edition, 1990
Published in the United States by
Paragon House
90 Fifth Avenue
New York, N.Y. 10011

Designed by Deirdre C. Amthor

Library of Congress Cataloging-in-Publishing Data
Markides, Kyriacos C.
    Fire in the heart: healers, sages, and mystics/Kyriacos C. Markides.
    —1st ed.
        p.   cm.
    ISBN 1-55778-160-5
    1. Sathi, Spyros.   2. Healers—Cyprus—Biography.   3. Mental
healing.   4. Psychical research.   5. Occultism.   I. Title.
RZ408.S37M35   1990
615.8′52′092—dc20
[B]   90-32661
                                                                           CIP

10 9 8 7 6 5 4 3 2 1

The paper used in this publication meets the minimum requirements of American National Standard for information Sciences—Permanence of Paper for Printed Library Materials, ANSI Z39.48-1984.

Contents

Author's Note

Fire in the Heart is part of a trilogy, a continuation of my earlier volumes *The Magus of Strovolos* and *Homage to the Sun*. It also stands on its own. One can read *Fire in the Heart* without any familiarity with the other volumes. Those who have already read *The Magus* and *Homage* will discover that *Fire in the Heart* provides material not previously presented or developed. The first chapter can be read primarily as a summary and review of the central ideas of the first two volumes. The density of that chapter and the new vocabulary must not overwhelm or intimidate the uninitiated reader, however. These ideas and concepts are further developed and clarified in the subsequent chapters through extensive dialogues, anecdotes, stories, and experiential vignettes. For a better grasp of this material the first-time reader should make good use of the glossary at the end of the book.

For the sake of consistency I have employed the same

Author's Note

idiom with male Greek names. When I talk about someone
I say Daskalos, Kostas, Yiannis, Antonis, Stephanos. For
example: "Daskalos was not home when I arrived." But
when I address male Greeks I say: Daskale, Kosta, Yianni,
Antoni, Stephane. For example: "Tell me, Daskale, how do
you leave your body at will?" (Female Greek names do not
offer this linguistic peculiarity.)

All names in the book are fictitious with the exception
of historical names and those of my family. *Daskalos* is not
a given name but a title. It means "master" or "teacher"
and is commonly used in the Greek world when one ad-
dresses schoolmasters or priests.

The list of people I am indebted to for the completion of
this and the previous volumes is too long to mention by
name. It includes all the dear friends who are part of this
book as well as my relatives in Cyprus. Needless to say, I
am profoundly grateful to Daskalos and Kostas, the Greek
Cypriot spiritual masters, for their friendship and trust in
offering me the opportunity and the honor to bring these
extraordinary teachings to a wider audience.

I am thankful to the University of Maine for a leave of
absence and a summer grant that made my ongoing work
in Cyprus possible. All my colleagues in the sociology department have been very helpful and supportive in my research effort, for which I would like to express my most
sincere appreciation. In particular I am grateful to my
friends and colleagues Professors Steve Cohn, Stephen
Marks, and Kathryn Grzelkowski for their involvement
with my work, their moral support, and their readiness to
offer helpful advice and critical comments. I am most grateful also to Susan Greenwood for her enthusiasm with the
material and her generous offer of time and energy to carefully read the first draft. I cherish Michael Lewis' art and
extensive involvement with the substance of these books.
During the last few years, and thanks to these teachings, I
have become a most privileged beneficiary of Michael's
friendship, artistic advice, and spiritual sensitivities.

My wife Emily has been part of this work from the very beginning. We have grown together in our spiritual and existential struggles as we tried to cope with the formidable challenge of Daskalos' and Kostas' mystical cosmology. A native of Cyprus herself and trained in the rigors of German and French literature, Emily brought to our meetings a dignified and critical perspective that triggered some of the best dialogues. Emily alerted me to the necessity of "resurrecting the Goddess" as a precondition of the spiritual renaissance of humankind. Above all, she has been a balancing keel in my life's voyage. Without her presence it is doubtful whether I would have had the energy and peace of mind to pursue my long-term adventure into the mysterious world of the Greek Cypriot spiritual masters.

Στούς Ἐρευνητές τῆς Ἀληθείας

1 The Erevna

I had barely arrived in Nicosia in May 1987 when Stephanos called me on the phone. "I have something to show you," he said. "It is about Daskalos. I must see you right away." There was excitement in his voice and a sense of urgency, and, although I had not slept the night before because of the long flight from Maine, I asked him to come right over. Regardless of my fatigue I was more than happy to see my good friend and confidant Stephanos.

"Things are getting out of hand," he said, smiling as he took a deep breath and handed me a newspaper with a two-page article on Daskalos.

I shook my head in dismay. In spite of my promise to protect Daskalos' privacy there seemed to be no way to keep his identity secret any longer. I had already written two books about him, and Cyprus is too small an island for anyone to remain anonymous, particularly a person like Daskalos. When he performed a healing "miracle" in front of some astounded journalists it was inevitable that his story would soon appear in the papers. Stephanos happened to be present when the extraordinary healing took place and therefore was able to elaborate.

"I was chatting with Daskalos," Stephanos said as we settled down with cups of iced tea, "when these journalists with their cameras and tape recorders entered the house requesting an audience with him. They had heard about what he was doing and wished to ask him a few questions. Daskalos invited them in and talked to them for over an hour."

"That is quite a change of heart," I marveled. I knew that until that time Daskalos had never given any interviews to journalists.

"They were asking all sorts of questions, about life after death, reincarnation, healing, clairvoyance, and the like. I don't think those fellows had ever heard about such matters before and they were listening with obvious fascination in their eyes.

"Then at the point they were ready to leave," Stephanos continued, "an Englishwoman came in, holding her three-year-old son in her arms. What happened after that is pretty much the way it is reported in the news."

I looked at the weekly paper in front of me once more as I reread the large Greek letters: "In front of several witnesses Spyros Sathi [Daskalos] healed a three-year-old English boy suffering from polio." I read further: "Was it a miracle? Was it suggestion? I really do not know what to say. I know only what I have seen with my own eyes: A small child, who a few minutes earlier could not stand on his feet, could now run around the room." The journalist went on to describe how Daskalos carried out the healing: "I stared with curiosity at the Englishwoman holding her child. Only when she placed the boy in Spyros Sathi's arms did I notice that his left leg was covered with a heavy plastic brace. It was atrophied and clearly shorter than the other leg. . . . Spyros Sathi sat on a chair with the child in his arms and began to speak to him with a sweet, very sweet tone in his voice. As he was doing that he began to gently stroke the sickly leg. 'What is the problem with your son?' one of my companions whispered to the woman. 'He has polio,' she said. 'He can't stand on his feet. If we leave him standing by himself he will fall.' In the meantime Spyros Sathi continued to stroke the atrophied leg. He pulled it a few times as if to make it longer. . . . Ten, twenty minutes must have passed—I don't remember. I had my eyes glued sometimes on the child and sometimes on Spyros Sathi. Suddenly the child made a pained grimace. At that point he raised the boy up, gave him a light slap on his buttocks, and said 'Now run, my boy.' And the child began running around the room! Was it a miracle? Was it suggestion? One can make whatever conclusions one wishes. I just describe what I saw."

"The time of anonymity is over," I said to Stephanos, who had been sharing my experiences with Daskalos for almost a decade.

I had first met Spyros Sathi, a retired civil servant, in the summer of 1978. He was a tall, ordinary-looking man no different in appearance from any of his compatriots. One could find them in abundance in the all-male coffee houses of Cyprus, killing time with backgammon and cards, reading newspapers, gossiping, and lazily sipping Turkish coffee.

But Spyros Sathi was no ordinary man and was hardly a patron of coffee houses. In his spare time he preferred to look after his plants and cacti, paint strange out-of-this-world landscapes, and listen to Beethoven. Had he lived in Siberia or Nepal or some African village anthropologists would most probably have pronounced him a shaman, and had he been born a Mexican or a Peruvian he would have certainly earned the title *curandero*. Indians and Tibetans would have venerated him either as a yogi or a lama.

Spyros Sathi is a healer and a master of metaphysical knowledge and unimaginable psychic powers. He claims to

3

have the capacity to fly out of his aging body at will and in the company of other "invisible helpers" travel to faraway places and other dimensions in order to be "of service" to those in need. He can do this in full consciousness, and, as shamans are reputed to do, report back to his followers about his *exomatosis* (out-of-body experience).

People from all walks of life, after exhausting the potency of conventional medicine, have discreetly sought him out to conduct exorcisms and to cure their bodies and souls of all sorts of physical and psychological disorders.

For a long time his name on the island was synonymous with occultism, and the devoutly religious shunned him as a magus of Mephistophelean proportions. "Don't ever mention that man's name in my house," a deeply religious and wonderful aunt of mine once commanded me. Earlier efforts on the part of the clerical hierarchy to excommunicate him faltered thanks to the spirited opposition of the current Archbishop Makarios. It was rumored that His Beatitude was himself a sort of disciple, secretly provided with taped talks and lessons from Sathi. The prelate surely recognized that the man was no threat to Christianity and was certainly not a menacing sorcerer. He must in fact have realized, as I did, that the unusual man from Strovolos was a Christian mystic.

For nonbelieving sophisticates Spyros Sathi was not to be taken seriously. He was perhaps a rogue, definitely a charlatan. Or at best an amusing curiosity, a harmless anachronism for the gullible and the naive, someone for those soft in the head and unschooled in the ways of studied reflection and scientific objectivity. "Do you really wish to waste your time with this man?" asked a concerned cousin, an accomplished social scientist, shaking his head when I first mentioned my intention of spending a sabbatical leave studying the world of Spyros Sathi. "Why don't you study the class structure of Cyprus and the relationship between voting behavior and political party affiliation? Nobody has done anything like that yet."

4

Spyros Sathi spent most of his life a pariah in his own society, viewed with deep suspicion by believers and non-believers alike. That was not the case, of course, for those who had been seeking his help or for his growing circle of disciples who risked their reputations to attend his lectures at the Stoa, a room turned shrine in the back of his house. There they gathered and practiced the mystical arts, including the meditation exercises he assigned for their psycho-noetic and spiritual development. For this group of people Spyros Sathi was not only The Magus of Strovolos but Daskalos, master and teacher of esoteric wisdom.

I told Stephanos I would go to see Daskalos the following morning, after I had a good night's rest. When I arrived at his house the next day there were several visitors who, as usual, had sought his assistance for one reason or another. He was in a jovial mood and was happy to see me after the more than eight months since our last visit in August 1986.

Far from being annoyed at his exposure in the press, he was actually pleased, even deeply amused about the astonishment of the journalists. "There was nothing miraculous and extraordinary about what happened," he chuckled. "I just became a vehicle for the Holy Spirit, that's all." He repeated what he had said to me many times, that what makes a miracle a miracle is our ignorance. If we knew how Nature works we wouldn't call such phenomena miracles. "The only miracle there is," he said emphatically, "is life itself. Nothing else."

In his mischievous mood Daskalos characteristically cracked several jokes about the episode, spreading hilarity among his small audience. Since he had company and work to do I stayed only briefly. We made arrangements to meet again later in the week. In the meantime I spent a few days in the booming port city of Limassol. There I reestablished contact with Kostas, Daskalos' most advanced disciple and designated successor.

The newspaper article had created a stir all over the island, even among those who normally ignored such matters as healing, psychic abilities, and the like. Since I was considered some sort of expert on the subject I was approached by friends and acquaintances for my "informed opinion." Among them was Sophia, a sociologist of Cypriot heritage who worked at a Canadian university. She had come to the island for a summer visit and after learning of my presence on the island contacted me.

We made arrangements to meet late Saturday at the Elefthere Karpasia, a restaurant next to the Green Line, the boundary drawn by the United Nations Forces in Cyprus (UNFICYP) to keep the peace between the Greek and Turkish Cypriots. It was actually a bombed-out abandoned government building constructed of sandstone during the British colonial period. I liked the place in spite of grim reminders of the tragic state of affairs between the two ethnic groups and the catastrophic invasion of the island by Turkey in the summer of 1974.

The restaurant was basically four walls with only half a roof overhead, the other half having been demolished by shelling. There was open space, a yard with jasmine and palm trees and old Venetian arches overlooking the Turkish-occupied side of Nicosia. Refugees from the Karpasia Peninsula, now occupied by Turkey, took over the building and operated it afternoons and evenings as a modest, makeshift venture during the hot summer months. A favorite of some of the local intelligentsia and some radical political activists, it was a good spot for long, quiet conversations.

"Frankly, I am at a loss to understand what you have been doing all these years," Sophia began with a smile as we settled at a table under one of the Venetian arches. "I have to be honest with you; these matters you are dealing with make me uneasy. They go contrary to all my training and values."

"I fully sympathize with you." I laughed and reassured her that such reactions do not bother me in the least. I was almost certain that Sophia knew of my research only vaguely. She knew me as a political sociologist; on several occasions we had participated in seminars about the solution of the Cyprus problem. It was difficult for her to understand how I could make such a radical shift in my writing career and preoccupy myself with the life and work of obscure healers and mystics. Trained as I had been in the scientific, positivistic tradition of the social sciences and schooled in the notion that any form of religion is a projection of either society or psychopathology, Sophia naturally questioned my sympathies for Daskalos, Kostas, and their circles of disciples. I could sense what must have been going on in her mind: Poor Kyriacos. He means well, but what on earth got into him?

"When I started my research with Daskalos almost ten years ago, I was a thorough skeptic like you," I said. "But after all these years I have come to recognize that there may be something very authentic here that cannot be dismissed lightly."

"But what about your scientific objectivity?" Sophia asked, friendly irony in her voice.

"I assure you that my approach is not contrary to the aims of science. I just employed a more phenomenological approach in this particular study." I told her that my aim had not been to explain (or rather explain away) the world as experienced by people like Daskalos and Kostas.

"Instead of me, the American academic," I said, "entering the world of Daskalos with set, preconceived notions about his reality, I chose instead to let him tell me about it himself. In situations where the reality of your subjects is so radically different from your own it is unwise to impose your views, no matter how scientific they may appear to be, before you offer your subjects the opportunity to present their case in their own language and categories of understanding. I had to be careful not to impose my own prejudices and limitations."

"Don't you think, Kyriaco," Sophia said thoughtfully, "that the method you have used and apparently continue to use has drawbacks? In other words, isn't it a drawback that your method is descriptive and not based on a critical predisposition?"

"On the contrary, in my encounters with Daskalos as well as with Kostas I have always played the role of the Doubting Thomas. I have maintained a critical predisposition all along, sometimes more so than was called for under the circumstances. In other words, I felt compelled to explore the validity of what they were saying on the nature of reality. In fact, my relationship with them has been easy precisely because I have been accepted as a skeptic."

She persisted. "On the other hand, your approach implies that you really do not question their version of reality. You do not confront them with an alternative view."

"Had I stayed on the level of confrontation I would not have gone very far. I would not have been able to collect during the past decade the voluminous material about the extraordinary world within which these mystics live and work. They would have dismissed me by now as hopelessly dogmatic and rigid."

"But again," Sophia insisted, "isn't there a risk of your being identified with these people—what we call in sociology 'going native' and forgetting about your role as a critical sociologist?"

"But is this a risk or a prejudice?" I countered. "The risk of being identified with them implies that you as the researcher refuse to enter into the situation to really understand your subjects. Instead you prefer to maintain your scientific detachment, treating the others as objects of study. I do not think in cases of this type such an approach would lead to any fruitful results or to any real understanding. On the contrary, it leads to bias and lack of real insight into the matter under investigation."

Our brief and friendly debate on methodology ended when the waiter came to our table. Sophia ordered tea and I asked for a glass of beer. It was getting dark—the sun had set almost an hour earlier—but we could still see people moving on balconies on the other side of the wide dry moat separating us from the Turks living within the city walls, fortifications built by the Venetians in the sixteenth century, when they were the overlords of the island.

"Are you saying, Kyriaco," Sophia asked as she gazed at the Turkish side of the divide, "that this Daskalos has so-called metaphysical abilities?"

"I will tell you what he himself says, and what in fact all authentic mystics say: that there is really nothing metaphysical in the world. It is the limitation of our awareness that would classify certain phenomena or abilities as metaphysical. Had our awareness been different, perhaps such things as nonmedical healings, psychic abilities, and so on would have been considered perfectly normal and natural.

"In fact, I have come to realize that our awareness about what Nature is all about is grossly limited. Whatever is outside these limitations we tend to call metaphysical and then define as something beyond the scope of science and reason. Once we make this categorization in our minds we consciously or unconsciously reject what we have so labeled. We either consider it unreal or at best not amenable to human understanding. The underlying message is 'Don't bother.' In other words, we consider natural and real only what is accessible to our ordinary sight, hearing, touch, taste, and smell. But what if we are actually endowed with 'supersenses,' as mystics and even some scientists of today are claiming? And what if we can develop and master these supersenses and employ them for a more profound understanding of the world?

"We take it for granted," I continued, Sophia now listening with obvious interest, "that the evolution of human consciousness proceeded from the point of no consciousness to superstition and primitive magic. Then on to reason, climaxing in the triumphs of nineteenth- and twentieth-century scientific thinking. But there is no logical basis for assuming that the growth of consciousness has reached its final home and destination in the mechanistic science of today. Perhaps, as the great mystics throughout history have been telling us, there are transrational and transscientific stages yet to be attained by the human species. In fact, this is precisely what transpersonal psychologists are claiming today."

Sophia, thoughtful and silent, sipped her tea. "Are you suggesting, then," she said finally, "that people like your friends Daskalos and Kostas have extraordinary abilities over and beyond the five senses?"

"All I can tell you," I told her with a smile, "is what I have experienced with these people over the past decade. Then you can draw your own conclusions. I started this project suspicious of any claims to so-called paranormal abilities. However, exposure to Daskalos and Kostas over the years and my reading about such matters forced me to reevaluate my earlier positivistic biases. I have reached the tentative conclusion that such abilities are not only possible, real, and normal, but may in fact be our species' philogenetic inheritance. They are dormant, to be sure, in the average human psyche, but manifested within some gifted individuals such as Daskalos and Kostas. People like them have been branded with such names as psychic, clairvoyant, shaman, mystic, and so on.

"I must admit that my former skepticism suffered considerable erosion over time, once a string of extraordinary healings and coincidences began happening in front of my eyes. You see, what took place the other day in front of the journalists was not surprising to me at all, since I have observed such phenomena so often that I began to take them for granted."

"Can you give me some examples?" Sophia asked.

"There was this British healer who came last summer to offer 'workshops' in her specialty. It was while I was getting ready to return to Maine. She visited Daskalos after reading my books. When they ended their conversation Daskalos and Kostas healed her chronic spinal problem. When she realized what had happened to her she spent some time sobbing by herself in the Stoa. Later that night she called my wife Emily to tell her that when she went to bed she discovered that her two legs were even. She no longer had a problem walking. And she went on sobbing on the phone. 'Here I am,' she said. 'I came to Cyprus to give workshops on healing and instead I got healed myself.' "

Then I described to Sophia a number of other cases— including the spectacular one of Mrs. Katina, who was paralyzed and in bed for months, also suffering from spinal problems. Daskalos healed her in front of our eyes. That woman has been able, since that time, to live a normal life without a relapse. What was important about that case was the fact that after her sudden recovery she visited her radiologist, who took X-rays of her spine. The new plates showed a normal spine while the X-rays taken a week earlier had shown a diseased spine.

"On another occasion I was driving around with Daskalos. Then quite unexpectedly he began to describe to me the inside of our house in Maine and joked that we should install a telephone upstairs. 'As you rush down to pick the phone up you may break your neck, Kyriaco,' he said. No one had ever described to him the inside of our house in Maine and certainly not the location of the phone."

"Perhaps," Sophia argued with reluctance in her voice, "all that can be explained as just coincidence."

"It would be difficult for me to dismiss them as mere coincidences. When such cases take place frequently you begin to pay attention to them. Then the notion that they are just coincidences begins to lose its power."

I then gave further examples. "A student of mine had suffered physical problems for the last twenty years. The doctors could not locate the source. I took her picture to Daskalos. After holding it for a few seconds, he diagnosed that the problem was in her brain. He suggested an electroencephalograph. She followed his advice and had an expensive examination of her brain. Indeed there was a problem there. She avoided telling her doctors how she had come up with the idea that she needed a brain examination.

"In another similar case I brought a picture of a New York woman to Daskalos. She had chronic physical problems and again the doctors were at a loss to locate the cause. Daskalos told me to tell her that her problem was in her rotten teeth. She must take them all out, he said, because they were infecting and poisoning her entire body. With great hesitation I wrote what Daskalos prescribed and mailed the letter from Cyprus. Six months later I received a phone call. It was the husband of this woman. He wished, he said, to just let me know what happened. His wife did not take Daskalos' advice seriously and of course did not visit a dentist to extract her teeth. In six months four of her teeth literally exploded and fell off. The infectious mucus dripped down her mouth. Then she did go to a dentist and had all her teeth removed. Her physical problems disappeared."

"If what you have been telling me are real cases," Sophia said, looking perplexed, "then, since you exclude coincidence, how do you explain such phenomena?"

"Throughout history great philosophers, mystics, and scientists have been saying that in reality there are no coincidences. Carl Jung, for example, developed his famous and controversial theory of synchronicity arguing just this point, that there are no coincidences. Daskalos and Kostas have also been working from within a highly developed system of knowledge that can explain the nature of coincidence."

Just then I spotted an old friend at the entrance. I waved at him and after our greeting each other for the first time in years he joined another table with his friends. Then Sophia and I settled down to a hearty dinner. All the tables at the Elefthere Karpasia were full by now and the waiters were busy rushing from the outdoor kitchen to the tables bringing their patrons *mezedes,* an assortment of different Greek and Turkish hors d'oeuvre accompanied by beer and chilled local wine.

"I am ready to hear more about the world view of your

friends," Sophia said after we had spent some time eating and catching up on personal news.

"Our thoughts and feelings are energies that we project out into the environment." I began my attempt to introduce Sophia to the basic principles of the teachings. "These are the elementals every human being incessantly creates."

"What do you mean, elementals?"

"Elementals are thought-forms that can assume a variety of shapes and colors; an advanced mystic and clairvoyant can perceive them coming out of the subconscious of a person. These elementals have power, energy, and a life of their own. Their energy can be positive or negative. For example, a benign thought and feeling toward another person is an elemental charged with positive energy. Likewise, a negative feeling or thought is a negative elemental."

"Where do these elementals go?" Sophia asked.

"It is the nature of elementals to live within what Daskalos and Kostas call the psychonoetic dimensions of existence, influencing people who vibrate on the same frequency as these elementals in a subconscious way. They return to their source sooner or later. Therefore, whatever elemental we project out into the environment, good or evil, eventually returns back to us seven times stronger. This is the way karma works."

"*Karma?*"

"Yes—the law of cause and effect. They claim that nothing in life is accidental. All existence is governed by the law of karma, of cause and effect. 'As you sow so shall you reap.' These injunctions, they claim, are based on the law of karma. Whatever we do, good or bad, in reality it is to ourselves that we do it."

I explained that the law of karma works within the context of repeated incarnations. "The elementals we project outward will return back to us either in this or in a future life. This is how we weave our destiny."

"Are they suggesting that we are totally responsible for our fate?" Sophia asked.

"This is exactly what they say. Our thoughts, desires, and emotions are elementals that make up our subconscious. It is in fact these elementals that structure our subconscious. We carry the sum total of our subconscious from one life to the next."

"Now, look. This notion of reincarnation is a tough idea for me to swallow," Sophia said with nervous laughter.

"Daskalos claims that these notions are not matters of beliefs, likes, dislikes, but facts of life. And, with a serious investigation into the nature of existence one can discover them to be so."

"Go on. Tell me more. What happens to us from one life to the next? What do your friends say?"

"To understand what happens to us after death you must realize that we don't have only one body; we actually have three."

"Three?" The disbelieving look on Sophia's face made me chuckle.

"Yes, three," I confirmed. "In addition to the gross material body we also have a psychic body and a noetic body. The psychic body is the body of our feelings, sentiments, and desires that has as its center the heart. The noetic body is the body of our thoughts and has as its base the center of our head. Each of these three bodies exists in different dimensions of reality, and together they compose our present personality. The gross material body exists within the three-dimensional world, the psychic body within the fourth-dimensional world, and the noetic body within the fifth-dimensional world. They are three bodies in one, together composing our present personality.

"These bodies are linked together by their corresponding etheric doubles, the energy field that permeates them and maintains their vitality. Daskalos and Kostas claim that at the point of death it is only the gross material body that dies. We as self-conscious personalities continue to exist within the psychonoetic dimensions with our feelings, sentiments, likes and dislikes. We can do so because we have the other two bodies, the psychic and the noetic."

"So what is the difference between life within this dimension and life after death?" Sophia's voice continued to betray deep skepticism mixed with fascination about the matters we were discussing.

"The only difference is in regard to the laws that govern these other dimensions. Daskalos and Kostas claim that there are worlds within worlds and that all the worlds are different in terms of their vibrational frequencies. For example, the gross material world appears solid to us because when we are within our gross material bodies we vibrate on the same frequency as gross matter. The other worlds are also worlds of matter but have higher levels of vibration. For example, within the psychic world space is transcended. One can move instantly from one side of the earth to another.

"They claim that if we learn how to raise our vibrations we could, while still living within a gross material body, leave it behind and travel to these other dimensions with our psychonoetic body. The gross material body and the gross material world will not be an obstacle in such a state, which they call exomatosis or out-of-the-body travel. Our consciousness can travel instantly not only in those other realities but also move about on this gross material plane and get information and knowledge about other parts of the world, such as the inside of my house in Maine," I said, laughing.

Sophia listened with a puzzled look on her face. I felt that what I had been saying must have appeared to her a fascinating fairy tale. Her persistence in her questioning reminded me of the way I had related to Daskalos during the early stages of my research almost ten years earlier.

"Would you say that the psychonoetic body is what people usually understand as the soul?" she asked.

"No, not at all," I said. "The psychic and noetic bodies are also material bodies at higher levels of vibration. When we abandon the gross material body at the point we call death, we will continue to live with our other two bodies —with our emotions and thoughts. We would look pretty much the same way as we looked on the gross material earth. We will continue to live within these other dimensions for a period of time until our new incarnation. At that point, our psychic and noetic bodies will be absorbed by what they call the permanent personality."

"What is that?" Sophia asked, folding her arms on the table.

"It is that part of our inner self upon which the incarnational experiences are being recorded. And it is through the permanent personality that the sum total of our incarnational experiences are being transferred from one life to the next.

"You see, nothing gets lost. At the start of a new incarnation a new noetic and a new psychic body will first be constructed. They will enclose within them the sum total of not only the experiences of the previous incarnation but of all past incarnations. At conception, then, assuming that circumstances permit, a new present personality will begin the journey into the three-dimensional world in order to receive new experiences and lessons within the context of the law of karma."

I went on to explain that the process by which the psychonoetic body attaches itself to the new present personality is, according to what Daskalos and Kostas teach, gradual —starting at conception and going all the way to about the seventh year of life. Until then children usually live partially within the psychonoetic worlds. After that age, the average individual becomes fully focused within the three-dimensional world and becomes forgetful and oblivious of the other realities.

"So, is the permanent personality the soul?" Sophia asked again.

"No, not quite," I replied and laughed as I looked at Sophia's puzzled expression.

"Perhaps we should continue this conversation somewhere else," Sophia suggested in a low tone. Several people at a neighboring table were taking great interest in our conversation.

It was ten-thirty, and we decided to take a walk within the old walled city, the part still controlled by the Cyprus government. We drove to the Famagusta Gate, parked next to the moat, and began walking through the narrow and almost-deserted streets.

"So what is the soul after all?" Sophia asked as we walked along the rampart of the Venetian walls.

"To answer your question we must first discuss a few things about what Daskalos and Kostas understand about God, whom they prefer to call by the more impersonal term of the Absolute or Absolute Beingness. For them the Absolute is the unfathomable reality behind all the worlds. We can make only tentative statements about it, since our language and reason are insurmountable obstacles. One will know God, they claim, only when one becomes God, when one reaches the state of Theosis.

"They teach," I continued, "that the Absolute Beingness is composed of myriads and myriads of Holy Monads. Each Holy Monad in its turn is made up of myriads and myriads of spirit entities. It is one God, one Absolute in Its plurality, multiplicity, and self-sufficiency or what they call Divine Autarchy. The Absolute has everything within It and It lacks nothing. To manifest Itself the Absolute created Mind, the infinite ocean of vibrations from the most rarefied, unformed levels all the way down to the gross material."

"Are they saying that God is Mind?" Sophia asked. I detected a growing interest in the subject we had been discussing.

"No. Mind is the means by which God or the Absolute manifests Itself. Now, every Holy Monad radiates spirit entities that must pass through the Worlds of Ideas. This is perhaps similar to the Platonic notion of Ideas. One such idea is the Human Idea. The moment an irradiance of a Spirit-ego or entity passes through the Human Idea a soul is constructed."

"I thought that the soul is immortal," Sophia said as we continued our walk.

"It is, but it has to be constructed first. The real Us is the Spirit-ego that is beyond the soul, beyond the Human Idea, what we call in Greek the *Pneuma*. The core and essence of every human being, therefore, is *Pneuma* or spirit. It is the God within. Remember what they chant in the Greek church—'Πνεῦμα ὁ Θεός' [God is Pneuma].

"The moment a soul is constructed," I went on, "it must inevitably extend itself all the way down to the gross material level to acquire experience of the lower worlds, the worlds of polarity, of good and evil, of life and death, and so on.

"The soul as soul is uncolored. It has no experiential knowledge of the lower worlds. The condition of the soul before experience is that of Adam and Eve before the Fall. To acquire experience of the lower worlds the soul must extend itself further down, so to speak. At that point the permanent personality is being constructed. The latter is that part of the soul upon which the incarnational experiences will be recorded. Then, at the moment of the first incarnation, a present personality will be constructed— which, as we discussed before, is made up of a noetic body, a psychic body, and a gross material body.

"Every human being is a multidimensional being. As Daskalos says, it is one line with two points. The point of the Spirit is radiant and the other end-point, the present personality, is the dark side. The aim of existence is to join the two points and form one brilliant circle."

"How is that done?" asked Sophia.

"Through the awakening of the lower self to its divine origin. Our descent into the lower worlds and the start of the incarnational cycles in reality meant the entrapment of our Divine Self, the Pneuma, into a state of ignorance."

"You are saying then," Sophia admitted with a reluctant smile, "that in reality we are all gods."

"We are gods in exile," I responded, "who suffer from self-inflicted amnesia. Our ultimate and overarching purpose in life is to recover our memory. This is what Daskalos and Kostas have been teaching."

"The next question that comes to mind then," Sophia said, "is How can we recover that memory?"

"There are several ways. Daskalos and Kostas teach that whether we recognize it or not, whether we are conscious of it or not, we are all in fact on the path of self-discovery and self-realization. Through experience resulting from repeated incarnations within the context of the give and take of karma we shall all mature and begin our return to the point of our origin, the Spirit-ego within. In this way all human beings will eventually become self-realized. This is the path of pain and suffering, the unavoidable result of ignorance.

"The other way is through a conscious and disciplined process of a research for the truth, through what they call *The Erevna* [Research]. You become a Researcher of the Truth and consciously embark on the journey of self-discovery. You begin the return journey to the palace of the Loving Father, according to the parable of the Prodigal Son that Daskalos is so fond of referring to. The Erevna is the methodological side of the injunction 'Know the truth and the truth shall set you free.' "

"But how do you start this Erevna? How do you become a Researcher of the Truth?"

"Through contemplation, meditation, self-observation and service." I then introduced Sophia to some simple meditation exercises that Daskalos and Kostas had been assigning their students. "Self-observation and service are most important in that effort. They aim at killing what Daskalos is fond of calling 'the Minotaur within,' our egotism. Our egotism, they say, is our worst enemy because it prevents us from realizing who we truly are. And it is our egotism that keeps us trapped at low levels of awareness. Therefore, like Theseus, we must kill the Minotaur.

"When we systematically cleanse our subconscious from egotistical desires, then we accelerate the evolution of our awareness. We speed up the process of our return to the state of our God realization, of Theosis."

"I have a problem with this incarnational theory," Sophia said after a while as we walked by Ayios Savvas, one of the many ancient churches in the heart of old Nicosia. "If we are gods to begin with, and if our destiny is to re-awaken to our godly state, why then did we start the incarnational cycles to begin with?"

"This is a great question! It has generated all kinds of speculation throughout the ages among amateurs and serious mystics alike.

"A popular notion that springs from a specific branch of the Buddhist tradition," I went on, "is that the ultimate state of consciousness is a form of nihilism of the ego-self, that our selfhood becomes enmeshed and diluted within the totality of God. At that state the separate individual as such ceases to exist. This idea appealed to many secular intellectuals in the West whose agnosticism was more compatible with such notions than the idea that individual consciousness is immortal. In fact, the other day I was reading a very interesting book on *Lucid Dreaming* by Stephen LaBerge, a researcher at the Sleep Research Center of Stanford University. Toward the end of his book he speculated on this very issue. I was intrigued by what he said and jotted down on a piece of paper some of his statements so that I could discuss them with Daskalos or Kostas. In fact, I have it right here in my wallet."

We walked toward a street lamp. I unfolded the paper and read: "Your transpersonal identity transcends your personal identity. This, your transpersonal individuality, may in the end prove identical with the nature of ultimate reality. . . . 'Possessed of all possession, Knower of the All-Knowledge, Creator of All Creations—the One Mind, Reality Itself.' Now, from the point of view of The Erevna, so far so good. I don't think either Daskalos or Kostas would have any quarrels up to this point. But hear what this dream researcher is saying further." Sophia had come closer as I read.

" 'Thus it may be that when death comes, although you are annihilated as an individual and the dewdrop is lost in the sea, you at the same time return to the realization of what you have always essentially been: the drop recognizes itself to be not merely the drop it thought it was, but the Sea.' So to the question 'What will we be after death?' the answer may be given, 'Everything and nothing.' "

"If I had read this to Daskalos," I said as I folded the paper, "I am certain he would have rolled with laughter. He would have said that if death could give us enlightenment, then the surest way to wisdom would be suicide.

"First of all," I explained as we resumed our walk, "death does not change our awareness. The only change that takes place, Daskalos and Kostas would say, is that we leave behind the gross material body. But we continue to live as self-conscious beings with the other two bodies, the bodies of our feelings and thoughts, the psychic and the noetic. We enter these other vibrations at the level of awareness that we had at the moment of our death. It is through repeated incarnations and karma that we will eventually mature spiritually and reach our destination of Theosis. And of course we can speed up our return through The Erevna.

"You see, Daskalos would say that most people are not aware of the reality of the psychic and the noetic bodies. That's why they arrive at such erroneous notions about our ultimate destiny."

"You still haven't answered my original question," Sophia reminded me. "Why the incarnations to begin with?"

"I will come to that. Daskalos and Kostas teach that the aim of the incarnations is precisely to develop individuality, to develop uniqueness within the Oneness of the Absolute, not to abolish it. Before we descended into the worlds of polarity we were gods without the experience of the lower worlds, without a distinct individuality. We were all alike. We lived an archangelic existence beyond time and space. The lower worlds of polarity, of time and space, are created for the purpose of offering spirit-egos or Pneumata the opportunity to acquire experience that will eventually lead to their Ontopeisis."

"Now what is *that*?" Sophia asked, hands raised in feigned desperation.

"Unfortunately," I sighed, "I could not find a term in English that could offer the precise meaning of Ontopeisis. As you know, the term is a composite of the Greek noun *on*, which means 'Being,' and *peisis*, which derives from the verb 'to become.' Briefly, *Ontopeisis* means the process by which the Pneuma attains this individuality after the cycles of incarnations have come to an end (once the karma of the lower self has been exhausted). Ontopeisis is the end-product of Theosis. If the latter designates the final illumination and liberation of the lower self from the cycles of incarnations and its assimilation with the Spirit-ego, Ontopeisis is what the Spirit-ego has gained by projecting itself through the Human Idea and into the worlds of polarity, of time and space.

"This great truth, according to Daskalos and Kostas, is beautifully expressed by Jesus in the parable of the Prodigal Son. Ontopeisis means the state of the Prodigal Son after his return to the palace of his father, after he had gone through the experiences, the trials and tribulations of time and space.

"It is experience within time and space," I continued, "that offers us our individuality and uniqueness. No two human beings are precisely alike because no two human beings undergo the same experiences within the worlds of opposites, of good and evil. To me at least, this notion makes much more sense than the idea that our ultimate aim is to abolish the 'I AM I', that is, our self-consciousness. What we must abolish is our egotism, not our self-conscious individuality. Daskalos would say the 'I AM I' is our immortal underlying Spirit-ego, the Pneuma, which is our true self, our beingness and the very fountainhead of our existence. It has never been born and it will never die. It is the god that willfully and divinely entered the realms of polarity and ignorance for the sole purpose of accumulating experiential knowledge of the lower worlds that would lead to Its Ontopeisis."

Sophia gave me a thoughtful smile. "You are suggesting that when we as scientists and scholars struggle to accumulate knowledge and unlock the secrets of nature, deep down what we are actually struggling for is our own Theosis and Ontopeisis?"

"According to The Erevna, that is precisely what all human beings are really doing, be they scientists or longshoremen, Communists or capitalists. They are just not conscious of it."

"Who then is conscious?"

I chuckled. "Only a few mystics. The rest of humanity, Daskalos and Kostas would say, are fast asleep, locked up within the cocoon of their limited awareness."

As we passed through a narrow pathway dating from the Ottoman years and found ourselves in the middle of the square facing the Archbishopric, Sophia said, "But from the little I know there are so many differences among mystics, so many disagreements. How can one rely on what they say?"

"According to Daskalos and Kostas, we should rely on nobody's word. Rather, we should embark on our own research for the truth. To them The Erevna is not a set of dogmas but a method of personal exploration for self-discovery and self-realization. They would argue, however, that authentic advanced mystics do discover the same truths in the same way that advanced scientists reach consensus about their explorations of the outer world. Besides, they would say, all knowledge is tentative and relative, whether it is scientific or mystical. Ultimately we shall know the truth only when we ourselves become the truth, at Theosis.

"Therefore, when knowledge of higher worlds passes down to the lower levels there will always be a certain amount of distortion, depending on the state of development and awareness of the mystic conducting that knowledge. You see, not all mystics are created equal, in the same way that not all physicists are Nobel laureates."

We found ourselves back at the Famagusta Gate, from which we started our walk. We had been so engrossed in our discussion that we had completely lost track of the time. It was already after midnight and there was little movement in the mostly deserted streets. Only a couple of soldiers were keeping guard at a barricade close to where we had parked.

I drove Sophia to Kaimakli, a nearby suburb, where she was staying during her visit to the island.

"Tell me, Kyriaco, how has this material affected you personally?" she asked as we rode toward her home.

"This is a question people have been asking me ever since I got involved with this subject. It is a long story." I smiled at her.

"Just like you, I was very skeptical of any claims to realities other than the one apparent to the five senses. I must confess I was not a happy and enthusiastic scientific materialist. Like you, I grew up within the Greek Orthodox religion and I was enamored with its liturgical beauty. However, with time I felt I had no choice but to move in the direction of agnosticism. My university experience gave me few other options, since it was founded on the belief that this is the only real world there is, the world of our everyday consciousness. I was led to believe the scientific method was the only road to any authentic knowledge. Everything else was nothing more than a matter of opinion, therefore unreal. I became a reluctant convert to rational, scientific fundamentalism.

"You see, I assumed that if there were other worlds they must be beyond human comprehension anyway. Therefore any inquiry in that direction would be fruitless, a waste of time and energy. I made peace with myself by focusing on this three-dimensional reality, trying to understand through my profession as a sociologist the social world I found myself in. It may interest you to know that for a brief period as a graduate student I even flirted with Marxism as the answer to everything."

"And what happened then?" Sophia asked. I sensed a certain irony in her voice. I knew she had historical materialist sympathies.

"I got a job at the University of Maine and everything began to change." Then I told her how through a colleague I was introduced to Eastern methods of meditation "for the relaxation of body and mind" and to a body of literature I had no idea existed.

"What literature are you referring to?"

"The perennial philosophy," I replied, using Huxley's famous term. I then went on to explain that the perennial philosophy, or "the primordial tradition", as philosopher Huston Smith prefers to call it in his book *Forgotten Truth*, is the esoteric teaching considered to express the wisdom of the ages, which is revealed to serious practitioners and explorers of consciousness throughout history.

"This primordial tradition," I explained, "is grounded in human nature itself and is independent of the various philosophical trends, fads, or fashions that may prevail at any particular culture or period in time. It is said that great mystics and teachers of all epochs and civilizations have been expressing this tradition.

"For the first time in the history of the world the masses of humanity have access to this primordial tradition."

"How?"

"Through paperbacks."

"What do you mean?"

"Until now this mystical knowledge has been the privileged domain of few initiates who, with great difficulty and often personal risk to their lives, pursued and sought it in secret brotherhoods. But times have changed. We are now fortunate to live in relatively more open, tolerant times. Everything surfaces in print.

"You see, Sophia," I said, "my involvement with these

Cypriot mystics further triggered my interest to explore these matters in greater depth. And I have come to realize that we are perhaps on the verge of a major revolution in human consciousness more profound than the Renaissance and the Enlightenment combined.

I stopped the car outside her mother's house. "Perhaps," I said, "we are not the helpless creatures doomed to ignorance we assume we are. Perhaps there are worlds to discover inside us that are as vast as, if not vaster than, the space of the astronomers."

I then mentioned the American astronaut Edgar Mitchell —who upon stepping on the moon underwent a mystical experience so profound that when he returned to earth he founded the Institute for Noetic Sciences in California, a research foundation for the exploration of this new frontier of "inner space".

"The greatest reward for me in writing these books," I went on, "is the response I get from people all over the world who write to me about how these teachings are offering them a map and a guide to the other worlds they claim they are experiencing or have experienced.

"Perhaps at this point the issue for me is no longer whether there are other realities that interpenetrate our ordinary three-dimensional world. The issue now is how to explore and investigate these worlds, how to develop a science of these spiritual dimensions. This is what the Tibetan lamas have been doing for thousands of years from their mountaintops."

"I assume," Sophia said, "that you believe your friends Daskalos and Kostas have access to these other worlds, that they teach this primordial tradition."

"I believe Daskalos and Kostas deserve to be heard and taken seriously in what they tell us about worlds that lie beyond the reach of our ordinary senses.

"You know, Sophia, by now I am convinced that good nondogmatic science is not the enemy of the spiritual but one of its great allies. This is what makes the contemporary scene so fascinating and promising."

"I will think about that," Sophia replied with a smile. I then suggested Marilyn Ferguson's *The Aquarian Conspiracy* as a start for an overall summary of how "frontier science" is offering indirect credibility to many of the spiritual claims of the great mystics.

"I have one last question," Sophia said as she was leaving the car. "How do these people know? Where did they learn about the things you have been telling me tonight?"

"Both Daskalos and Kostas claim that the knowledge they possess on what they call the 'higher worlds' comes from two sources. One source is their own direct experience into these other worlds. They claim that they developed these abilities and knowledge not only in this life but in previous incarnations. Once you become a master of your three bodies you can use them in exomatosis and visit those other dimensions. Then you can get knowledge about these other worlds and be of service there to human beings who are in need. You become an 'invisible helper,' possessor of superconscious self-awareness, a *Hermes Trismegistus.*"

"Become a *what?*" Sophia inquired, eyes widening.

"A Hermes Trismegistus," I repeated with a chuckle. I explained that the Hermetic Philosophy dealing with esoteric, mystical wisdom is believed to have been started by a Greek named Hermes Trismegistus who lived in ancient Egypt hundreds of years before Christ. Hermetic Philosophy is part of what Huxley called the 'perennial philosophy'.

"When I mentioned that interpretation of the origin of the Hermetic Philosophy to Daskalos," I said, "he shook his head and laughed. He claimed that Hermes Trismegistus is any human being who reaches the state of superconscious self-awareness. Anyone who has mastered his or her three bodies—the gross material, the psychic, and the noetic—is a Hermes Trismegistus. The winged god Hermes symbolizes flight—that is, the mastery of exomatosis, or what others call 'astral travel'.

"As you know, the word *trismegistus* in Greek literally

means 'the thrice-great'—that is, the one who has attained mastery over the three bodies and therefore can travel freely in these other dimensions of existence, accumulating knowledge and wisdom and disseminating it to those, like us, who carry on a life confounded within the lower levels of awareness.

"So you see, my dear Sophia," I said, "eventually you and I and every other human being can and will become a Hermes Trismegistus. When we do so then we can experientially verify like good spiritual scientists what they are telling us about the higher worlds."

"Is the state of Hermes Trismegistus another term for Theosis?"

"No, Theosis is at a much higher level of awareness. Theosis is the final destination of every soul, the final stage of the evolution of consciousness. The stage of superconscious self-awareness is one of the several stages that will lead to Theosis. They say that Theosis is a one-way avenue. Once you enter you never come back in the ordinary human way—birth, death, rebirth, and so on. Kostas, in fact, told me that great masters who reach the doorsteps of Theosis, and could enter there any time they wish, avoid doing so precisely because they want to stay behind and help others on their spiritual path. 'The higher you ascend,' he told me, 'the greater your love and compassion for others, therefore the greater your readiness to be of service.' He told me that in reality 'the first will probably go last.' "

"What is the other source of their knowledge?" Sophia asked as I prepared to drive away.

"This is going to startle you even further. They claim that they can enter into a state of complete attunement with the consciousness of great masters who carry on a life at the highest levels of consciousness and wisdom. These are masters who are inside the Divine Autarchy of the Absolute. One such master is Yohannan, John the Evangelist, the Beloved Disciple of Christ. They insist that what they teach is under the direct guidance of Yohannan. Therefore,

The Erevna as a system of spiritual practice is the Research for the Truth according to the teachings of this archangelic entity who once lived on planet earth as Saint John, author of the Gospel.

"Daskalos and Kostas claim that any person, once he or she reaches a certain level of spiritual development, of superconscious self-awareness, can become a conduit of Yohannan, that 'super-intelligence' who oversees, as they say, the spiritual evolution of our planet."

"Do these people ever read any books?" Sophia asked. I had already turned the ignition key but noticed the increased incredulity on her face after my mention of the name Yohannan.

"They don't read to gain spiritual knowledge," I told her. "Their emphasis is experiential. However, both Daskalos and Kostas are educated people. Kostas is a British-trained engineer and Daskalos graduated from the American Academy at Larnaca and later, although he never left the island, managed through correspondence to get several higher degrees with distinction from British institutions."

"I would like to meet these people," Sophia said.

During the following few weeks Emily and I accompanied Sophia to several meetings with Kostas and Daskalos. By the time she left Cyprus for Canada I could sense that those encounters were beginning to make an impact on her view of the world. In fact, after our last meeting Daskalos winked at me and murmured "She is ready." Her time had come for the beginning of the long process of her own awakening. Sophia promised to return to Cyprus for a more prolonged stay that would offer her an opportunity for a deeper familiarity with Daskalos' and Kostas' world. I could certainly understand Sophia's reactions. In her I saw myself ten years ago, when I first confronted the extraordinary world of Daskalos and Kostas.

2   Hells and Paradises

Stephanos and I reached Daskalos' home at Strovolos at nine-thirty in the morning. The front door was open wide and the sun filled the entrance hall with its intense mid-summer radiance. Daskalos was sitting alone in a shady corner. He appeared exhausted, as if all energy had some-how been drained out of him.

"Daskale," I exclaimed anxiously, "what has happened to you?"

With half-opened eyes he waved his right hand and asked for a glass of water. "I will tell you later," he whispered.

"I have just returned from a hell," he said as he drank the last drop of the water and sighed with relief. "I had a job to do there. It is so unpleasant to visit those spaces." He gri-maced; then, noticing our inquisitive looks, he proceeded to narrate his experience. Daskalos was regaining his strength.

"While you are still living on the earth plane it is easier

to coordinate your consciousness with the lower psycho-
noetic conditions because the vibrations there are closer to
the gross material level. So an acquaintance of mine on the
other side, an invisible helper, sought my cooperation to
assist one of his friends who lived at the lowest levels of
the psychonoetic worlds. You know, of course, why I call
them psychonoetic—because the psychic and noetic levels
interpenetrate. When there is no thought there is no sentiment. And we have these worlds here on the gross material
level also. I made contact with this invisible helper at a
luminous space and we carried on a conversation. It was
beautiful up there.

   " 'Come,' he said, 'let us go and help my friend. I have
visited him there so many times but so far I have not been
able to do him any good.' 'But it is not easy to help him
when he himself is unwilling to move out of his own hell,'
I pointed out. 'Anyway, bring him to your mind and we
shall be there.' As you know, within the psychonoetic
realms we can transport our consciousness through coordination. Either we can move like lightning and be where we
want to in a split second or go there gradually. It would
depend on our preference. Well, it was terribly dark.
Ghastly. I focused my attention, trying to perceive whatever I could. In terms of shape and form that world was
beautiful, with hills, trees, valleys. I noticed a sea but it
was still and mute. I said to this invisible helper that I
rarely descend to such spaces. It seemed like a dark night
with a barely visible half moon. 'This space,' my friend
explained, 'cannot be filled with greater luminosity because
the entities that live here cannot tolerate it. It is Divine
Mercy at work. This darkness that you see comes from
within themselves and it affects the surrounding landscape.' 'The atmosphere here,' I complained, 'suffocates
me. It is something like rottenness.' 'They are the ones who
create these conditions,' he explained again. 'It suits them.'

   "We found ourselves," Daskalos continued, "in front of
a house four times as big as mine. We knocked at the huge

31

iron door. Nobody answered. It seemed to me that that invisible helper was not too experienced because I had to urge him to go through the walls. I had to remind him that we did not have to knock. We entered and saw a man sitting in a semidark living room. I presume Divine Mercy must have placed the dim light I noticed there. It had the power of a twenty-watt bulb at most, and for a huge room the light it gave was barely sufficient. He was sitting in a dark velvety armchair. He kept asking how we entered his house. 'We are friends,' I replied. 'I understand,' he murmured angrily. 'You are like those troublemakers who keep bothering me all the time.' 'I am sorry,' I replied. 'But are you pleased to live in here?' 'Why shouldn't I be?' he answered. 'This is my home. Get it out of your mind that you are going to steal from me. Nobody can steal from me.' I tried to reassure him. 'We have not come here to steal from you. We have come for a different reason. This fellow is a friend of yours.' I pointed at my companion.

"The man grinned. 'Yes. I know what kind of a friend he is. Leave me alone. I don't need any friends.' 'But why not?' I persisted. 'Is it better to live by yourself, all alone?' 'Yes it is better,' he answered with spite. I communicated to my companion that there was nothing we could do to assist him and that the best thing for the time being was to become invisible to him and stay around to observe what happened. We did just that. We changed our vibrations and became invisible to him even though we remained right there. I had to help my friend become invisible because of his inexperience with these matters. You see, it takes a lot of practice to be able to change your vibrations at will from one state to another. You must learn how to ascend beyond the meaning of images and shapes and without being affected by them become invisible. So we stayed in that condition and observed that man. We heard him say 'Thank god they are gone to hell. But how did they get in here?' He started screaming. Then we saw someone dressed in dark clothing coming into the room. He looked like a servant.

The man kept shouting at him. 'How did they get in here? Why did you leave the door open?' Then I understood what was happening. The servant was in reality an angel who was trying to help him come to his senses. People like him preoccupy even angels to serve them. Of course, the angel could not have appeared to him as a luminous angelic entity. He looked like an ordinary servant dressed in the clothes that man created with his thoughts and hatred.

"He continued screaming," Daskalos went on. " 'Sit right here,' he ordered the servant-angel. Then he opened some squeaking iron doors and pulled out a rusty case. He opened it and continued shouting demands to know who stole from his treasure. Then he began counting some gold coins. I started laughing to myself. That was his punishment, his hell, I thought. He counted his gold pounds, the type that had the king of England on one side and Saint George on the other. He counted and counted. Then he would forget and start all over again. He would mix them up and begin counting from scratch. His mind would get tired and lose the count and start from the beginning once more, over and over. And he was obsessed with the notion that thieves were stealing from him and kept staring at his piles of gold.

"I said to the servant who was there—he was able to notice us, which is why I said he must have been an angel —'How long has this been going on? Do you create them for him?' 'Yes, but he keeps losing them. Then I recreate them for him and again he loses them. He just won't disentangle himself. He constantly worries about his treasure, that thieves will steal it from him. He is the one who creates the conditions that cause him to feel that he loses his coins.' 'What do you do to help him out?' I asked. He replied that he was doing everything possible to help him understand the illusory nature of his obsessions, but to no avail. Then I proposed that perhaps I could try with powerful thoughts to let him realize that he is dead, that his coins have no value, and that he should come out of that dark room and into the sunshine to meet other people. 'Do you suppose I haven't done that?' the angel replied. 'I have done it a thousand times but he would not listen. But you go ahead and see what happens.' I tried. He rebelled and again began counting his gold pieces. I discovered then that in his last incarnation he was a very wealthy miser who ended his life by committing suicide. Well, this fellow will be tormenting himself until he decides to come out of his own hell, which he alone has created."

"When did you have this experience, Daskale?" I interrupted.

"This morning."

"You mean while you were asleep?"

"No. While I was awake. It is not necessary to be asleep in order to work." Daskalos then proceeded to offer further details about his encounter with the servant-angel. By now he was full of energy again and there was no trace of the fatigue we had noticed earlier.

"Well, after we got out of that house I tried to enter inside that angel and make contact with him. He was indeed luminous. I asked him why everything was so dark. 'Suppose,' he replied, 'you are in a beautiful place and some people begin to burn tires and the whole landscape is full of stinking smoke. Will it be pleasant?' 'Of course not. But your example of burning tires makes me realize that you know a lot of things about our world, about the earth.' 'Naturally I know,' he replied. 'The minds of people here in this space are like burning tires that poison the atmosphere. The landscape turns black because of the thoughts and feelings of the people who live here.' 'Is it pleasant for you to be here?' I asked. 'And who told you that I am here?' he replied. 'I am also elsewhere.' 'That explains it,' I said, and went on to say 'I do want to get to know you better.' 'I know you very well,' he responded. 'Don't worry, you will get to know me also at some point because you will be coming down here to help these people who are in need.'

" 'I am disappointed,' I said, 'that I have not been able to

accomplish anything with this fellow.' 'The love you have brought with you here is your accomplishment,' he replied. 'Gradually he will mature and come to his senses. When you eventually come on this side he may still be counting his gold pounds and we will continue to come down together to offer our assistance. Only God knows when he will disentangle himself from his predicament.'

"You get the feeling," Daskalos told us, "that the hell this man was in was somewhere below the earth. Of course he himself has created the environment within which he lives, engrossed within his thoughts and his feelings. If you ask him whether he is pleased with his situation he will most probably reply that he is. He does not wish to abandon it. In fact, all he has to do to get out of his hell is to wish it himself."

Stephanos asked about the nature of the boundaries between the various dimensions and Daskalos explained. "The boundaries between the various planes and subplanes of the psychonoetic world is a question of vibrations and harmonizing your consciousness with those vibrations. For example, with a radio I can tune in a symphony transmitted by the BBC. Without moving myself or my radio and by just turning the knob a little farther I get Greek bouzouki music, a radically different reality. Therefore, on the basis of earthly time you can move in and out of a hell or a paradise in a matter of a split second. To get out of a hell you simply raise your vibrations, so to speak, and enter into spaces filled with vibrant luminosity. The higher you move upward the more light you experience and the more clearly you perceive Reality.

"On the basis of my experiences," Daskalos said after a pause, "I have noticed that as you move higher on the psychonoetic ladder people live closer to one another, are more united. On the other hand, those at the lower levels, even though there may be many of them, usually do not take notice of each other, do not feel one another and carry on a solitary psychonoetic existence."

I recognized that what Daskalos stated made perfect sense both on the basis of my own experience and from the perspective of conventional sociology and psychology. "Therefore, the higher you raise your consciousness the less your alienation from your fellow human beings and the lower your self-estrangement," I responded and then, venturing another proposition, "the higher you raise your vibrations the closer you come toward unity both with other human beings and within your self." I was carried away now and continued: "The lower you are on the consciousness scale the weaker the manifestation of love within your present personality. The higher you are on the psychonoetic consciousness scale the stronger and more focused the expression of love, until you reach total unity when you *become* love."

"Very good." Daskalos nodded with satisfaction, then went on to elaborate further on the various characteristics of the psychonoetic dimensions.

"People create their world as they knew it on earth. You will see, for example, that they live the same kind of life as they did while on the material plane. You will see them cook their favorite foods, drink their favorite wines, enjoy themselves in their festivals as they did on earth. And they walk exactly the way they were accustomed to on earth."

"All these things you mention," Stephanos observed, "are there to satisfy the material needs of the body. But the body is no longer there."

"After death, as I said many many times, people do have bodies. They live with their psychonoetic bodies. People's character and perceptions don't change simply by moving to the other side. They live with their psychonoetic bodies, and since they have not transcended their desires they construct a world on the other side which is a replica of the world they were used to while on earth." Daskalos explained that within the psychonoetic dimensions thoughts and desires more easily become solidified as elementals. They exist within the consciousness and the subjective environment of those who create them.

"Daskale," I asked, "do people on the other side experience the same kind of pleasures they were accustomed to while within their material existence?"

"Certainly."

"Such as sex, for example?"

"Yes. But, of course, as you ascend higher within the psychonoetic dimensions your sexuality is gradually transcended. At the lower levels you do have it, however, just like on earth."

"But don't you have to have a material body to experience sexual pleasure?" I asked, somewhat puzzled.

"But how can you say that?" Daskalos responded. "Is the source of sexual pleasure the gross material body or the psychonoetic body? Is it not the body of sentiments that makes intercourse possible? So you do have a material body. It is right there." He pointed at the floor. "But when a person is psychonoetically inadequate . . . it doesn't even move." He smiled and pointed his forefinger. "We continuously face so many cases of people suffering from impotence.

"So, within the psychonoetic dimensions you will find everything that you find on the gross material plane—including sex, violence, kindness, and so on. It is the character of those present that determines the nature of the subplane."

"Do they also have the fear and meaning of death? And what about murder?" I asked.

"Yes, they do. With one exception, though. Suppose a violent person attacks another and feels that he has killed him. The murderer will discover after a while that his victim has returned to life. Then he attacks again and the cycle is repeated. You cannot kill the psychonoetic body. Do you understand what is happening? People who engage in wars and battles here often repeat them within their psychonoetic dimensions once they pass on the other side."

"When someone attacks someone else does he or she cause pain on the other person's body?"

"No. On the other side there is no bodily pain. For example, one may experience a bomb blowing him to pieces. He has this experience, which gets imprinted within his consciousness. But he feels no bodily pain. And then he realizes 'Look, I am okay.' Later on he may bring to mind this incident and he will have the experience all over again. He will not experience any physical pain. He will realize that he continues to exist. Then he will imagine that that experience was a bad dream or a nightmare. Again, you see, you will find all these experiences at the lower levels of the psychonoetic worlds. And I am speaking on the basis of personal experience. I have lived through such experiences. Those who die on the battlefields in the Iran–Iraq war move to the other side and continue their war. I would in fact argue that the battles begin on the psychonoetic levels first and then are projected downward on the gross material level. We do not carry on wars only on the material surface of our planet. Wars take place whenever there is the desire to attack and start a war. And those who go on the other side bring along their desires to kill, to subjugate, and to conquer just like on the material plane."

Daskalos then noted that one of his tasks as an invisible helper is to visit battlefields and to help those who suffer. For example, with strong visual imagery he would try to control a hemorrhage until the medics arrive. And if the karma of the person is such that death is inevitable, then as invisible helper he will—along with other invisible helpers—assist him to make the transition to the other side.

"When a person gets killed in battle and finds himself in such a condition he is in a state of shock and confusion. 'What is happening to me? Where am I now?' is the usual reaction. He checks his body and finds that there is no wound. You see, the wounds of the psychonoetic body heal instantly. The invisible helpers are always present to assist such individuals. Then, with their assistance, the person will develop within himself the appropriate psychological condition that will guide him to the subplane of the psychonoetic world in which he must live until his next incarnation. Nobody takes him there. It is not you as an invisible helper who decides where one will go. At the moment of his transition into the other dimension you simply help him to come out of this confusion. He may be a good fellow paying for an ethnic, collective karma. And we can never know the reasons why one gets killed on a battlefield, for example. Only the Absolute Beingness knows, the force behind the law of karma.

"The great majority of the invisible helpers are archangels. Just imagine the great tolerance of these archangels, to always be of service to insane humanity. They constantly work to help people calm down and guide them to the appropriate subplane of the psychonoetic world that suits them. So, in a battlefield you may notice three hundred people getting killed and no one will enter the same psychonoetic condition as the person who is killed next to him.

"There is something else I have discovered," Daskalos said. "I have seen Armenians speaking their language and carrying on their church services in Armenian. I have seen Greek Orthodox carry on their *Kyrie Eleison,* and I have seen Catholics and Mormons do likewise with their languages and traditions. It means that all those who bring along to the other side the same mentality and psychological state will gather together at the analogous subplane of the psychonoetic world. Therefore you will find there all the denominations and all the religions of the world. And I have also noticed something else. Our religious celebrations and ceremonies on this side affect those on the other side who tend to vibrate approximately like ourselves. At the lower levels you will also find the fanatics. I call these spaces the hells."

"In other words," I interjected, "the earth upon which we live is a kind of hell."

"Exactly," Daskalos said. "Of course, as geographic space it is not a hell. Keep that in mind. It is the psychonoetic

conditions that human beings have created that transformed it into a hell. There are, however, differences. This
hell of the three dimensions is governed by natural laws
different from the laws that govern the psychonoetic
planes. For example, on our earthly hell light and darkness
is the product of the earth's rotation around the sun.
Within the psychonoetic dimensions the entities that live
there do not need a sun to provide them with light unless
they create it themselves with their thoughts. Even though
they don't need a sun, they bring along their experiences
from the earth plane and create a sun with their imagination. Within the psychonoetic worlds everything emanates
light—including the darkest hells, assuming that you wish
it.

"Now, suppose a fellow has a craving to build a beautiful
home. He has no money to construct it while living on the
three-dimensional space. On the psychic level he will be
given the opportunity to create one. And then he will wonder 'When did I build it?' It is his desire that created it. He
will be able to do that, assuming that he was basically a
good human being. Had he been an evil person karma will
place him, or (better) he will place himself, on the lowest
levels of the psychonoetic dimensions. On the other hand,
had he been someone who craved a comfortable house upon
arrival on the other side he would have it. He would have
created it with his thoughts. He would build it and he
would find himself inside, assuming again that he would
deserve it.

"But I have noticed something that we also observe on
the gross material level," Daskalos continued. "The satisfaction of whatever desire brings about saturation, fatigue,
and boredom. And the lack of satisfaction of a desire inten-
sifies the thirst for it. Similar psychological factors work
on the other side. There is something else. Human beings
are generally greedy; they are insatiable in their desires. I
will give you an example from personal experience. I had a
friend named Andreas. We were classmates at the Ameri-

can Academy, the high school at Larnaca I graduated from. He was very poor and was deprived of just about everything. But he was a dreamer. He grew up with shouts, anger, and abuse. His mother died when he was twelve. After we graduated from school we went our separate ways. I met him several years later. His great obsession was to build his own little house with a couple of rooms to 'find rest.' His ambition was to become a salesman. He attended some of my lectures and learned about the power of visualization. Then he stopped coming to the lessons. Years later he visited me. He announced that, among other things, through the power of strong visualization he managed to become quite wealthy. He bought two cars and he even built a house by the sea at Larnaca. There was no end to his desires. At the age of thirty-five he died. That was as far as karma would allow him to live. One day I met him on the other side. He considers himself very wealthy there. I thought that I should help him overcome his illusions. 'Hey, Andrea,' I said to him, 'are you aware of the changes? Do you realize that you have died?' 'Who, me?' He just could not believe that he was dead. 'I went through a terrible illness,' he told me. 'I remember I was urinating and defecating blood and I had a terrible dysentery.' (Possibly—Daskalos explained to us—he had typhus. They didn't know much about typhus during those days.) 'I went through a terrible illness, Spyro, but now I am completely well,' he said. 'Actually I feel much better now. Before I would wake up in the morning and I couldn't walk. Now I am like a bird. And I noticed something else. Instead of growing old with time I feel younger.' (That is what happens on the other side—Daskalos explained. You acquire a youthful appearance if you so wish.)

" 'You have always been handsome, Andrea,' I said. 'Come on,' he replied, 'don't flatter me like that. Let's go to my house at Larnaca.' 'So you imagine that you are in your house at Larnaca,' I said to him. 'Where on earth do you think we are, in London?' he replied with mockery.

" 'Andrea dear, you are dead. Now you live in an environment analogous to the one you craved. You have built all this with your imagination. You brought along everything from your experience on earth.''

" 'Spyro, are you trying to drive me crazy?' he said to me. 'My brain is not big enough.' ''

" 'No, my dear, your brain is quite big. I just want to show you that you must chase away every anxiety that you have about your property, your wealth, your houses. You have always been dissatisfied with whatever you had and always wanted more, Andrea. Your appetites were insatiable. Now you find yourself in a beautiful world—some would even call it paradise. But in reality, my friend, you live in a type of hell that you yourself have created. Let me ask you something. Do you eat now?' 'I just don't feel like it any more,' he replied. (You see, he started recognizing that he did not need food in order to live.) 'Before I ate whatever I wanted,' he said, 'but, Spyro, do you know what is happening? It is like magic. Whatever food I desire I find it in the kitchen ready-made. Who makes all that?' 'You, my dear; you make it by wishing it. You have learned so many things, why don't you realize that your desires and your thoughts become materialized here, whereas while you were still living on the earth plane you had to first shape things psychonoetically and then you had to get dirt, stones, wood in order to create them. In this place where you live now, matter—because it is matter—is shaped by your thoughts.' 'You mean to tell me,' he said, 'that all these are not real?' 'Here you go again,' I said. 'Why do you consider real that which could rot and which an earthquake can destroy in a few moments and you don't consider real that which cannot be destroyed? First of all these things that you are creating with your mind last longer, they will be here for as long as you wish them to be. And when you no longer desire them they leave you and others will find them and use them.'

" 'My brain is not big enough,' he said. 'No, my dear, you have enough brains,' I said. 'The problem with you is that your desire to understand is not strong enough. You have so many houses. You dreamed of them and you created them. You ride in your flashy car outside your properties and you admire them. You have been getting these experiences. You created all that. And do you know why? Because while you lived on earth you were neither a thief nor a dishonest person. You were basically just an average man who could use mind and create all these things that you so craved for. Fine. But for how long do you wish to live within your illusions?'

" 'You are really going to drive me crazy, Spyro. Look! How can you say that I created all that? The other day there was such a downpour, so much rain I have never seen in my life.' 'My dear, you are the one who brought that rain with your thought. It is not in the psychic environment that you are now inhabiting. You brought the rain within your own subjective psychic shell, which you have shaped in the same way as you knew it while you were alive. In your present state there is only that which you create with your thoughts and desires.'

" 'This business you are talking about, this side, the other side . . . you mean to say that we are dead?' 'No, *you* are dead,' I said. 'I am still on the other side but I can also come on your side whenever I wish to do so. I am still there because I have work to do. You, on the other hand, came here to stay. Are you not satisfied with your life now?' I asked him. 'Oh, absolutely,' he replied. I then asked, 'But why, Andrea, don't you try and focus your attention to understand the laws that are at work on this side?'

" 'Spyro,' he said and grabbed a handful of dirt. 'Are you trying to tell me that this is not dirt? It *is* dirt, damn it. Look at it.' "

.   .   .

"Well," Daskalos said to us to conclude his story, "what do you tell such a fellow? You see, he did not stay in the circles of the Erevna long enough to get a better under-

standing of the laws that are at work within the psycho-
noetic dimensions. I tried to explain to him that everything
is Mind at various levels of vibrations and that the four
elements are found in all the dimensions. But he just could
not understand. You see, a great advantage for the Researchers of Truth, those who have advanced in the teachings, is that they are aware of what is happening to them
when they move on to the other side. The knowledge you
gain here is not lost. A Researcher of Truth has a definite
advantage over ordinary people in that he or she lives more
consciously not only on earth but also after the transition
to the psychonoetic levels.

" 'You know something,' Andreas said to me," Daskalos
went on, " 'all these neighbors of mine speak Greek. There
are some Englishmen here but unfortunately my English
is not that great. I haven't been using the language for a
long time and I have forgotten much of what I learned in
school.'

"Whatever you learn on this earth plane you bring along
to the other side. The languages you learn, for example, you
can use within the psychonoetic dimensions. Now, suppose you were unable to learn foreign languages while on
earth but you did manage to develop yourself psychonoetically. Then, within the psychonoetic dimensions you will
be able to absorb the thoughts of others without the need
for the medium of language. Otherwise it will be necessary
for you to learn foreign languages in the same way as you
learned them on earth if you are to communicate with persons of different nationalities. I would also add that whatever you can learn on this side you can also learn on the
other side. Suppose someone, for example, had a great desire to learn how to play the piano but because of circumstances he was unable to do so while on the gross material
plane. In the same way that he would proceed to learn how
to play the piano in this life he could also get the training
on the other side. And when his time would come to reincarnate he will bring along to the new life the knowledge

and the talent he developed while living within the psychonoetic dimensions."

"When does one incarnate?" Stephanos asked.

"Two people never are incarnated under the same circumstances. The great masters of karma will decide when one is ready for a new incarnation. But, to tell you the truth, this issue of reincarnation puzzles me. Even though I know a lot of things as a result of my own personal experiences and investigations, I still cannot say that I really know how it works."

Stephanos said, "I wonder whether, as in this life, a person living within the psychonoetic dimensions more or less has a certain life span before moving out of these dimensions to reincarnate."

"No. It is strictly an individual matter," replied Daskalos. (Kostas explained to me at an earlier encounter that the time span of a person in the psychic dimension would depend on how violently the psychonoetic body vibrates. The greater the turmoil the individual brings along from the life just lived the longer the time needed for calming the vibrations in preparation for the new incarnation.)

Daskalos went on. "I am still struggling to help Andreas understand his situation and help him move higher so that he can experience greater light and begin appreciating loftier things than his house and his property. The higher you ascend the freer you become from material obsessions. They are the chains that keep you bound. You don't need houses on the other side to protect you from the elements. Do you understand? I am again speaking on the basis of my own personal experience. My life at the stage I find myself now is not confined within the restrictions of forms and images of the material world. I personally prefer spending most of the time coordinating my self-consciousness with something other than the body and the personality. It is really difficult to explain what is happening. These experiences that I am talking about are beyond the lower noetic world. In other words, you need to reach a stage where you can become one with Nature. To be transformed, for example, into the saltiness of the sea. Is there anything human in this? Is it in any way related to self-consciousness? Yes! What I am about to say is perhaps too audacious, but you can become a small god. Just as God feels within His creations so can you, as a small god, in a microcosm, feel like God. You can become a flower, the beauty of a flower. Or you can fuse in oneness with the beloved person. We have these ideas and meanings within the lower world, but can we put them into practice?"

"This unity that you are talking about, Daskale," Stephanos added, "is something that I have experienced myself momentarily and unintentionally, without being conscious of it. It is something like a gift from Divine Grace which catapults you in such states without you knowing how it happened."

"Now, just a minute. Everybody does this momentarily and subconsciously. For example, can you be preoccupied with yourself when your mind is absorbed with the thought of a loved one? In such cases you become that person. Subconsciously this is a form of coordination and oneness. And who does that? God himself, love. This attribute of love is God, as much as we can understand it—that is, within the limitations of the worlds of separateness. I would even go further and say that even our life within gross matter is a form of coordination with objects."

"I think I understand what you are saying," Stephanos said, "but when this coordination and oneness happens inside me it happens accidentally. I do not know how to consciously bring it about."

"Only through practice will you be able to accomplish this. Keep trying."

"But when I try it is as if I am creating something artificial which I cannot repeat."

"No. It is through the artificial that you will make your entrance into the real. You must practice. You need to become master of creative image construction. Do you understand? When I ask you to practice by constructing an image in reality I am asking you to become partially assimilated with that image. Such exercises will gradually help you overcome your attachment to your own image and become love itself. That means loving human beings without necessarily knowing them personally. To see Loxandra, a stranger, not as Loxandra but as an entity that incarnated as Loxandra in this life to gain certain experiences and will reincarnate again and again until the attainment of liberation."

I changed the subject back to the psychic dimensions. "Daskale, when people get killed in an accident, will they have memory of what happened to them while on the earth plane?"

"Most people will not remember anything. Whether they will remember or not will depend on their karma.

"Suppose I die now," I said. "Given that I have been exposed to your teachings for such a long time, will I be conscious of what will be happening to me? Will I be able to distinguish the differences between the worlds?"

"First of all, you don't die. How many times must we clarify this point?" The gentle tone of Daskalos' chiding betrayed his amusement. "But if you so wish you will be fully conscious." He then explained further that the great reward of the Researcher of Truth is the development of his or her consciousness and that what we gain on the gross material plane will be carried over into the psychonoetic worlds within which we will reside until our next incarnation. What you imprint within your consciousness, Daskalos had repeated many times, will always remain with you. He then proceeded to narrate another experience with an old acquaintance who lived within a hell of his own making.

"This fellow for many, many years now has been tormenting himself with a 'Why?' 'Why did she say this to me? Why?' 'For heavens sake, man,' I would implore him, 'forget her.'

"He was a librarian and was constantly dissatisfied with his life. In my youth I used to go to that library and we got to know each other. I remember I tried hard to let him understand that the reason I went to the library was to study and not to spend my time talking with him. My obsession at the time was modern Greek poetry and so was his. That is why he would not leave me in peace. Well, the fellow got engaged. But he was literally 'walking on the clouds' with his poetry and his aristocratic pretensions. His fiancée was getting bored having poetry recited to her day and night, something she was not the least interested in. One day while he was lecturing poetry of lofty sentiments to her she began cleaning her toes with her fingers. 'Listen,' she told him, 'if you go on like this and if this is how I am supposed to live my life with you I would rather break up right now. I want a man who is down to earth and not a foolish dreamer like yourself.' He was devastated, particularly at having been called a foolish dreamer. He decided to end his life. He climbed up on the roof of the library and jumped.

"I have struggled for many years to make him understand that at this very moment he does not live within gross matter. I tried to make him understand that the beautiful girl he was so madly in love with is now an old grandmother. 'She is no longer the one you fantasize about, your doll, your idol.' 'Why,' he keeps repeating, 'did she call me a foolish dreamer? She owes me an explanation and an apology.' 'For God's sake,' I said to him, 'calm down.' I told him what he had done. 'Yes,' he admitted, 'I did fall down. But nothing happened to me. I only felt a little pain in my bones. I got well very quickly.' 'So you got cured,' I said. 'And now what are you doing, my friend?' 'Now,' he said, 'well, now I am resting. I owe it to myself.' You see, he was by temperament lazy—that is why he ended up becoming a librarian so that he could relax and rest," Daskalos said with sarcastic humor. (At the time few people visited libraries.)

"Now, he reads some books that he carries with him and is still obsessed with the same 'Why?' 'Come,' I said to him, 'let me show you something. Let us go through that wall to help you realize that you do not live within the world of gross matter. You now live within what people call the lower world.' 'No wonder they call you the Magus. You just hypnotized me and made me see all these things.' 'For God's sake, man,' I said to him, 'you departed.' (I did not tell him "you died.") 'You do not live within the world of gross matter.' 'How can you say that,' he replied, 'since here I am, I live.' 'Yes, you do live, my dear, but you don't live the way you used to.' 'How can you say that? Am I not ———'[he mentioned his name]?' 'Of course you are, since you still desire to live within the worlds of your illusions and to imagine that you are the one you think you are. Come, let us go through that wall.' I passed him through without opening the door. 'Just try to understand you are living now within a different form of matter where you can rarefy yourself and you can go through walls and objects and you don't need to move like on earth, step by step. On this side the law of gravity as you knew it does not apply. There are other laws here. Why don't you just sit down and study these laws as you studied the laws operating on the material level. There is no need for you to live within the cocoon of your illusions.' But he ranted on: 'Why did she call me a foolish dreamer? Why? And I loved her, I adored her. She owes me an apology and she must ask for my forgiveness.'

"He got stuck there. To this day he is still obsessed with that 'Why?' That is his hell and his punishment. I tried to get permission from the masters to create an elemental of that woman. I could have picked her image from his own subconscious as he knew her. Then I would present that elemental in front of him. That would have been easy enough to do. But Yohannan did not allow me to do that. He explained to me that what I had in mind was fraudulent. 'But how is he going to disentangle himself from his illusions?' I asked. That elemental could have come to him and begged: 'My love, my darling, I made a mistake. I am asking for your forgiveness just as you are asking me to do.' " Daskalos mimicked and chuckled with mischief.

"Father Yohannan absolutely forbade me to do that. You see, we do have restrictions. We cannot do whatever we fantasize to be the right thing to do. That is why I personally never ignore the instructions of the higher masters whenever they offer it to me. Otherwise I would have been making horrible mistakes all the time. In this case had I acted strictly on my own volition I would have created that elemental without any problems of conscience because I would have thought that the trick could have helped him overcome his obsession and move a step higher. You must realize that the powers of the invisible helper operate within limits that must not be violated. Pay attention to this point.

"So, I was a young fellow when this man committed suicide. Now I am in my seventies. He still lives within this obsession of 'Why?' He may be in that state, in terms of earthly time, for another eighty or a hundred years—who knows?"

"Can one speak of time when one lives in such states?" I asked. "Can it be measured in terms of years?"

"You are raising an important question. Because time and space lose their meaning under such conditions. If you ask that man 'Where are you now?' he will answer most probably 'I am in my room,' or whatever he brought over from his experiences on the gross material level."

"I presume it must be the same with time. That is, an experience on the other side that gives you the impression of one year in terms of earthly life could be an entire century," I pointed out.

"Very true. I have noticed from experience that a lesson which would have taken me three to four hours to give on the gross material level I could give in three minutes within the psychonoetic dimensions. The difference is the speed with which time moves on the other side. Pay attention to the following point. What do you think space is? You know the dimensions of this room that we are in at this moment and you call it space. But before you can blink your eyes you are thousands of miles beyond this space since the earth is in constant motion. And the earth along with the sun move inside the galaxy, which in turn moves with unimaginable speed within the infinity of space. So which space are we talking about when we refer to the 'space in this room?' You see, in the final analysis space as such is the idea of space you possess in your mind. And you will possess this specific idea of space for as long as the walls of this house are around to give you this impression. So, strictly speaking, space is only an idea in your head, a phenomenal reality."

Daskalos' exposition on space and time struck a familiar chord. The eighteenth-century German philosopher Immanuel Kant first postulated within Western thought this idea—that time and space exist only in our minds and not 'out there' in the 'objective' world—and brought on a revolution in philosophy. I doubted whether Daskalos had ever heard of or read Kant. What he spoke about was based primarily on his own experiences and observations within the magical cosmos into which his consciousness traveled.

"So," Daskalos continued, "someone may be tormented for years within those dimensions, and if you pose to him the question 'When did this happen, my friend?' he will answer 'Yesterday,' or 'Today.' He will not be in a position to realize that so many years have passed."

"Had it not been so," I argued, "he would have been living in an intolerable hell."

"I imagine so."

"This, I suppose, is what you would call Divine Mercy."

"Very true. I meet so many people on the other side and they would say to me 'yesterday' and in terms of time on the gross material level sixty years may have passed since the time they refer to as yesterday," Daskalos said and remained silent for a few seconds. Then he remembered another encounter he had had with a man residing within the psychonoetic dimensions.

"This person was quite an intellectual of very high noetic spheres. One of his habits was to descend to the lower levels. When I asked him why he was doing that his reply was that he was accomplishing something he was unable to do during his life on earth. He would enter into a space like a twilight where water would flow very slowly, something like a river covered with beautiful water lilies. These were conditions he and others created with their thoughts, giving them the impression of a night on some Hawaiian island with palm trees, and so on. I went with him and saw all that. 'It is beautiful here,' he said to me, 'there is great peace and tranquility. Let us sit down and talk.' 'Talk about what?' I asked him. 'Let us talk about all this beauty. Don't you hear the music?' (You see, he was creating the music with his thought. Music of course does exist. It is a question of coordinating your vibrations with the kind of music you want to hear.) 'I want to ask you a question for which I need an answer. We enter,' he said, 'into a deep dreamless sleep.' (You see, it is the same phenomenon we have on this side.) 'I have gone through a very trying and painful experience in my life,' he said, 'and I still remember it—without pain, however. My memory about it is not very vivid. But when that memory comes to my mind I feel very sleepy.' (Divine Mercy at work, according to Daskalos.) 'I enter,' he said, 'into something like oblivion. At first I was afraid.' 'Why should you be afraid?' I replied. 'Were you not doing the same thing every night while you were alive on earth? Did you not experience this deep sleep every night you went to bed? Were you not entering then into something analogous to oblivion? And were you not the same person upon your awakening the following morning? As self-consciousness you enter into a phenomenal state of nonexistence, but in reality you are not lost.' 'You are right,' he said, 'but it is something else I have in mind.' 'What is it?'

'Suppose,' he said, 'that I enter into that state of phenomenal nonexistence for ten minutes, or one hour or ten centuries and then wake up. What is the difference? How am I going to know?' 'I am very happy that you thought of this,' I replied. 'Yes. That is how it is. Suppose you have the need to enter into this form of nonexistence for ten centuries and then wake up. In reality you will be entering into the *meaning* of the ten centuries because in truth it is the Eternal Present into which you will be entering. And it is inside the Eternal Present you will be reawaking. Within your own consciousness you will not recognize that ten centuries had already passed.' "

I interrupted Daskalos. "Perhaps this condition is part of the mechanism of karma and Divine Mercy—that is, not to be conscious of time so that the appropriate conditions on earth may develop to the point when the soul or entity will need to reenter into gross matter to acquire further experiences."

"Exactly. Well, I said to this man 'But why do you want to feel this phenomenal oblivion and inertia?' 'Just a minute,' he said, 'what inertia are you talking about?' It was as if I had planted an idea into his head. 'Since you have acquired so much knowledge,' I said to him, 'and you are capable of descending so low within the psychonoetic worlds, why don't you join other invisible helpers to be of service? Instead of watching the bluish water lilies in the moonlight, don't you think it is preferable to look around you and help people who are in need?'

"This fellow must have lived two to three centuries ago, because the kind of conversation he was carrying on belonged to that period."

"Was he Greek?"

"No. He was of a different ethnicity," Daskalos replied. "Do you know what the problem with that fellow was? He was an intellectual but impotent in loving anyone except himself. This is a great drawback. He expressed no desire to join in with the invisible helpers to be of service to other fellow human beings. It is a thousand times better, as far as I am concerned, for a person to love erroneously than be incapable of loving. I would prefer someone who loves egotistically and aggressively than one who is simply indifferent. Because, you see, under the suffering from his egotistical love he will be awakened. I would rather see a father, for example, angry at his son because he loves him who exchanges heavy accusations: 'the ungrateful contemptible son, I educated him and now he left us.' I prefer this kind of love full of anger and bitterness to no love at all. Within such a passionate psychological state there is inherently the self-punishment which will help the person mature and evolve. Do you understand what I am saying?"

At this point visitors knocked at Daskalos' door seeking his services and we had to interrupt our discussion.

Two days later when I met Kostas in Limassol I mentioned to him our encounter with Daskalos and the discussion we had with him. It was Saturday morning and Kostas had decided to take the morning off from his work and spend a few hours with me at the Famagusta Nautical Club. As we were sitting under the shady eucalyptus trees sipping beer and watching swimmers and boats go by Kostas began describing one of his own recent experiences within the psychonoetic dimensions.

"We were a group of invisible helpers traveling inside the static condition of time. We were floating over the sea when we noticed a small coastal city. It was within one of the psychonoetic dimensions. It was what we call a hell— a psychonoetic plane at low levels of vibration."

"Was that city the psychic counterpart of an actual city on the gross material level?" I asked.

"Let me proceed and you will understand. Well, we landed and began walking through the narrow streets, whitewashed houses, and so on. Suddenly our attention was focused on an elderly woman who was sitting on a bench outside her home. When she noticed us she looked surprised. She became curious and invited us inside. Upon

entering her house she began complaining about her son—
who, she said, was in a state of psychological confusion and
pain. She implored us to try and help him. She called him
and introduced him by the name of Kostas Papadakis. He
was, he said, an instructor of English, forty-five years old.
He also told us that he was in love with one of his students,
a twenty-three-year-old woman. He was desperate because
she was having an affair with another of his students, someone of her own age. 'And recently,' he said, 'as I was riding
my bicycle I had a terrible accident. They took me to the
hospital in great pain. My bones were all broken. I just
don't understand how I got well so quickly and found myself here.'

"Then someone asked him," Kostas continued, " 'How
old did you say you are?' His reply was 'Forty-five.' 'But you
look only twenty-five.' 'Come on,' he said, 'don't tease me
like that. I am forty-five years old. Why do you say I am
twenty-five?' 'But that is how you look. Are you certain
that after the accident you did not die?' 'What are you talking about?' he protested. 'How could I have died since I am
here talking to you?' Then he went on to tell us that there
are certain things that puzzle him. 'You see,' he said, 'here
I am in my house in Thessaloniki. A few years ago they
informed me that my mother, who lived in Italy—in Na-
ples—had died. I wonder why they lied to me. And how did
my mother appear all of a sudden here in Thessaloniki with
me?' 'Let me ask you something,' I said. 'What year do you
think you are now living?' 'But are you taking me for a fool,
Mister?' he replied angrily. 'It is nineteen twenty-three.'
Then he went on to tell us that he remembered that since
his accident he slept and woke up twice. Based on that
realization he went on to figure out the exact date. 'My
friend,' I said, 'the year today is nineteen eighty-seven.'
'Come on,' he said, and shouted an Italian curse which I
don't remember now. 'Why are you wearing white clothes?'
he asked later. 'Are you of this world or did you come from
another planet?' 'My dear,' I said to him, 'you have died and

now you are living within the psychic worlds, and that is why you have contacted your mother. Right now you exist within the environment of Thessaloniki as you knew it in nineteen twenty-three. Many years have passed since then. It is nineteen eighty-seven now. Had you been alive today you would have been a hundred and nine years old. In other words, you would have already died the natural way. And the student you fell in love with would have been by now eighty-nine years old.'

"You see," Kostas said as I finished my glass of beer, "he told us before that he wanted revenge against the student who took his love away. This man from nineteen twenty-three to nineteen eighty-seven has slept twice and lived and still lives within the illusion that he is within a gross material existence and wants revenge. We promised to visit him again."

"And you left him," I said, amused, "in his Thessaloniki of nineteen twenty-three."

"Right, and he still lives there. You see, we entered within the vibrations of his own consciousness and understanding. It was an environment of his own creation."

"Did you perceive that environment from your vantage point or from his?"

"From his, of course. We entered the awareness of that individual with the specific task of being of assistance to him, to help him move out of the hell he was in. We entered the environment of nineteen-twenty-three Thessaloniki within which his awareness was transfixed."

"Was that visit something you have initiated yourself, the product purely of your own volition?" I asked.

"Yes. This is our purpose as invisible helpers, to be of service."

I persisted. "I suppose that for that man you were something like extraterrestrials."

"For him we were certainly a paranormal phenomenon. Before we left we told him 'In order to realize that we are not of your world we will disappear right in front of your eyes,' and we did."

"Was he convinced?"

"Not quite. But we raised questions in his mind. We will need to visit him several times before we could have some effect on him."

"What about his mother?"

"We were not working on his mother. She was not of the same vibrations. Actually, to tell you the truth, it was with the elemental of his mother that he was in contact with most of the time."

I asked Kostas whether the invisible helpers who accompanied him in that psychonoetic space were members of various nationalities or simply members of Daskalos' inner circle. He said that they were members of many nationalities. There are no language or ethnic barriers, he said, at the higher psychonoetic spheres and communication there takes place directly, mind to mind. In these higher spheres, Kostas said, people may speak their separate languages. And you are aware that they do so. But at the same time you understand what is being said without yourself necessarily knowing the language. He also mentioned that Daskalos was present in that encounter. He checked, he said, and verified his experience with Daskalos upon their return to the gross material level. This has been a routine practice of Kostas', a practice that authenticated the objective validity of his experiences within the psychonoetic dimensions.

"How long did that visit last?" I asked.

"It must have lasted for over an hour—in terms of earthly time, that is. It was a very tiring experience because I projected myself within those spaces while maintaining myself in a state of semi-consciousness within gross matter."

"Does that mean that as you went through that experience you were simultaneously aware of the goings-on on the gross material level?" I asked.

"Yes. And that is the most tiring method of out-of-the-body experience. Incidentally, this is the customary way we project ourselves within the psychonoetic dimensions."

Kostas' comments brought to my mind the findings of

some contemporary anthropologists who studied the phenomenon of shamanism and the shamanic trance. Unlike their predecessors, who reduced the shamanic experience to schizophrenia or other pathogenic categories, anthropologists like L. G. Peters and D. Price-Williams have argued convincingly that the Shamanic State of Consciousness (SSC) is a reality sui generis, a reality unto itself, irreducible to other forms of consciousness (hypnotism, schizophrenia, ordinary trance, sleep, and so on). The scientific experimental evidence for this argument simply overwhelms the earlier notions. The authentic shaman is now shown to be master of a special type of trance whereby he or she willfully moves in and out of such states. During this unique type of trance the shaman becomes a vehicle bridging the gap between the world of ordinary consciousness and that of nonordinary reality. During this dissociative state shamans, according to this perspective, while visiting the realm of the spirits are in constant communication with their audience—that is, they are simultaneously conscious within both worlds.

"It is not so tiring," Kostas went on, "when you place your gross material body completely into a trance state and remove your consciousness from it. In such states your body gives the appearance of a corpse. A physician, for example, who would conduct a clinical examination will find there a pale and apparently lifeless body. The doctor in fact may need special instruments to detect whether there is any heartbeat. This happens particularly when the self-consciousness removes itself to vast distances away from the gross material body. The further away the self-consciousness removes itself the more the material body is forced to slow down its functions such as blood flow, heartbeat, and so on. The blood flow could slow down to such a degree that the body may feel almost as cold as a corpse." The functions of the body, Kostas explained, return to their normal state as soon as the self-consciousness returns back to the body.

Our discussion was interrupted when an acquaintance of Kostas', a member of his circle, came and sat at our table. Kostas introduced her to me and ordered another round of cool local beer. We switched our conversation to more prosaic issues, the perennial Cyprus problem and her husband's sensitive political post. But when she realized what we had been talking about she earnestly asked Kostas to clarify a question for her based on lessons he had given a week earlier.

"What happens," she asked, "to human intelligence after the death of the material body? Will it be maintained? In other words, will someone who today is a great genius continue to be so after the death of the material body?"

"As I have explained to you many times," Kostas replied, "the present personality will continue as present personality with the level of intelligence, knowledge, and awareness that it had in the life just lived. John will remain John, Maria will remain Maria, and so on. And in the event that the present personality becomes adapted within a reality of those other dimensions, it will be offered the opportunity to acquire more knowledge for advancement on the spiritual path. The subconscious of every human being will be given the opportunity to be enriched there as well."

"Will the tempo and pace of progress be analogous to what one would normally experience within the three-dimensional reality of gross matter?" I asked.

"If you manage to construct solid foundations on this plane of existence," Kostas replied, pointing to the ground, "then your progress within the psychonoetic dimensions could gallop in a geometric progression."

"Why is it so?" I wondered aloud.

"In this dimension you have many questions that you are unable to answer experientially. The confines of gross matter are an obstacle to the advancement of your awareness. Within the psychonoetic worlds, on the other hand, there are no such obstacles. The very moment you begin within those worlds to raise questions and become a Researcher of the Truth you are in a far better position to explore and discover for yourself what is real and what is not. For example, in this world you are characterized by curiosity and eagerness to witness so-called paranormal phenomena. Within the psychonoetic worlds you will not wait for others to perform phenomena for you. You will be able to carry them out yourself. You can more easily experiment there on the validity of these teachings."

"Therefore it must be easier," I interjected, "to be a Researcher of the Truth within the psychonoetic dimensions."

"Yes," Kostas said, smiling, "but with the proviso that the first steps must be made within this gross material world."

"Do you think the steps that we have made so far are sufficient for that purpose?" I asked playfully.

"They are," Kostas reassured us. "The further you are advanced in this world on the path for the Research of Truth the easier and faster will be your advance within the psychonoetic worlds."

3   Illusions

Emily, our children, Constantine and Vasia, and I spent
Sunday morning at Kourion Beach, a mile long and still-
unspoiled stretch of seashore west of Limassol. Lying
within the jurisdiction of the British bases nearby, it had
been spared the development of the rest of the coast. The
British, fearing international terrorism against their bases,
banned the construction of paved roads and permanent ce-
ment installations. Thanks to their concern the beach was
left by default to joggers, swimmers, and sun-worshippers.
The beach is at the base of a precipitous hill upon which
the ancient theater of Kourion lies, a spot from which one
can contemplate unparalleled sunsets. In antiquity Kourion
was one of the twelve kingdoms of the island. Recent ex-
cavations have shown it had a fate identical with that of
Pompeii. Around A.D. 365, when Christianity was becoming firmly entrenched in that part of the Mediterranean, a
devastating earthquake destroyed the city of Kourion, killing virtually all of its thousands of inhabitants.

In early afternoon we decided to return to my in-laws' apartment in Limassol to rest before the one-hour drive to Nicosia. On our way we stopped at Kostas' garage near the KEO wineries. Emily and the children went to shop at an outdoor fruit and vegetable market nearby while I went to pay a quick visit to Kostas.

Dressed in blue jeans (his most comfortable costume, he joked to me once), Kostas had been working since early morning remodeling an old Rover. Auto repair had been his business since his arrival in Limassol as a refugee from Famagusta. Although he was in the process of starting a new business related to tourism and a duty-free shop, he kept his garage. A British-trained mechanical engineer, Kostas thought of auto repair more as a challenging hobby than work, a relaxing diversion from the serious business of healing and The Erevna. The owners of the building where his garage was housed, however, had notified him that the premises must be evacuated because they were to be demolished to make room for apartment houses. He had just a few months left, he said, and that was the reason why he had been working even on Sundays. The west side of Limassol, where the old wineries and Kostas' garage were located, was rapidly being developed because of the construction of a modern harbor and the growth of tourism.

"Fixing old cars is really a pleasure," Kostas reassured me as he checked with an electronic instrument the newly installed engine in the antique automobile.

"But how odd," I joked, "a master like yourself wasting precious time fixing old cars!"

"Not so," he replied with a grin as he continued testing the engine. "I need a break too, you know. If you vibrate on a certain level of consciousness continuously, you get tired. Periodically you need to rest by getting yourself engrossed with activities at lower levels than the level at which your awareness ordinarily operates." Watching movies, Kostas once told me, is another way of relaxation for him, "even silly movies and cartoons." Being in his garage all day Sunday working by himself, without patients and seekers after wisdom looking for him, was a real treat. It was just him, his tools, and the cars.

As I watched Kostas bury his head under the open hood I marveled. Here was this unassuming, slim, forty-seven-year-old and ordinary-looking sage who assured me that since high school he had never finished reading a single book except the engineering texts assigned him by his professors while he was a student in England. Yet his intellectual acumen and philosophical sophistication always astonished me. "What I know," he had told me several times, "does not come from book-reading." His knowledge sprang from a direct access to the sources of wisdom that reside within every human being. When a present personality, he said, begins to enter the state of superconscious self-awareness, he or she does not need books. One can simply enter as a center of consciousness inside the Universal Memory, where all knowledge is found. "We have inside us," Kostas claimed, "all the knowledge of the universe. And it is inside us that we must enter in order to acquire true knowledge of existence and reality."

Kostas informed me—and I believed him—that he had not even read my two books that included my encounters with him. "I just placed my hands over the books," he said matter-of-factly, "and I knew the essence of what you had written."

At first I was shocked when I heard both Kostas and Daskalos speak along these lines. But later I began to realize that what they were claiming made perfect sense from within their teachings, from within their extraordinary epistemology. If we as human beings are unconscious gods suffering from self-inflicted amnesia and if our aim is to reawaken into our divine state, then book-learning is irrelevant once we begin to overcome our predicament. The great masters of humanity, after all, were not teaching out of books they had read or written. Perhaps reading and writing are relevant and necessary only at the lower levels of awareness.

I stayed with Kostas for no more than twenty minutes.

When I discovered that in a couple of hours he was to go
with Chrysanthos, a young jeweler, to a late-afternoon performance by a Greek magician I expressed a strong wish to
join them. Kostas wiped his hands with a rag and called his
disciple on the phone. We were informed that all tickets
were sold for that special performance. But Chrysanthos
had secured an extra seat because he "felt vaguely," as he
put it, that someone else was about to join them but had
no idea who that might be. Chrysanthos reassured me later
that his buying the extra ticket was not "accidental".

The Blond Magus, as he was called, was a Macedonian
wizard reputed for possessing superhuman powers. He
claimed on local television that he developed his special
powers during a six-year sojourn in a Tibetan monastery.
He was credited with several international awards for his
extraordinary skills at various conferences of magicians
and wonder-workers. The advertising posters presented
him as one of the foremost magi of the planet. In a newspaper interview he boasted "I learned all about meditation
and how to control my own body, how to do things and feel
no pain. I can tell a dentist to pull out a tooth from my
mouth and I won't feel a thing, just as I can stop my heart,
or prevent my blood from hemorrhaging through the power
of my mind." These secrets, he claimed, he had learned
from the Tibetans.

Kostas reluctantly accepted the invitation to attend the
special performance and attest the authenticity of this
magus after several of his followers pressed him to do so.
Apparently a lot of "paranormal" phenomena were taking
place on stage. The most shocking were some fakirlike
demonstrations when the magus allegedly pierced his body
with skewers, knives, and power drills. Emily was not the
least interested in the performance herself and preferred
instead to take the opportunity to spend time with her
aging parents.

Kostas went home, had a shower, and waited for me.
When I arrived at five-thirty Chrysanthos, who seemed to

be quite knowledgeable about stage magic, was already there. Kostas sat in the living room nervously puffing his pipe.

"If this fellow is for real," he said gravely, "he most probably does all these feats with the aid of demons. Only a black sorcerer would use such powers to impress audiences and make fortunes."

After puffing his pipe a few more times Kostas murmured that there was the possibility that the magician was employing a certain class of demons and mentioned the class, a strange word I had never heard before. "That would be very very dangerous," he said. "They will eventually eat him up. These demons are terribly powerful. With a few drops of blood they could create havoc."

On another occasion Kostas told me of a near-miss encounter he had with such a demonic force. Someone brought him an object that a local woman, a black sorceress, had created after she was hired by a man to destroy a rival family. Kostas showed me the object, a round piece of metal with various magical symbols on it. He also showed me a picture of the black sorceress, a smiling, ordinary-looking black-clad grandmother. "You can't imagine how much misery that woman created!" Kostas shook his head.

On that piece of metal, I was told, the grandmotherly sorceress entrapped one of the class of demons that Kostas mentioned in relation to the performance of the Blond Magus. That demonic elemental was so powerful that Kostas was hesitant to handle it on his own. After I pressed him further on the subject he revealed to me a few more details. Kostas had sought Daskalos' assistance. The two of them lit a white candle and through strong, intense concentration miniaturized the demonic elemental to the size of the head of a needle and forced it inside the candle flame. "We had to make certain," he said, "to bring the vibrations of that demonic elemental to the vibrations of the gross material fire." An eyewitness, a woman in Kostas' circle, told me that she actually saw with her material eyes the minuscule dark shadow image of the demon inside the flame of the candle. The moment Daskalos and Kostas entrapped him inside the flame they rushed to blow it out. That was how they liberated that object of its destructive energy and that was how they dissolved the demonic elemental. The moment they accomplished that feat the people affected by the diabolical object found immediate relief. "These demonic elementals," Kostas explained, "draw their energy from the believers themselves, and that is how their life is prolonged."

Kostas warned that what he and Daskalos had done that day was extremely dangerous and not something that amateurs should get involved with. Had their joined concentration not been powerful enough, the demon could have escaped from the flame. Had that happened, "the explosion that would have followed could have brought down the house and killed everybody in it."

When these considerations came to my mind I felt slightly uneasy about the afternoon performance. In a previous performance the magus allegedly disemboweled himself in front of a stunned audience. He proceeded to place his intestines in a bowl and then stuffed them back and mended the wound with his bare hands. It had also been rumored that a person sitting in the audience was instantly found outside the theater. My conventional skeptical mind, of course, had a difficult time digesting such extraordinary tales, although in the occult literature of both East and West such phenomena are considered perfectly possible. I was once told by a rational and sympathetic Indian professor of music who was on a visit to the United States that he himself had been a witness to the 'teleportation' of an Indian mystic. Daskalos too claims that such phenomena are possible. They are even chronicled, he told me once, in the Bible—as in the case of Saint Philip, who is said to have materialized instantly next to the Ethiopian king, baptizing the latter in the name of Christ.

Both Daskalos and Kostas, however, have repeatedly

warned that psychic abilities must be used only for healing purposes and never for profit, status, or power. It is for this reason that within The Erevna psychic power must develop gradually and parallel the development of one's level of consciousness and spiritual maturity. Otherwise, a person runs the risk of degenerating into a black magician. In such cases egotism takes over and the practitioner becomes a menace both to others and to himself or herself.

"Listen to me," Kostas said very seriously after a short, pensive silence. "When we go to the theater make certain that you place yourself inside a white, luminous five-pointed star. This will give you protection against possible assaults by demons that may be present."

For an instant I felt a lump in my throat as I pondered Kostas' dire warning. "Why," I asked with puzzlement, "would demons assault us?" Kostas explained that since we were practitioners of white magic demons that might be present would probably try to assault us because our presence would be a threat to them. Once we placed ourselves inside a five-pointed star there was nothing to fear from such evil psychonoetic influences.

"Also," Kostas cautioned us, "do not get emotionally engrossed with what you might witness there. Just be detached observers. And please don't ask me any questions while we are there. Wait until we return home."

The theater was packed with noisy people. The seats were numbered; we were to sit in the third row, a good spot to get a close look at the magus. In spite of NO SMOKING signs many in the audience were puffing away and ignoring the discomfort caused to the rest of us. Behind me a muscular mustachioed man, his shirt half-opened to display his robust hairy chest, kept lighting one cigarette after another, to my great annoyance.

I was astonished to see so many children in the audience and wondered whether there was any chance that some might be traumatized by what they were about to witness. Kostas' warnings of potential devils around did not make me feel very comfortable. I had come to have great respect for Kostas' magical abilities and healing powers to dismiss his caveats about dangers lurking within the psychonoetic dimensions regardless of how bizarre they might have appeared within my hopelessly conventional mind.

The lights went off and loud, deafening bouzouki music blasted through the megaphones, creating a hellish atmosphere of discordant sounds. When after five tortuous minutes the music was finally silenced, a tall, slim, burlesque-type comedian came onstage to prepare us psychologically before the awesome magus made his appearance. With a long monologue of the most lewd jokes I have ever heard uttered from a public forum he tried to entertain us and make us laugh. He moved his hips in a most inappropriate manner, waving with his hoola-hoop movements a five-inch plastic thing hanging freely from his belt, presumably for the symbolic purpose of accentuating his gender. I felt embarrassed for the sake of the children and was relieved that mine were not present. For more than fifteen minutes we were exposed to an avalanche of four-letter vulgarities pouring through his mouth like sewage. I thought to myself that had there been demons around certainly he must be one of them. He reminded me more of an ancient satyr with tail, horns, and goat legs than a contemporary Athenian performer. When after twenty endless minutes he completed his debauched number, he announced in a jolly good spirit and beaming pride that on our way out of the theater we might buy the performance we had just witnessed on a stereo cassette.

At last the magus made his appearance. He was a tall, muscular man with blond hair that reached to his shoulders. He appeared onstage almost naked from the waist up and carried along several skewers, a couple of large butcher knives, and an electric drill. Looking somber and, saying nothing, proceeded with his act. He pierced his limbs with the skewers, blood dripping through the wounds. He then began with seemingly masochistic gusto to cut with a knife his left wrist—the blade of the knife reached halfway through the bone apparently without causing him pain. It was as if a butcher were working on a leg of lamb. A couple of children in front of us bent down, covering their eyes with their folded arms in a desperate effort to spare themselves the macabre sight. He then proceeded to pierce his belly with the electric drill, inducing some moaning sounds among the audience. Then he went on to plunge the knife into his arm, and half of it appeared on the other side. He moved it up and down his arm while walking in the aisles of the theater for the audience to have a closer look. With wide-open eyes the archetypal macho man behind me fainted. Four people rushed to carry him outside for some air. A woman in the back of the audience followed his lead and had to be rescued. The magus, undisturbed by the commotion he created, kept gleefully working on his body with his knives, skewers, and electric drills.

"Do you think this is for real?" Chrysanthos, on the other side of Kostas, whispered excitedly.

"Not now, not now, please," Kostas reacted with discomfort as he fixed his gaze on the performer. Noticing Kostas' nervous reply I began visualizing once more and with greater concentration the luminous five-pointed star. I made certain that I stayed inside it and that it covered every single cell of my material and nonmaterial existence.

The performance lasted for about fifteen gruesome minutes. The Blond Magus walked offstage as thick black blood ran down his muscular arms. As soon as he was out of sight I was aware of Kostas laughing silently. I looked at him with astonishment, thinking for a moment that he had been overtaken by some nervous reaction.

"What's going on?"

"He is just a bloody magician," he whispered smiling, and shook his head.

"You mean he is not for real?" Chrysanthos asked as his face dropped with disappointment.

"Of course not," Kostas waved his hand. "He is just a

good magician, a first-rate illusionist. He may have some abilities, like the ones that the fakirs of India demonstrate in the streets. These kinds of demonstrations do not interest us."

"Phew," I said. "What a relief. You mean there are no demons around here?"

"Certainly not," Kostas replied, chuckling. He reassured us that the Blond Magus was not a dangerous sorcerer after all but a highly skilled artist and wonder-worker.

"What about his claim of a six-year apprenticeship in Tibet?" I asked.

"Tibet!" Kostas scoffed. "Do you think that had he spent six years with the lamas he would occupy his time with this nonsense? Or even be allowed to use psychic power for show and money?"

Before we could say anything more the Athenian satyr made a triumphant reappearance to shower us with another outpouring of sexual jokes, presumably to relieve us of the strains and tensions of the performance we had just been exposed to. After twenty more minutes of four-letter aphorisms the Blond Magus returned. There were no wounds on his body, only a few scars. The rest of the performance was regular but first-rate magical illusions, including hypnotic feats, levitation, and the traditional cutting-the-woman-assistant-up-into-pieces act.

Just as the show was coming to an end the magus spoke to the audience briefly, claiming that most of the feats he had performed that afternoon were not tricks and that we could not explain them rationally, at least not through ordinary logic. Therefore he advised us that it would be unwise to waste our time trying to figure out how he did it.

"Prior to my performance," he explained, "I meditate backstage for some time and incorporate the audience within my magnetism." These, he said, were secret techniques the Tibetan monks taught him.

I felt great relief as we left the stuffy and noisy atmosphere of the theater. We decided to walk toward the waterfront. Kostas seemed to be equally relieved. The moment we stepped on the asphalt he stretched his elbows a few times, breathed deeply, and sighed with satisfaction.

The mile-long promenade covered on both sides with newly planted palm trees was ideal for leisurely walks and conversation. It was exactly what we needed, to move our limbs, smell the saltiness of the sea breeze, and indulge in conversation.

. . .

We paced silently for a few minutes as we marveled at the full moon rising above the Mediterranean. Ever since I became involved with Daskalos and Kostas the moon had acquired a different meaning for me. According to them the moon, regardless of how beautiful and inspiring it has been for poets and lovers throughout the ages, has been nevertheless a psychic prison house for planet earth. It is the place where extremely destructive human entities are being isolated by archangelic entities assigned to oversee the evolution of our planet. These destructive human entities are kept imprisoned for long periods of time within the psychic counterpart of the gross material moon. Being confined in this manner they yearn to return to earth and always try unsuccessfully to escape. They do so when the psychic counterpart of the moon and the earth touch each other at certain periods of the year. Then these entities attempt to take hold either of animals or of human beings who are susceptible to their influences. The phenomenon of epilepsy, Kostas claimed, is in fact a form of temporary possession by such entities. It stops when the psychic counterparts of earth and moon no longer touch. Then these entities are pulled away by the moon and the epileptic seizure comes to an end. Kostas further taught that a Researcher of Truth can help an epileptic during those moments by placing and pressing his or her hand at the side of the patient's liver, visualizing the therapeutic hand covered with white luminosity. The Researcher of Truth must simultaneously make a strong wish that the diabolical human entity who took temporary possession of the patient be ejected. The moment this procedure is followed the patient is relieved of the seizure. Kostas claimed that it is through the liver of the susceptible patient that the moon residents are trying to take possession and escape their prison. It was reassuring to learn that these demonic humans cannot escape before their time is up as determined by the masters of karma.

We sat on a rock and gazed at the reflection of the moon on the calm water. "Daskalos once mentioned to me," I said, breaking the silence, "that our five senses are the most unreliable means to explain reality."

"That's right, that's right." Kostas nodded, puffing his pipe. "They can so easily deceive us. That is the lesson one can derive from performances like the one we have just witnessed. It is for this reason that within The Erevna only healing is allowed as phenomena. No magician can with tricks heal a wound, remove a cancerous tumor, or straighten a crooked spine. A skillful magician can duplicate with illusions just about anything that an authentic master can accomplish with real power. But an authentic Researcher of the Truth will not indulge in power feats to impress audiences and the curious."

"For many people," I commented, "there is no distinction among impostors, tricksters, and authentic healers. They are all lumped together under a single category."

"That is why we must be extra-cautious not to scandalize people who cannot understand what we are doing," Kostas added. "It is necessary to protect The Erevna. In a manner of speaking, of course. The Erevna does not need anyone's protection."

We continued walking. I mentioned that a group of famed authors in America, including such stars as Isaac Asimov and Carl Sagan, alarmed by the mushrooming interest in matters pertaining to spirituality, had joined forces with The Amazing Randi, a celebrated magician to expose tricksters and healers who (according to them) threaten the very foundations of our rational Western culture. "The trouble is," I went on as Kostas and Chrysanthos listened with interest, "that they make no discriminations. For Randi and company all healers and all psychics are a priori impostors and tricksters."

I went on to lament my tribulations with a good friend and colleague, an Indian mathematics professor, a diehard convert to Western scientific rationalism who found it hard to understand why a rational being like myself would be interested in Indian spirituality, in the sutras of Patanjali, and in Daskalos. This otherwise good-natured and well-meaning professor was instrumental in organizing a lecture at our campus by the Amazing Randi to warn us of the deadly dangers of allowing charlatans to undermine our rationality. My two companions erupted in laughter.

"In what way does the five-pointed star offer protection?" I asked after Kostas and Chrysanthos had calmed down.

"Whenever you find yourself in a difficult situation," Kostas replied as we continued pacing leisurely up and down the promenade, "try to see yourself covered with an all-white luminosity and create with your mind the five-pointed star."

"What do you mean by 'difficult situation'?"

"I mean when you find yourself facing psychonoetic dangers coming from your everyday environment, such as persons assaulting you with their thoughts or feelings and from similar intrusions from other psychonoetic dimensions."

"Kosta, can you show us more precisely how to construct the five-pointed star?" Chrysanthos asked. Kostas thought for a few seconds, toked on his pipe a couple of times, and proceeded to answer Chrysanthos.

"Make certain," he cautioned, "that the topmost angle is above your head. The two horizontal angles should cover your arms as you have them stretched out like the horizontal sides of a cross. The tips of the two angles must be at the edge of your two hands, respectively. The other two angles of the five-pointed star should have inside them your two legs spread out and their tips will be at the edge of your two legs."

"I suppose," I said, "that we must imagine ourselves standing with our arms spread out in a horizontal position and our legs opened up, as in the classic design of Leonardo da Vinci?"

"Exactly. The five-pointed star is the symbol of the psychic world. It is also the symbol of the transference of human consciousness from the five senses to the five supersenses."

"In what way is the five-pointed star different as a form of protection from the egg-shaped all-white luminosity we visualize covering us up during our meditations?" Chrysanthos asked.

"The five-pointed star is more concrete. Once you are inside the five-pointed star, nothing—but nothing—can touch you. The only one who can overpower the five-pointed star is the six-pointed star. But whoever is master of the six-pointed star can do only good and express only love. Do you understand?"

"You mean to say that an evil person can master the five-pointed star?" I asked.

"Yes," Kostas replied, "but an evil person will use the five-pointed star upside down, which is the symbol of Lucifer. But the very moment the Researcher of Truth dresses himself or herself with the protection of the five-pointed star no negative thought or influence can have any effect."

"You are saying, if I understand you correctly," I said, "that whoever uses the five-pointed star in the proper way is invoking powers of protection."

"But of course. The five-pointed star itself is an invocation."

"Should we construct the five-pointed star with closed eyes?" I asked.

"Construct it mentally in any way that suits you," Kostas replied. He then demonstrated with certain bodily movements how we must mentally draw upon ourselves the lines as we construct the noetic talisman.

He placed his pipe on a bench and looked around to see whether there were any people on the promenade. He wished to be certain that no one was watching us making strange movements as we tried to master that mental technique of spiritual and psychic protection.

No one was in sight. Kostas stood still facing the sea and the rising moon. Then he spread out his legs as he stretched his left arm to the left and his right arm straight upward. He held himself in that position for a few moments as he waited for us to follow his motions.

"Now start with the top spot over your right arm. Begin to draw the line linking that spot with a straight line to the back of your right leg. Okay?"

We followed his instructions awkwardly. "Now move the line from that spot behind your leg and bring it mentally straight to the edge of your left hand. Now move the line from the edge of your left hand to the edge of your right arm, having both hands stretched out.

"Now you must draw the line from the edge of your right arm to the end of your left leg and then bring the line all the way up over your head to join the spot from where you started.

"Now you have completed the five-pointed star!" Kostas resumed a normal posture.

"Do it once more," he directed us. After a few more tries Chrysanthos and I were both confident that we mastered the technique of drawing the five-pointed star and placing ourselves inside it. Kostas explained that we need not stand up and move our limbs in the way he had just showed us every time we wish to construct the five-pointed star. We should perform those movements mentally, he said. Otherwise we run the risk of being misinterpreted, with possible unpleasant consequences.

"Is it necessary to draw the lines mentally?" I asked.

"Isn't it enough to visualize ourselves inside the five-pointed star?"

"No. The protective power of the five-pointed star is activated in the process of drawing it. It is not sufficient to just see yourself inside it. By repeatedly drawing this protective elemental, because it is really an elemental you are creating, you energize it and give it solidity and substance. Then, once that is done, you can simply focus on it and it will be there to offer you protection at any moment."

I pointed out that while in the theater I constructed the five-pointed star the wrong way, without drawing the lines. Kostas reassured me that since I was with him in reality I had nothing to fear from the possible presence of demonic furies. "Besides," he said, "The Erevna protects you anyway. But in the event that for whatever reason you encounter the *anapodos* [the five-pointed star upside down], just get inside your five-pointed star. Then the anapodos cannot touch you."

"How is that so?" I asked.

"The one locks inside the other like this." Kostas brought his two hands forward, interlocking his fingers. "The summit of your five-pointed star penetrates the anapodos and neutralizes its power."

I asked Kostas to clarify further what kind of dangers the five-pointed star was good for as protection. He explained that whenever we experience any psychonoetic threats, such as bad vibrations coming from whatever causes or dangers that we may encounter in our conscious dreams, the five-pointed star is our best protection. "The moment you notice in the form of a vision or in the form of a symbol the anapodos," Kostas said, "enter at once inside your five-pointed star. But, again, as an initiate of The Erevna you do have protection anyway."

These tips of protection are important to a Researcher of the Truth, Kostas added. When we begin to open up our psychonoetic centers or chakras, he said, we must be ready to protect ourselves from evil intrusions coming from other dimensions.

Kostas repeatedly mentioned that having our chakras closed is a form of protection; "our bodies are our castles," he used to say. Opening our psychonoetic centers prematurely, before mastering thought and emotion, may expose us to negative vibrations and elementals that could disturb our mental and emotional equilibrium.

We had been so engrossed in our peripatetic conversation that I had not realized that it was already past nine in the evening. We had been walking up and down the promenade for more than an hour. I bade Kostas and Chrysanthos goodnight and walked briskly along the road by the sea toward my in-laws' apartment.

The following morning I drove to Daskalos' home and described to him our adventure with the Macedonian wizard. Daskalos roared with laughter as I told my story.

"From what you tell me, this fellow seems to have some abilities," Daskalos said, "but he is not using them properly." Then Daskalos reminisced about Tahram Bey, a Sufi wonder-worker Daskalos knew and respected for his yogic abilities.

"When Tahram Bey came to Cyprus I recognized that the man had power. He himself claimed that although he could make his audiences see whatever he wanted them to see he was going to demonstrate something real and authentic. 'But pay attention,' he warned us. 'No noise whatsoever, because it can cost me my life.' Well, he used to go into a special kind of trance that is unknown to contemporary hypnotists. In that state he used to tell his audience 'You can pierce me with knives and nothing will happen to me. You may shoot me and the bullets will come out the other side without killing me.' He really shocked many doctors in Europe with his demonstrations. They used to pierce him with knives, and the moment they would pull the knives the wounds would automatically heal."

"It sounds totally incredible," I said. But having read about such extraordinary cases as that of the Brazilian villager Arigo [as presented in John Fuller's impeccably documented study *Arigo: Surgeon of the Rusty Knife*] I could not dismiss Daskalos' story as sheer nonsense, as I would have ordinarily done in times past.

"But how did Tahram Bey do it?" I asked.

"He learned how to rarefy his etheric double, to semi-dematerialize his body so that it was not quite solid. The knives could then go through without causing damage to his flesh and bones. There was no gross material resistance to cause wounds. Simply, once the knives were out, the cohesion of his body's cells returned to their normal state." Daskalos joined his two palms to emphasize his point. "Tahram Bey used to do these things. He always warned his audiences to be absolutely silent because what he was doing was extremely dangerous."

"Can you do these feats yourself?" I asked with a light tone. "I mean, can you rarefy the tissues of your body to the point that they could not be affected by knives or bullets?"

"No, I can't. I have never preoccupied myself with this type of fakirlike phenomena. But since I work on the body's tissues I could master such abilities had I spent the time to develop them. But for what purpose? My specialization is different, my job is different," Daskalos concluded with mild laughter.

"What happened to Tahram Bey?" I asked.

Daskalos' face turned gloomy. "Unfortunately, he was killed during one of his performances," he said, and sighed. "While he was in that special trance state pierced with knives some idiot fired his pistol in the air without a silencer. Tahram Bey was shaken out of his trance and immediately there was hemorrhage caused by the wounds on his body. The tissues of his body reacquired their normal state of density and cohesion while knives still pierced his body."

"Did Tahram Bey employ the help of demons to accomplish these feats?" I asked only half-seriously.

"No, no." Daskalos waved his right hand as a way of dismissing that suspicion. "Tahram Bey was a good man.

He accomplished those feats on his own individual effort. There are many methods one can employ to accomplish a certain psychonoetic feat. I witnessed his performance twice and I came to like and appreciate him. I really felt great sadness when I heard of his tragic death. He was a real angel. You see, the purpose for which he performed those phenomena was for the sake of educating and alerting, particularly the doctors on the impact of mind over body. His purpose was the advancement of human knowledge and consciousness, not money or fame.

"Now that magician whose performance you witnessed in Limassol," Daskalos went on mischievously, "revealed to us an aspect of magic that we did not know about."

"What?"

"Until now I thought that there is just white magic and black magic. But this fellow informs us now that there is also blond magic," Daskalos puffed and roared with laughter that I quickly joined in.

When our laughter abated I told Daskalos that the Blond Magus claimed that he meditates backstage and brings the audience inside his magnetism. "That is perhaps how he makes his audiences see things that in reality do not take place," Daskalos said.

"How so?"

"It is possible to spread your aura and through powerful visualizations to make everybody within your aura see as objective facts what you actually create as elementals with your mind. It is, you might say, a form of deception."

"But it implies incredible psychic powers!"

"Of course. Such phenomena support what we teach about the nature of mind. But why abuse such abilities in this manner? Why misuse this supersubstance of mind for the purpose of impressing audiences? Instead of making people see that he is spilling his guts into a bowl it would have been wiser to use such abilities for healing."

"How?"

"He could, for example, help a woman dissolve a tumor

79

in her breast. By visualizing that he is dissolving the tumor with his mind he could induce that visualization within the patient's consciousness. I am telling you it could work. You can really do miracles through this form of autosuggestion. The woman herself could visualize her tumor disappearing and it could very well disappear. He prefers instead to entertain people and make money. What a waste of time and energy.

"Of course," Daskalos continued, with a pensive expression, "this method of autosuggestion is not very orthodox, and we as Researchers of Truth try to avoid it."

"In what way is it unorthodox?" I asked.

"There are possible dangers with autosuggestion in healing. Through this method you may undermine the will of the other, which is an undesirable state. You make the other enter into a state of semihypnotic stupor whereby the will plays little role if any."

"But why not, if it is a question of healing?"

"I prefer the method of persuasion rather than suggestion. In certain cases we do of course use suggestion, but it is more desirable to use persuasion if possible."

"What is the difference between suggestion and persuasion in healing?"

"Through persuasion you engage the will of the other. Not so with suggestion. When a patient comes to me and I say 'Here is where the problem lies, look!' and I touch the place and I tell the patient that now I will dissolve, say, this tumor, then I involve the patient in his or her own healing. Because if I do not involve the patient's will so that the patient can take an active part in his own healing there is the danger that after I detach myself from the patient the symptom may return. But through persuasion the patient believes in his own healing."

"But isn't this a form of suggestion or auto-suggestion?" I asked.

"No, it is persuasion. You don't force another to believe in his own healing. Do you understand?

"Let me make it clearer to you," Daskalos continued as he sensed my perplexity. "Suppose there is a barbarous husband who abuses his wife. One way of dealing with him is to construct an elemental enclosing within it the injunction 'Thou shall not beat up your wife because it is beastly and dishonest.' This is a form of suggestion even if he is not aware of it. This is not the best method to deal with the problem, because his own will is not engaged in the process of change. It may even create such guilt feelings that the person, in extreme cases, may commit suicide, for example."

"Well, what would be a better method under the circumstances?"

"I am coming to that. In the event ordinary persuasion through ordinary counsel was impossible I would do the following. I would leave my body, project an elemental, and enter inside him. Through the process of *at onement* I then become *him* and with my thought I, as himself now and not myself as a separate ego, I say 'I will never repeat this beastly act because of this and that.' And then I would retreat out of him. Through this process he will not realize that his thought, which *is* his thought now, did not originate from himself. But now he will not react against it, because it will be his thought for all practical purposes. The point of this method, you see, is to prevent him from reacting adversely. Otherwise, if you force your suggestion without your consciousness becoming one with the other's ego, he will accept what you suggest as a form of compulsion since he would have no other alternative. Do you understand now what is happening?"

"But isn't what you are saying a more subtle form of compulsion?"

"No, my dear, no. This is what advanced invisible helpers do day and night. Through this method you engage the will of the other. There is no order coming from the outside. It is he who would decide now and not the result of external compulsion.

"Now you may ask me," Daskalos continued, "is it pleasant to enter inside another person, a pathological person, and become that person? And feel like that person during moments of at-onement with him? The answer is no." Daskalos spoke emphatically and tapped my knee. "But so what? If someone is drowning inside a cesspool, shouldn't I enter there, get dirtied, and offer help? Of course I should. I could then come out of it and have a bath. The dirt will be washed away."

"Are there dangers in this method?" I asked.

"Yes, grave dangers. You must be very strong and know what you are doing. Otherwise," Daskalos said with raised eyebrows, "you can end up becoming like the other yourself. If you have the slightest inclination of the other's problem you may take it up yourself. You see, there is always the danger of what I would call psychical contamination that is worse than contamination with viruses. Unless you are advanced and know what you are doing you run the risk of attuning yourself to the vibrations of the other and staying there.

Daskalos leaned back in his armchair and folded his hands over his belly. "Besides," he continued after a momentary pause, "is this not what is happening in society day and night? So we must be very, very careful when we deal with such matters."

"You are suggesting then that one can develop psychic abilities of this sort and the kind that the blond magician claims to possess without necessarily being a particularly spiritually advanced person."

"Yes, of course." Daskalos nodded. "These are the dangers of knowledge. Because knowledge is dangerous for someone who has not gotten rid of egotism. This is why I insist on relentless self-analysis and self-mastery of thought and emotion. Kill egotism completely," Daskalos said, his eyes beaming and his fist clenched, "and let your Spirit-ego that needs neither money nor glory to express itself as Will and be of service to fellow human beings."

Daskalos stopped for a few moments. Then he leaned forward and whispered earnestly, "Don't you think it is time for some coffee?"

I walked to the kitchen chuckling to myself and prepared two cups of Turkish coffee, Daskalos' great weakness. He instructed me to make his very light. His physician had given him strict orders to cut down on caffeine.

Sipping lustfully from his cup, Daskalos, now in a buoyant mood, reminisced of experiences in his youth with magicians who visited the island.

"There was this hypnotist that my father invited for dinner. I was in my early teens at that time. There were several guests in our house that day and the magician wanted to demonstrate his skills. So he asked me whether I would volunteer to be hypnotized. I said okay. He was using a pendulum. I pretended that I was in fact being hypnotized but in reality I was silently projecting hypnotic elementals at him. In no time he dozed off. Then I went to the kitchen and fetched a large onion. I offered it to him as an apple, golden delicious. He ate it with pleasure. When he came back to consciousness he was unaware of what had happened and proceeded to move his pendulum trying to hypnotize me. Everybody in the room was laughing." Daskalos chuckled as he shook his head.

My conversation with Daskalos came to an abrupt end as we heard steps on the front verandah and a knock at the door. I left Daskalos sitting in the living room and let the visitor in. She was an attractive blond woman in her late thirties who spoke English with an accent. She asked whether Daskalos was home. After I invited her to sit in the hallway she briefly told me of her problem. She was a Norwegian artist married to a Greek Cypriot from Paphos. With some hesitation and obvious awkwardness she told me that some friends had urged her to visit Daskalos, who could allegedly assist her in discovering the whereabouts of her lost dog. I tried to keep a straight face as I went to the other room to inform Daskalos of her request.

"My dear," Daskalos said as he came to the hallway rubbing his palms, "we don't do this sort of thing. It is not our specialization. But if you so wish we could try to help you with the problem of your shoulder."

The Norsewoman's eyes widened and her body stiffened for an instant as she realized that this complete stranger had discerned the chronic ailment afflicting her right shoulder. She mumbled in obvious confusion that she didn't know much about Daskalos and that all she was told was that he could discover lost objects, and dogs. After some silent facial encouragement on my part she reluctantly followed Daskalos into the living room.

"Take off your blouse," Daskalos commanded casually, waving upward with his hands. The bewildered woman looked at me aghast, not knowing what to do. She whispered quickly that she was wearing nothing underneath. After reassuring her that that was no problem, I left the room, closing the door behind me and trying my best to control a torrent of giggles.

Twenty minutes had passed when Daskalos emerged from the living room, beaming triumphantly. "It was the blessed moment," he announced with a wide smile. The Norwegian visitor followed him, looking confused about what was happening to her. She had difficulty believing her cure as she kept moving her arm round and round—a motion that she had been incapable of performing, she reported, for years. She thanked Daskalos and left hurriedly. Daskalos kept shaking his head, laughing silently as he pondered the incident. "The Holy Spirit," he said, "works in mysterious ways. Sometimes a patient will come in here with all the faith and eagerness to get healed. And nothing happens. This woman came searching for her dog and got herself healed instead."

"How do you explain that?" I asked.

"Ask God," Daskalos replied and shrugged his shoulders innocently. "Perhaps her time has come for her own awakening. Perhaps this experience will create for her question marks that will lead her on the path of knowledge and the research for the truth."

"I wish, Daskale," I said with a sigh, half seriously, "that I could also cure people just like that. Just the way you do it."

"Kyriaco," Daskalos responded with a grave look as he grabbed me by the arm, "what is really important in life is not so much to spread our hands and heal people but to help them develop their awareness. This is our true mission. If it is allowed for a healing to take place on this material plane it will take place sooner or later. It may take perhaps a little longer without our intervention, but in the final analysis it is the Holy Spirit that does the healing, not us. But what we *can* do is to assist others to move out of their ignorance and embark, consciously now, on the journey of self-discovery. That is why all of us as human beings have descended into these worlds of polarity to begin with. And this is what our real mission as Researchers of the Truth is, to help ourselves and others to awaken from the stupor of unconsciousness and ignorance."

For an instant I felt an almost irresistible urge to weep. Daskalos' words touched me deeply. Given my occupation as an academic and a writer of this material, I felt filled with a sense of unsurpassed purpose.

When we returned to the living room and sat down Daskalos resumed his reminiscences of magicians and wonder-workers.

"During my youth there was this famous German psychic by the name of Hansen who performed at the Magic Palace [a theater in old Nicosia]. If I am not mistaken, Hitler later killed him because he was unwilling to cooperate with the Nazis. Well, I went with my father to the Magic Palace to witness his performance. We were sitting in the second row. He spotted me from my aura, he claimed, and asked me whether I would be willing to participate in an experiment. Even though my father was not very happy about it, I agreed. This German psychic gave me a piece of jewelry that a woman in the audience was wearing. He asked me to feel it with my hands. Then he hid it on an olive tree five miles away from Nicosia. That olive tree was next to Chrysospiliotissa [the Golden Madonna of the Cave, a cave turned into a holy shrine for the Virgin]. I was not aware of the location or the place where he hid the jewelry. He then blindfolded my eyes and got me into a taxi. Someone from the audience unrelated to Hansen sat in the back seat to make certain that there was no fraud."

"What happened?"

"With my eyes closed I guided the driver to the exact spot where the jewelry was hidden."

"No wonder," I joked, "people come to you to find out about their lost dogs!"

Daskalos said that these experiences, which he had from early childhood, made him realize that he was different from other boys of his age.

I pointed out that the experiment he had just described reminded me of the scientific experiments of two American physicists, Russel Targ and Harold Puthoff [*Mind-Reach: Scientists Look at Psychic Ability*], who have demonstrated under controlled conditions the truly extraordinary abilities some psychics possess.

Daskalos repeated what he told me many times, that he was no longer into psychic phenomena like the experiments of his youth or the discovery of lost objects. Yohannan, he said, had given him clear directives that he was supposed to employ his psychic abilities for the sole purpose of healing his fellow human beings.

4 The Understandable and the Real

My conversation with Daskalos was interrupted by knocks at the front door. An aspect of Daskalos' traditional way of operating was to have his house perennially open to anyone seeking his help. It was an approach, however, that became increasingly impractical as his reputation began to expand.

Daskalos was particularly pleased as he welcomed these visitors, an Indian family. With an expansive smile and the traditional Hindu gesture he escorted them into his living room. Judging from his disposition toward them and their demeanor I realized it was not their first visit to Daskalos. Kostas in fact had informed me earlier than an Indian family was seeing Daskalos for spiritual guidance. He told me that Daskalos had been able to help them understand that evolution does not proceed from the animal stage to the human. And certainly not the other way around either, as it is erroneously believed by some sects in the Orient. He explained to them using rational arguments that once an irradiance of a Holy Monad passes through the Human Idea then the entity will embark on an evolutionary trajectory specifically appropriate and unique for that archetypal form. Therefore, no human being as such ever evolved out of an animal and no human being will ever regress to an animal state, the holyspiritual state. When I discussed this issue with Kostas I mentioned that Socrates taught otherwise; in one of his dialogues he sets forth the argument that it is rational to assume that the good and the just will evolve and be reborn into another human body, whereas the unjust may regress and be reborn into the body of an animal—a sort of divine punishment for their transgressions. Kostas scoffed at the idea and with self-confidence argued that Socrates, great teacher that he was, was simply unable to penetrate deep enough into the mysteries to recognize the fallacy of his position.

Daskalos introduced me to his guests. The father, an ebullient and talkative man in his early fifties, was an employee of the Indian Embassy. His middle-aged wife, dressed in her traditional sari, was no less gregarious. Like her husband she was of less than medium height and slightly overweight. They were accompanied by two of their children. Their daughter, an attractive, bright-eyed twenty-year-old was visiting the island from London, where she was a student. Their teen-age son was preparing to fly to the United States to begin his university education. After the happy greetings the father proceeded to explain the cause of their visit.

"The reason we have come to you, Daskale," the man began gravely, "is to ask for your advice about a serious family matter."

"I am listening," Daskalos replied as we sat around. (I had been invited to stay.)

The visitors proceeded to explain that their eldest daughter, who was completing her graduate education in business administration in America, had been asked to marry by a successful and wealthy Indian engineer, a permanent resident of the United States. The daughter so far resisted her parents' pressure; she was not in the least interested to wed that particular suitor. Daskalos promptly told them that the wishes of their daughter must be respected.

"You mean we must not force her to marry him?" the father asked, showing surprise at Daskalos' quick reply.

"Certainly not," Daskalos responded with emphasis as his eyes widened. The faces of the parents dropped gloomily, but I noticed a broad smile on the face of the younger daughter.

"But, Daskale," the wife protested, "we have already gone to dinner with that boy and we have promised our daughter to him. We have given our word of honor and we have accepted his offer. He is so fond of her. I am afraid if we now tell him that we have changed our minds he may commit suicide. What can we do?"

After a few moments of silence Daskalos asked "Do you have a picture of him?"

"Yes, yes! Here it is," the mother replied, hurriedly pulling a photograph from her purse.

"Oh my God! Oh my God!" Daskalos reacted as he looked at the portrait of the would-be bridegroom. He made such a theatrical grimace that I was forced to control potentially explosive laughter.

"My dearest lady," Daskalos said earnestly, "let me ask you a question. How would you like to be in bed with this man and wake morning after morning to gaze at him snoring next to you?"

The Indian woman, obviously embarrassed by Daskalos' forthright question, moved several times with marked discomfort within her sari but said nothing. Daskalos passed the picture to me. I could see his point.

"Daskale, I am afraid you do not understand," the man protested. "We Indians have different customs and we are not as good-looking as you Europeans."

"Nonsense! Just look at your daughter and your wife.

And just look at this handsome son of yours, and yourself."
A smile appeared on the face of the father.

"But Daskale," the wife implored, "this boy may not be handsome but he has such a good heart."

"Now look here," Daskalos said, a serious look on his face. "Had your daughter not minded his appearance and had she really cared for this man, I would give my blessing to this marriage. But your daughter is vehemently against marrying this man. For the sake of the happiness and well-being of your child I would advise you not to exert pressure on her to marry him. And frankly," Daskalos continued with a mischievous grimace, "had I been your daughter I would have preferred to marry a man who would attract me physically and let him not be perfect."

"That does it," the husband announced. "The issue is closed. We shall not force her to marry him."

His wife did not seem to be too happy but went along with the decision of her spouse. The daughter and son, however, were beaming. Daskalos told me later he was pleased that he managed to rescue a woman from being forced into a miserable marriage.

I left Daskalos' house in the early afternoon. I tried to isolate myself at home for several hours so that I could catch up with my note-taking. In a society where privacy is a totally alien concept it was not an easy task. Acquaintances, relatives, friends, and close friends would routinely move in and out of our house talking about politics, Daskalos, and anything else that would offer an excuse for socializing. Being a product of that cultural setting myself and therefore easily seduced by local habits, I had to exert an extra conscious effort to find myself alone with my typewriter. I planned to meet Kostas the following afternoon when a meeting of one of his Limassol circles was scheduled and I needed to catch up with my writing before new field material began piling up.

I worked until late in the evening. Emily and the children were already asleep. Before joining them I decided to take a short walk and refresh my mind and body with the cool evening breezes. Upon my return, the moment I entered the house I began feeling an excruciating pain in my right leg. I could not understand what could have happened. I had never had any problems with my legs. The pain reached a point where I could not walk and was intensifying. It was as if someone was torturing my leg. I tried to rub it with alcohol, but to no avail. The pain was so intense that I felt my eyes getting moist. I thought for a moment that I was going to become permanently crippled and was ready to wake Emily so that she would rush me to the hospital. But I changed my mind. With great effort I reached my bed and lay down. I closed my eyes and began breathing deeply. I thought to myself that this was perhaps a good opportunity to practice some of Daskalos' teachings. When that idea crossed my mind my despair began to vanish. I began to view my pain as a challenge. I knew that visualization can be effective in healing, but I was not certain whether I had the necessary power of concentration. This was an opportunity to test it, I thought. I also knew that many determined and terminally ill patients cured themselves through appropriate visualizations. I have heard, for example, of cancer patients cleansing themselves by systematically directing certain color visualizations to the afflicted area of their bodies. A boy cured himself by visualizing Pac-Man [character in children's computer games] eating up the cancer cells.

I was surprised to discover that the pain itself helped me concentrate and focus my attention. My strong desire to have my leg healed was too powerful to allow any other thoughts to intrude. I visualized my leg covered with a pulsating and vibrant all-white luminosity. As I was doing that I made a strong suggestion to myself that by morning my leg must be cured and no trace of my pain remain. I am not certain what actually happened after that. I must have fallen asleep while I visualized my leg swimming within that all-white irradiation. I did remember, however, that the moment I began the deep breathing and the mental exercise I began feeling a partial relief, as if I had placed on the afflicted area some magical potion. When I woke up in the morning there was no trace of my ordeal.

The following afternoon I met Kostas in Limassol and described what had happened the night before. He smiled. "It was just a lesson for your spiritual growth." He shrugged and left it at that. I never learned what the problem with my leg was, nor did I care to find out. I did, however, learn that the key to self-healing, and nonmedical healing in general, is undistracted and focused concentration combined with a powerful desire for healing.

After a light dinner together Kostas and I drove to the industrial section of Limassol where he was scheduled to offer his weekly lesson. One of his disciples, a small-scale industrialist, provided a room in his factory as a temporary accommodation for the Limassol branch of The Erevna. The circles were becoming larger and the seventy or so participants in each of them could no longer be accommodated within private living rooms.

The factory atmosphere was a most unlikely spot for a spiritual gathering. But as far as Kostas was concerned it served the needs of The Erevna even though the environmental ambiance was more appropriate for a local labor union gathering. Kostas even suggested that there were advantages in having the circles meet in the industrial section. The meetings took place after hours, when the factories were closed and therefore there were no nosy bystanders to create potential irritations.

Kostas spent about forty-five minutes in another room carrying out healing and providing counseling to those in need, his customary procedure before any meeting began. His followers would either carry pictures of friends and relatives for diagnosis or healing from a distance or seek advice and healing for themselves. The meeting began after everybody gathered and after Kostas managed to give a private hearing to anybody who wished to have one.

"Today," Kostas began, "we shall pay special attention to the distinction between the Real and the understandable or comprehensible part of the Real. What is reality? People use this term constantly yet rarely ever delve into its great meaning.

Kostas paused for a few seconds. "We have said repeatedly that reality is another word for the Absolute. It is life itself, the expression of which are the laws, the causes, the ideas. Reality is our inner self as Holy Monad; that is, ourselves beyond time and space. However, to become understandable to human consciousness it is imperative that its projections and manifestations must first be studied.

"We are now aware of two situations, the Real and the understandable. To repeat, the Real is the unchangeable, eternal Absolute, the expression of which is the phenomenon of life.

"Now, we have identified the Absolute with life itself. And *it is* life. However, life behind the phenomenon of life is beyond the comprehension of ordinary human consciousness. Life in itself, not the phenomenon of life, cannot be comprehended through the construction of meanings and noetic images. It will become understandable only by the Holy Monad itself and its projection, the soul self-consciousness. It will happen at the point when a given self-consciousness becomes disentangled from the limitations and constraints of understandable reality and penetrates into the truly Real, its inner self, the Pneuma. And I must remind you that ourself as reality is not only that part which we call the Holy Monad but our self-realized soul as well. I mean by that the part of ourselves which has descended into the worlds of separateness and polarity, accumulated experiences resulting from repeated incarnations under the laws of karma and finally returned to the point of its origin. When that happens—that is, at the point of Theosis—every self-consciousness will have knowledge of God and of its own godliness. It will have knowledge of the Real."

Kostas paused for a few moments and looked at his audience with characteristic intensity to see whether his disciples were grasping the ideas he was projecting. After answering a few questions he proceeded.

"Now, in order to eventually acquire knowledge of the Real we must exhaust our exploration into phenomenal reality or the understandable expression of the Real. We must carefully study the projections and effects of the Real. And if reality can be identified as the law, cause, and idea, the understandable parts of the Real are its projections of Mind. And we have said many times that Mind is that supersubstance that the Real employs to manifest Itself. Remember that all the universes, including the gross material, are manifestations of Mind."

Someone interrupted: "What you are really saying, Kosta, if I understand you correctly, is that phenomenal reality is understandable reality. The cause behind all the phenomena is reality in itself and is beyond the understanding and comprehension of ordinary consciousness."

"Well said. But keep in mind that the Absolute as reality is even beyond the causes, the laws, the ideas that are themselves Its manifestations. Perpetually meditating within the Eternal Present, the Absolute expresses Itself as causes, laws, ideas. There are really no words to describe this divine condition."

"Can we perhaps assume," Andros (an architect in his late thirties) interjected, "that this condition is equivalent to a state whereby God enters into a form of dreaming?"

"No! From the perspective of the truly Real this is tantamount to blasphemy," Kostas blurted, then laughed lightly at his use of the anachronistic term. "Some schools in the Orient have taught that God, dreaming within Himself, within His meditation, projects dynamically and logoically the universes. A dreaming God?" Kostas asked and raised his eyebrows, sharp irony in his voice.

"We know that on the basis of The Erevna dreaming is the pulling up from within the subconscious or memory, including even Universal Memory, already-existing conditions which we experience in a given manner. This is what we understand as dreaming. It is a different condition, however, when we ourselves focus our attention and consciously meditate by utilizing Mind and deliberately forming noetic images. This is no longer dreaming but conscious, positive, and purposeful work.

"By studying these two radically different conditions we can arrive at the realization that the Absolute within Its self-sufficiency is not dreaming. Rather It projects Itself and creates the universes through purposeful and superconscious meditation, call it divine reasoning if you will.

"There is another mistake," Kostas went on as everybody listened attentively, "that a lot of people commit in reference to the nature of God. They assume that a static God is the cause of everything. But God is behind all causes. That is, it is His divine will that becomes the cause. God is not a cause. Here is some advice. For the time being do not try through arguments and the formation of meanings via our material brain to understand what the Absolute is really like. It is equally fruitless to attempt to comprehend through the formation of noetic images, and even through meditation, what our inner selves as Holy Monads are really like."

"What then must we understand with the term Absolute and Holy Monad?" someone asked, puzzled and with some agitation.

"Consider both the Absolute and yourself as a Holy Monad The Reality without attempting through such words to stimulate the construction of meanings and interpretations.

"As we have explained many times before, through Its divine reasoning, through Its meditation, the Absolute has the power within Itself to create Mind, the supersubstance with which and through which the universes are constructed. The Absolute creates. Pay attention to this word. Is creation possible through dreaming? Or is creation the product of divine reasoning and meditation through Will, Power, and Wisdom?

"We observe that this entity on planet earth which we call the human individual has constructed with the limitations of his reasoning marvelous things. Of course in no way can human intelligence match the creative intelligence of the Absolute. Yet humans have utilized their minds and brought about wondrous creations. And I ask now: Is it possible for the effect to be greater than its cause? Can this creation which we call the human being express a form of self-conscious reasoning, creating conditions and wondrous things, be the product of a cause lesser than itself?

"Consider it axiomatic," Kostas said after he let his audience assimilate for a few seconds the ideas he was presenting, "that the cause can never be weaker or smaller than its effects.

"Let us be realistic. Only one cosmic day separates human beings from the condition in which they lived while in caves holding clubs and sticks. Humans today are still at the infantile stage of their development. However, as souls and not as intoxicated present personalities they will inevitably come of age and will eventually express their divine self-consciousness within all the realms of creation—the gross material, the psychic, and the noetic."

"How are human beings going to be centuries from now?" someone asked. Kostas answered that human beings will be expressing themselves through an increasingly expanded circle of awareness until they reach total awareness with the attainment of God-realization. He then proceeded to elaborate further on the relationship between the Real and the understandable.

"Human beings today, including most of the scientists, study phenomena which they assume are products of accidents. This is incredible. They study these phenomena, which are really the expression of a deeper reality, without having the slightest desire or inclination to penetrate into this reality. Some day, you see, human beings will become conscious of the Real. For the time being we are all within the worlds of the understandable. We live within a gross material world, on the surface of this planet. After studying this situation deeply serious mystics through the centuries have arrived at the following conclusion: The understandable is the product of time and space, a nonexistent condition within the Real. Time and space, however, are the expression of a reality which we have called the Eternal Present. Therefore, past, present, and future expressing the succession of events and phenomena within time and space belong to the understandable projection of the Real. Only now some scientists, very few in number, are beginning to approach these truths."

Kostas then further explained the meaning of time and space, which are, he claimed, subjective conditions. Every human being perceives time and space differently.

I pointed out from my front-row seat that indeed this idea is not new and that with the development of anthropological literature it has been demonstrated that human beings are conditioned to perceive time and space in culturally unique ways.

"Fine," Kostas responded. "Yet again, behind the understandable there is the Real as the source that offers us the various impressions of time and space that we study and try to comprehend.

"Now where do I want to arrive at? When you develop on The Path and you begin to live more consciously within the psychic dimensions you will discover that the problem of the distinction between the Real and the understandable is more or less identical with the one we face within the gross material world. The psychic worlds are also worlds of the understandable. The psychic world, as well as the noetic, is a product of the same deep reality that is beyond conceptual understanding. It is the same deep reality that offers us the understandable reality within the gross material universe. For there really are not two, three, or four worlds. In reality there is only one world, with the same deep center but expressed in variable ways. Yes, as Christ said, it is the house of our father within which there are many mansions. Pay attention to this point."

Someone asked: "If the worlds of the psychonoetic dimensions are also worlds of the understandable and not of the Real, then what are the differences between the understandable within gross matter as compared with the understandable within the psychonoetic dimensions?"

"Good question," Kostas responded. "There are differences, of course. Here, within gross matter, the comprehensible—that is, the noetic images and meanings—are created through impressions which we receive via the five senses from outside our gross material body. We then interpret these impressions that come from the outside with psychic and noetic light. In other words, the outside impressions entering our body through gross material light cause a vibration on our psychic and noetic bodies.

"Now, both the psychic and the noetic light are much more intense and much more complete in their expression than light within the gross material dimension. When you as a self-conscious personality acquire knowledge, let us say, of an object or a landscape through gross material light, time and space are of paramount significance. Time and space are, as we have said, of central importance as impressions within the gross material universe. Within gross matter impressions move from the outside toward the inside, generating within us meanings and psychonoetic images. However, when we enter the psychic worlds we no longer get impressions in this manner—that is, from the outside toward the inside. Rather it is from *within* us that we acquire these impressions.

"Most people," I pointed out, "are not aware of this dynamic."

"True. Most people live within the psychic dimensions carrying along the illusions of the gross material level," Kostas said. "However, it is quite different. Within the gross material world we need to approach things in order to know them. Within the psychic worlds everything comes to us. And we have said many times in the past that with the psychic and noetic light we can see everything beyond the phenomenon of time and space. Haven't we said that within the fourth dimension the meaning of space is transcended? All we have to do within these dimensions is to focus on something within ourselves and we are there. Everything is within us. Inside the fourth dimension we need not move our psychic body to go here and there as we do within the gross material universe. Within the psychonoetic dimensions, as we said, everything comes to us by simply focusing there."

I asked: "Could we assume, then, that the experiences within the psychonoetic dimensions are closer to the Real than experiences within gross matter?"

"Definitely. The higher we move within the psychonoetic dimensions the closer we are to what is truly real. But remember that all these worlds are worlds of the understandable and not of the Real. However, within the psychic and the noetic light we *are* whatever comes to our awareness. Therefore, within these dimensions we can explore and become more conscious of the Real that is behind everything comprehensible or understandable. We do not have the obstacles and the limitations of the gross material universe that makes it much more difficult for us to get glimpses of the Real. Within gross matter people become seduced with the enchantment of the four elements far more readily. They become engrossed and blinded by the interpretations—or misinterpretations, to be more accurate —that are provided to them by the five senses. They perceive this world of gross matter as the paramount reality. They see it, touch it, feel it as solid and assume that this is reality. In truth it is not. What they misinterpret as real is only the understandable, the perishable and ever-changing manifestation of the Real."

Kostas stopped for a moment and gazed at his audience.

He answered several more questions and then proceeded with the lesson.

"When one penetrates from the understandable into the Real then one acquires power over the worlds of the understandable. The phenomena that many advanced mystics have been demonstrating through the aeons and which have been called 'miracles,' like materializations, dematerializations, and so on, are possible when these mystics manage to enter into the realm of the Real. Such phenomena are possible only when we transcend the worlds of the understandable that limit and constrain the power of our Will springing from our innermost Self. When we advance and enter into the world of the Real, anything is possible for us. We can then express ourselves in a fuller and more complete manner through the power inherent in us as divine beings whose true and inner core, the Pneuma, is always grounded within the Real.

"The advanced mystic," Kostas continued, "the advanced Researcher of the Truth acquires certain psychonoetic abilities that appear inconceivable to ordinary human beings by penetrating into the realm of the Real. The mystic, for example, can enter inside the psychic worlds any time he or she wishes through superconscious self-awareness without closing the doors of perception to experiences that are taking place in the gross material world. Additionally, the mystic, by entering into the Real, moves beyond time and space and therefore is capable of acquiring impressions and experiences simultaneously from all the dimensions of life—from the gross material, the psychic, the noetic, and beyond."

Responding to a question, Kostas elaborated on time and space: "They are understandable realities within the gross material universe as well as within the psychic and noetic dimensions. It is from this vantage point that we must begin our research. Meanings of time and space are not static. They are variable and relative."

He then illustrated this point with more concrete examples. "Let us say an event is taking place and we perceive it in a certain way. Time and space are dressed with meaning derived from the gross material level. If we unearth the same event from our memory we will have the meanings of space and time as they are related to that event. Nevertheless, these meanings are markedly different from the meanings we had formulated earlier while we were experiencing that event.

"Let me explain. Suppose we have gone for an excursion the day before. Say we went to the mountains and then down to the sea. During the journey we focused our attention and absorbed certain experiences. Ordinary human beings, as we said before, absorb only a very small fraction of possible experiences because they do not relate to their surroundings in full consciousness. They don't know how to focus their attention consciously and consequently they carry on their daily lives in monotonous routines and mechanical ways. Yet during such an excursion every human being would have certain experiences.

"Today someone who had those experiences yesterday can bring forward from his memory the experiences of that journey. He can see himself getting off the bus, making so many steps forward, and so on. And within his consciousness he relives the meaning of space within the context of his experience. The time element now is very different. It is so because he can stop his concentration on that experience, move to something completely different, and then return if he wishes to the original experience of the journey. Therefore, motion within time inside the psychic and noetic dimensions is experienced differently than within the gross material reality. Within gross matter one does not have the capacity to return to events that have taken place. However, through memory one can relive and reexperience the earlier sentiments—feelings and thoughts associated, in this case, with the journey.

"The event has taken place only once within the gross material world. However, within time we can repeat the

same event as a set of meanings within our memory. And
if we wish we can even alter or distort the experience we
have had earlier within the gross material world.

"Later we will practice certain psychonoetic exercises
designed to increase our ability to understand the impact
that the meaning of space and time has over our selfcon-
sciousness. (By that I mean our self-consciousness as present personality.) We want to widen our limited awareness
of the present personality so that it will become assimilated with the inner self and radiate its soul-self-conscious-
ness. And when finally as complete self-consciousness, as
masters of the meanings of the understandable in relationship to time and space, we enter inside the Real we shall be
one of those who shall 'not taste' death, as the Most Beloved One has said once to His disciples. Death is a meaning. It is a meaning of total transformation from an
immortal and immutable center which absorbs impressions and experiences. Death is not the end of the inner
self, which ultimately is the one that absorbs and interprets
these impressions. When we reach that state we will understand Saint Paul's words that 'the perishable puts on the
imperishable, and the mortal puts on immortality.' "

With these remarks Kostas, eyes beaming, completed the
lesson on the understandable and the Real. He concluded
with his customary saying, "Στῶμεν καλῶς ἐν Κυρίω
Πάντοτε" [With purity in our hearts we stand by the Lord,
always], a saying similar to what is routinely chanted in
Greek Orthodox liturgies.

"Now let us proceed with the meditation exercises,"
Kostas said after a few moments. "Let us start with the
exercise to replenish our body's energy."

We closed our eyes and sat as comfortably as we could.
Someone turned most of the lights off to facilitate our meditation.

"Be calm and tranquil. Remove from your mind everything that preoccupies your present personality," Kostas
began in a slow, firm tone. "Begin by repeating for a while

the word *Love*. Do that many times and with a tempo that is most suitable to you. Love . . . , Love . . . , Love. . . . Kostas lowered his voice while muttering the word. "Feel and loosen every muscle in your body. Prevent any other thoughts from entering your mind. By repeating the word *Love* you are invoking complete coordination with the Love of the Absolute. You now reach a state of complete peace and serenity. Nothing occupies your thoughts any more. You reach a point now of real peace and tranquility.

"Now begin to visualize yourself glowing within an all-white irradiance and begin to feel that you are within every particle and every cell of your material existence. You can feel completely the confinement of your form and shape.

"Begin now to breathe deeply and comfortably. Deep and comfortable breathing. You reach a point now that you feel yourself breathing from every cell and every particle of your material existence. You are breathing from each particle and from each cell. Energize this particular form of breathing. Fill yourself with living etheric energy from every cell and every particle of your body.

"With each breath you become whiter and whiter. Visualize it. You are becoming whiter and whiter. Feel it. Each time you exhale you breathe out every impurity that tends to stain your whiteness."

We kept our eyes closed and continued our meditation. "Offer your gratitude to the Holy Spirit which builds and maintains your material body," Kostas instructed. "Wish good health to reign within your bodies. Wish for calmness and tranquility within your present personality. Wish for good judgment, wisdom; wish for the right use of the divine gift of thought.

"That will be all. This exercise can fill you with energy every time you feel drained," Kostas said. Our exercise had lasted roughly ten minutes.

After we stretched for a few moments Kostas guided us through another meditation exercise, one he said was important for the mastery of the various properties of etheric vitality which would help us become healers and promote the harmonious development of the three bodies.

Daskalos and Kostas have taught that etheric vitality can be classified into its four primary functions, which must be mastered if one is to become a conscious healer and an initiate into superconscious levels of self-awareness. The functions of etheric vitality are the *kinetic* property, which makes movement and vibration possible; the *sensate* property, which makes feelings, sentiments, and sense experience possible; the *imprinting* property, which makes the construction of thought forms and noetic images possible; and the *creative* property, which makes life itself and the phenomena of materialization and dematerialization possible. The aim of the Researcher of Truth is to master the first three through meditation exercises. Then the fourth will develop naturally as a consequence of the mastery of the other properties. The creative property of etheric vitality is within the province of the Holy Spirit that makes healing itself possible.

We closed our eyes as Kostas repeated the instructions to place ourselves in a state of total relaxation: "You are now at a state of real calmness and tranquility. Employing the sensate property of etheric vitality, feel the soles of both your feet. Now employ the kinetic property of ether and feel the movement upward through your feet to your ankles. The kinetic and the sensate property of ether combined should make you feel as if you are putting on your socks. Continue the movement upward through your knees, up through the thighs, and arrive at the point where your legs join the pelvis at the hips. Using the sensate property of ether, feel your legs up to the hips. It feels as if you have put on tights. Now, employing the imprinting property of etheric energy, visualize both your legs within an all-white irradiance. It is an irradiance of white light. All-white legs. But pay attention: the all-white irradiance you visualize is the color of white snow, of clean cotton wool.

It is not something smooth or marblelike. It is an irradiance of light. Make a strong wish for good health to your legs.

"Employing the kinetic property of ether again," Kostas continued, "move upward through the pelvis. You now begin to move upward inside your abdominal region. Advance slowly upward; advance until you reach the rib cage. Employing the sensate property of etheric vitality, feel the region to the cage of the rib. Now, using the imprinting property of etheric vitality, visualize inside and around the abdominal region a white-blue glow of misty light. See an irradiance of white-blue light in and around the abdomen. Wish good health to your gross material body. Right here is the center of life for your gross material body. It is your solar plexus.

"Employing the kinetic property of etheric energy again, move upward and begin to penetrate inside your chest. Movement upward inside the chest. Advance slowly, slowly, and now—using the sensate property of etheric vitality—feel inside and all around your entire chest area. Employing the imprinting property of etheric vitality, visualize now inside and around the chest an all white-rose misty light, a radiance of white-rose light, and wish good health to your psychic body. Wish good health to the world of your emotions. Wish calmness and tranquility to your present personality in its totality.

"Using the kinetic property of etheric vitality again, move upward through your shoulders and then down inside your two arms and hands. Move down inside your arms. The movement is downward. Advance slowly downward inside both your arms, elbows, and reach the wrists, palms, fingers. You have now reached the tips of your fingers. Using the sensate property of ether, feel inside both your arms, elbows, and reach the wrists, palms, fingers. You have now reached the tips of your fingers. Using the sensate property of ether, feel inside both your arms to the tips of your fingers and using the imprinting property visualize both your arms within an all-white irradiance. Wish good health inside both your arms. Wish your two hands to become agents for healing the pain of your fellow human beings. Wish that their touch will bestow upon your fellow human beings the blessings of the Absolute.

"Employing the kinetic property of etheric energy, proceed toward your thyroid. Using the imprinting property of etheric vitality, visualize that a misty orange light surrounds the thyroid. An irradiance of orange color surrounds the thyroid. This is a center for the circulation of the energies within your three bodies. Wish good health to your three bodies.

"Employing the kinetic property of etheric energy again, move upward. You now begin to enter inside your head. Slowly upward, inside your head. Employing the sensate property of etheric vitality, feel your head. Now, employing the imprinting property, visualize a misty white-golden light inside and around your head. An irradiance of white-golden light inside and around your head. Wish good health to your noetic body. Pay attention to what will be said now. Wish right use of the divine gift of thought, wish for right thinking, right judgment.

"Employing the sensate property of etheric energy," Kostas continued, "you now find yourself in every particle and every cell of your material existence. By employing the imprinting property of etheric vitality you visualize white-golden color inside and around the head, white-rose in and around the chest, white-blue in the abdomen, and all-white arms and legs. In addition, now visualize simultaneously yourselves surrounded by an all-white irradiance. Wish this all-white misty irradiance to protect you from anything that may wish to harm you. Shield your present personality with this all-white egg-shaped irradiance. Will that it protect you, that it dissolve harmful thoughts and elementals created by those who may wish you harm. But you must not allow these elementals to return to their source. If they did return they would grow seven times their original force as they hit the other person. You must not wish that. Focus your mind on this to give you protection by dissolving these elementals the moment they hit your aura. Contribute to the clearing up of our planet from evil, from the pollution of ignorance. Wish good health to your present personality as a whole. That will be all."

We gradually came out of our meditation, which had lasted close to twenty minutes. Kostas told us it is essential that we practice this meditation daily. It will help us, he said, to master the various properties of etheric vitality as well as contribute to the health and general well-being of our three bodies, the world of our thoughts, feelings, and gross material body.

After the meeting a group of us, including Kostas, went to a seaside fish restaurant far from the tourist traffic, to spend the evening eating and talking. We ended up discussing politics, an unavoidable subject of conversation in any gathering on Cyprus.

5 Artist of the Heart

I brought a chair from the living room and sat next to Daskalos. I watched him complete a painting he had been working on for about a week, on and off. He had been painting since six o'clock in the morning in his makeshift studio, a small bedroom turned atelier. It was 9 A.M. when I met with him.

"I was inspired to make this painting after I watched a ballet performance of *Swan Lake*," Daskalos said after I lowered the volume on the tape recorder blasting classical music. "The bowing ballerina," he said as he continued to work on the canvas, "symbolizes the ego soul as she completes her dance, the life cycle. She is ready now to leave this world. The swan over the ballerina is the material body that must die, and the background hills and cypress trees are the psychic worlds the ballerina will enter upon leaving this life of gross material existence."

"I like this painting," I exclaimed, and we discussed art

as Daskalos worked with his brushes. He seemed pleased with my reaction since on many occasions I had criticized his artistic productions. I pointed out to him before that his painting could in no way be compared with his profound and awe-inspiring insights into reality and human nature. Knowing the depth of his self-confidence, I was not worried about offending him with my irreverent remarks about his art. In his younger years he had produced, in my opinion, noteworthy pieces, usually landscapes of the psychonoetic planes, he claimed. Some of them were truly impressive. But of late I found Daskalos' paintings rather rough and hastily put together—certainly not candidates for museum collections.

Daskalos informed me once that in one of his incarnations he was a professional painter during the time of Leonardo da Vinci. "In this life," he explained to me, "I chose to focus my attention and channel my energies elsewhere.

"Hey Kyriaco"—with a smile he gave me a light nudge with his left elbow—"in this life I prefer to paint on people's souls. To put fire in their hearts so that they may awaken to their true nature and develop their capacity for love and compassion. Out of a hundred artists only two or three are real artists. The rest are just painters. I am one of those." He applied a heavy dose of green paint on one of the cypress trees.

In fact, Daskalos painted to supplement his very modest pension and support needy relatives as well as to raise some money for charities. That was apparently his main concern rather than the artistry of his work. Many of his paintings were placed in raffles by his students and the proceeds were used for various charitable activities.

"There is so much pain in this world of ours," Daskalos lamented, "that we must be ready as Researchers of the Truth to help and be of service."

A few weeks ago I found him furiously hand-washing army blankets he had bought for a refugee family from Lebanon. They had been expelled from Germany, then from

France, and finally a boat had literally dumped them on Cyprus. They were living in the open air under some olive trees. Their case came to Daskalos' attention after the mother of four went into a church in Strovolos and in her despair began screaming for help. She cried that they were Christians too and asked for help because her family had neither food nor a roof over its heads. In Lebanon they had been a rich Protestant family, but the war wiped out all their wealth and they became refugees wandering from country to country. The woman went so far as to proclaim that they were willing to be baptized Orthodox. The local immigration officials were ready to follow the examples of the Germans and French, but with Daskalos' energetic intervention the family was given permission to stay. He found a job for the man as a painter of automobiles and offered regular Greek lessons to the three teen-age boys.

"Sometimes," Daskalos said with a sigh as he continued painting, "I just don't understand why God allows so much pain and suffering. Look what is happening in the Middle East. So much bloodshed, so much destruction. It is hard even for masters to cope with so much savagery."

At the start of the meeting of the inner circle the previous week Daskalos took off his white robe and with unusual agitation began protesting at the insufferable conditions prevailing at the war front between Iran and Iraq. While in a state of exomatosis, he claimed, he witnessed a battle that cost the lives of over a thousand young soldiers and blood was flowing "like a river." He then said "I stood there with my etheric body stupefied at what I witnessed. Then I raised my hands upward and cried out 'Why, my God, why?' And at that very moment I felt Father Yohannan behind me. He closed my mouth with his hand and whispered to be quiet. I asked myself what kind of human beings send those children to be maimed and blown up carrying around their necks keys to paradise? Can you please tell me?" The rest of us remained silent.

Daskalos' sudden outburst was uncharacteristic. It was

also interesting that during the following morning I heard on the news of a battle at the Iran–Iraq border described by the announcer almost as Daskalos had: blood running "like a river."

"Sometimes I ask myself," Daskalos continued as I watched him paint, "why did God give man so much freedom to cause such incredible suffering to his fellow human beings?"

"And you cannot explain that?"

"No, I can explain it theoretically, but I am a human being and it is difficult for me to accept it emotionally. After all, man is God and no one can deprive him of his divine properties of freedom."

"But what you doubt is why human beings should have such capacity to inflict so much pain and evil."

"Yes. Why should human beings have such a right? And then that endless jogging through the aeons: I do you in, you do me in; I kill you, you kill me; and on and on. Of course I accept the law of karma. No human being suffers without deserving that suffering. But you cannot know the reason behind the suffering. And when at a certain stage of your spiritual evolution you are in a position to penetrate into reality, then you will be able to understand the reasons. The law is absolutely just, but it does not cease to be painful." Daskalos momentarily stopped his painting as he turned toward me. "Now you may raise the question 'and why doesn't God intervene at a certain moment to silence the pain?' He has done something far superior. He created human beings in such a way as to be incapable of remembering pain. This is very, very significant. It is Divine Mercy at work. I understand Divine Mercy as God's intervention to subtract from the individual the *anamnesis* [remembrance] of pain. God has offered the individual anamnesis of events and incidents but not the pain experienced during these events. And this is true for pain suffered on the gross material body as well as on the psychic and the noetic bodies. This is indeed a great attribute of Divine

111

Mercy," Daskalos concluded, an expression of awe on his face.

"But the pain offers you lessons for spiritual growth."

"Yes, of course." Daskalos carefully put some finishing touches on the swan's white neck with his brush. "Let me ask you a question. Have you ever undergone an operation?"

"No."

"Have you ever gone through some kind of illness or something that caused you a lot of pain?"

"Well," I said, "in my early teens I broke my right arm as I jumped from a tree holding an umbrella. It was very painful."

"Today," Daskalos continued, "you remember the breaking of your arm, but no matter how much you may try you can never remember the pain you experienced during that incident."

"If I was capable of remembering that I would feel the pain."

"Exactly. This is Divine Mercy. It does not allow you to remember your pain. And the more intense the pain is, the easier it is for you to forget it. So many things human beings can remember, so many things they can shape with their mind and thoughts, but never pain. And I ask the question now, Does God feel pain whenever we feel pain? What do you say?" Daskalos stopped painting for a moment to turn and look at me.

"I suppose God must feel pain, since everything is inside Him."

"Of course. However, His pain is not the same as ours. It is analogous to pricking a child with a needle, causing a lot of agony and crying. For an adult the same needle will hardly be felt. This is a great principle within creation."

"I suppose this is what you told us before—that the Christ Logos can absorb and nullify the painful burdens of humanity. It is that which allows human beings to be able through love to bear each other's burdens. The greatest portion of karma can then be nullified and only a small fraction of the actual pain is experienced."

"Exactly."

"While we are talking about pain, Daskale," I said as he continued painting, "what is the relationship of pain to joy, laughter, and happiness?"

"Well, when the pain is over you simply remember it as an event. Of course, you avoid those events that caused you pain in the first place, and then you feel a certain relief. It is part of your experience."

"Why is Christ presented in many of the icons as one who does not seem to have joy, laughter—or sadness, for that matter?"

Daskalos abruptly lifted his brush from the canvas. "Who told you that Christ didn't have joy and laughter?"

"That is how He is portrayed in many of the icons."

"It is precisely because those who painted Christ never met Him or knew anything about His personality. If you would ask someone who had experienced Jesus Christ during His lifetime he would have reported to you that He did indeed laugh, had humor, and had the sweetest smile that any human being could possibly have."

In an earlier encounter Daskalos had described to me in great detail a life he lived during the time of Jesus. During that incarnation he used to be taken to Jesus with other children by Yohannan, John the Beloved. That is how he knew, he claimed, of the personality of Jesus.

"Had Jesus been incapable of laughter and joy, then why did He frequent the various events associated with joy and merrymaking such as weddings and banquets. Of course He did not need all that. Yet He participated and shared the happiness and joy of His fellow human beings. And just remember that His first miracle was to turn water into wine so that the guests at the wedding feast could celebrate and enjoy themselves. Jesus Christ was not an austere puritan as He is often portrayed in the icons of ignorant monks."

"Within Christianity," I said as Daskalos resumed painting, "we notice a great emphasis on the notion of suffering. In the Eastern religions, on the other hand, we find the idea of *maya*, that suffering (along with everything else) is in fact an illusion."

"We have this idea within our own Christian tradition," Daskalos responded. "We say, for example, that the gross material world is the world that offers us the meaning of past, present and future, a form of maya. And in order to prove that it is maya, just bring to your memory an episode that made you feel good or caused anger yesterday or the day before yesterday. Is it not that which you experienced yesterday and remains in your memory as anamnesis a form of maya? What did the yesterday offer you other than anamnesis today? It is based on this observation that the Indians called the world of experience maya and the ancient Hebrews called it chimerical and illusory.

"And yet," Daskalos went on, concentrating on some detail on his canvas, "it is not exactly this way. The world of gross matter is neither chimerical nor illusory. It is not so because it offers us lessons and experiences. It offers us, for example, the sum total of our experiences in order to draw the appropriate lessons for our spiritual development.

"And then I ask the question If maya means illusion and nonreality, then where were my past experiences stored, experiences that I can bring back to my awareness as memory and anamnesis? If we sit down and study this issue carefully we will realize that what we call maya is really not as illusory as is commonly assumed, because what is called maya and illusion remains as anamnesis within the subconscious. And if the world of experience is just maya and illusion, then how could it be imprinted within Universal Memory that can be recovered at any moment by advanced masters?

"After all, the world of maya is the world of elementals that every human being incessantly creates. And elementals have the power of reality since they keep us accountable. You may have forgotten them somewhere in your subconscious, but sooner or later you will have to confront them since you are the one who has created them. Maya, you see, is a way of perceiving things. For if all these things," Daskalos waved his hand at the various objects in the room, "are just maya, then God too is fantasizing and dreaming. The Absolute is meditating, not dreaming. And we are within Its eternal meditation. Everything unfolds and takes place within Itself.

"So," Daskalos continued as he turned back to his painting, "we must be careful how we use this word *maya*. Something that has happened is over as an event but it remains as an elemental. And the world of elementals, as we have said many, many times, is not illusory because they keep us accountable. Christ did not speak of maya, of illusions. On the contrary, He placed great emphasis on urging people to watch what they were doing. He told them 'What you sow so shall you reap.' He was not referring to chimeras and illusions."

Daskalos put his brush down and looked at his painting. "It is done," he pronounced with satisfaction.

"Daskale," I said, "Kostas told me the other day that early in your life you created some very beautiful art pieces but you burned them."

"Did he tell you that?" Daskalos' gaze was pulled from his painting and he looked at me with an expression of mild shock.

"Why did you do that?"

Daskalos smiled, shook his head, and without any further words from me he proceeded to offer a rational exegesis for his rather bizarre action.

"Fifty years ago, when I was about twenty-five years old, someone asked me to paint for him the sacrifice of Abraham. In fact, I remember he was sent to me by a priest, an archimandrite. I was in great need of money at the time and he offered me about two hundred pounds. In those days such an amount was a small fortune. It was really an excellent painting, one of the best I have ever done. Some called it a 'masterpiece.' I painted Abraham getting ready to sacrifice his son Isaac."

Daskalos began cleaning his brushes and putting his paints away. "When the time had come to deliver the painting I felt uneasy. I rebelled. I just could not tolerate the fact that a god was asking a father to sacrifice his son. God could not have given such an irrational command, I said to myself. Abraham's story was an insult to the all-loving God. In my agony over this issue I tore the painting into pieces and burned it."

"How do you explain, Daskale, Abraham's intentions? What must have gone on in his mind that led him to proceed with the sacrifice?"

"Obviously Abraham created an elemental of God of his own fantasy and imagination. His god was an arbitrary god playing tricks with his people. Old man Abraham simply lost his wits. Psychologists today would have called his case temporary insanity. Fortunately, at the end his innermost self intervened. Abraham came to his senses, wisdom triumphed, and poor Isaac was saved. There was no angel with feathers outside of himself grabbing his hand," Daskalos stated with a slightly mocking tone.

"Well, with a single stroke you have canceled out Kierkegaard's venerated thesis on Abraham's sacrifice," I quipped. "His readiness to sacrifice Isaac was viewed by this thinker as the supreme act of faith and laudatory obedience to the Divine."

Daskalos shook his head and winced. I explained that Sören Kierkegaard, a nineteenth-century Danish philosopher, is considered one of the most influential Christian existentialist thinkers of the West, respected by philosophical theists and atheists alike.

"In Christ's teachings," Daskalos said, "you will never find such nonsense. God is not an arbitrary ruler up there playing tricks with his people. There is nothing irrational in what Christ taught."

"Sociologists would argue," I said, "that Abraham's sacrifice symbolizes and reinforces the values of an authoritarian patriarchal culture. It celebrates obedience to authority as the highest good, regardless of how irrational that authority may be. An authoritarian culture created a myth that fitted its structural needs for self-maintenance. In this case sociology is at par with the Research for Truth and quite compatible."

"To tell you the truth," Daskalos said, "since the incident with that painting I don't feel good talking about Abraham and Isaac and the way that insane act has been treated by religion."

"Did you make any other painting that had the same fate as that of Abraham?"

"Yes. During the same period somebody else brought me a copy of Milton's *Paradise Lost* with a black-and-white print inside showing Archangel Michael with a large sword chasing Adam and Eve out of Paradise. Well, he asked me to do a painting based on that theme. It turned out to be a very impressive painting. It showed Adam and Eve barefoot and terror-stricken holding each other by the hand as they left Eden. Over them Archangel Michael majestically holding his fiery sword chasing them out. I painted God overlooking them from the sky like an angry overlord of the universe banishing them from his kingdom. Again I felt upset as soon as I finished it."

"And you tore it into pieces." I sighed.

"That's right. And then I burned them. The whole thing seemed blasphemous to me. Archangel Michael chases no one out of Paradise. He is the master of the element of fire. He is inside us working incessantly to give us our body's warmth. And God is not a wrathful and jealous lord. Do you understand now why I rebelled? I burned this and another painting of Cain and Abel because they were not compatible with my conscience, with my inner self and personal experience."

"Kostas told us the other day," I said as Daskalos began

117

cleaning his hands, "that the condition of Adam and Eve is an archetype, the state of the human soul before its descent into the worlds of separateness and gross matter. We should speak more accurately about Adams and Eves in the plural, since that state is beyond time and space and infinitely repeatable over the entire creation. He said that the paradise they were in and are still in are the psychonoetic dimensions just prior to the first descent of a soul into the gross material universe."

"Precisely."

"Kostas also told us that the apple Eve offered to Adam symbolizes the gross material planet and that their descent into the material universe was not an expulsion from the Garden of Eden but the product of the human soul's urge to acquire the experiences of a gross material existence."

"This is exactly how our Research for the Truth interprets the Adam and Eve myth. God does not punish and expel them out of His Kingdom. God supports the soul's wish to acquire a gross material existence. And God,fj according to the Old Testament, offers Adam and Eve 'tunics made of animal skins'—that is, gross material bodies."

"Kostas," I went on, "did not explain the role of the Serpent. He passed it casually and said that that was for another time. Can you tell me what the Serpent symbolizes?"

"What do you think?" I noticed a wry grin on Daskalos' face, suggesting to me that what he was about to reveal might prove a bit of a shock.

"A serpent has a head and a tail, right? And it moves like this." With his right hand he mimicked the way snakes move on the ground. "It is the way a spermatozoon with its head and tail moves up a woman's vagina to fertilize the ovum. Do you understand now? The Serpent is not the devil and does not symbolize a Luciferian force. On the contrary, Christ admonished that we should become innocent as doves and wise as serpents. The Serpent symbolizes the essence of life and not a tempting demon. And one more thing. Eve's apple does not only symbolize the material earth but also, on the microcosmic level, the female ovum.

"The myth of Genesis is analogous to Christ's parable of the Prodigal son, the soul leaving the paradisiac level willingly, entering the material universe willingly for the sole purpose of acquiring earthly experience, and eventually returning back to the palace of the loving father.

"Do you see now why I rebelled and burned those paintings? They were representing and perpetuating falsehoods on the nature of life, existence, and the relationship between humanity and God."

"So you are implying, then, that art should be in the service of assisting people to raise their consciousness to higher levels of awareness and not just appeal to aesthetic sensitivities."

"Absolutely!"

(I discussed Daskalos' paintings with my friend Michael Lewis, a professor of art at the University of Maine who had the opportunity to meet with Daskalos and examine his paintings. Michael pointed out to me that Daskalos' artistic productions should not be judged on the basis of their aesthetic appeal or technical precision. They should rather be appreciated and valued as the art productions of someone who has a privileged access to spiritual realities that he tries to portray on canvas.

("Suppose," Michael told me, "that I can only speak enough Greek to express myself in very simple sentences but I could attune myself with this spot with the kind of superconsciousness that Daskalos is capable of. I could then tell you about it, but only with a limited vocabulary. Somewhere behind the limitations, though, would be the profound experience and content. On the other hand, suppose someone who was eloquent in Greek but without special spiritual consciousness came and described to us the appearance of this spot as it looks on the surface. It would be a very impressive description, especially when compared to the limited Greek description. But the eloquence would not necessarily make up for the lack of deeper content found in the first description. If Daskalos' paintings are not eloquent statements they seem to me nonetheless to contain the emotional and spiritual intensity of his vision."

(I will never forget the reaction of Petrovna, a British medical scientist and clairvoyant who, though she had never met Daskalos and didn't know that the large painting in my office was one of his, stood looking at it in wonder. She claimed that the painting was emanating white luminosity and that it served for her as a stimulus to enter into 'the other world'. I tried unscientifically to check her claims with a couple of other psychics and they reacted in parallel ways. When on a visit to Cyprus I mentioned this to Kostas he explained that Daskalos' vibrations and elementals are embedded in his paintings, which therefore often function as talismans.)

"It is time for a break and some coffee," Daskalos announced. He finished cleaning his brushes and hands and took off his heavily paint-spattered smock. "But first we have some important work to do."

I wasn't sure what he meant. Daskalos took his painting out onto the front porch to dry. Then he nonchalantly asked me to help him burn some books.

"Burn books?" I jumped as if bitten by a cobra. The thought crossed my mind that perhaps the discussion of the fate of his paintings brought to the surface of the aging master's mind some deeply suppressed desire for pyrotechnics. Was he really asking me to commit such an unspeakable act? To violate such a sacred taboo? I shuddered slightly as scenes of Nazi book-burnings flashed through my mind.

"Yes, books, Professor!" Daskalos, noticing my astonished look, stressed the last word sarcastically.

"Do you see these books here?" he said, pointing to some old, dark, hardbound volumes lying on the top of his piano. "You can't imagine how much evil they have caused. That is why we must burn them."

I picked up the books. They were carefully handwritten

Arabic texts. The leaves were beginning to turn yellow from age and use. They were heavy, seven-hundred-page-monographs.

"These books are texts of black magic," Daskalos said gravely. "That is why they must be burned lest they fall into the wrong hands. They were brought to me a few days ago by an Egyptian hojah [muezzin] who used them for sorcery, causing a lot of pain to a lot of people."

Daskalos said he had discovered what this Egyptian mullah was doing while out of his body. Then, with intense visualization and concentration, Daskalos forced him to come over to his house, bringing along the magical books. "This fellow came to Cyprus and made a living by practicing magic and black sorcery. I ordered him to gather whatever gold and silver he had made so far and immediately return to Egypt. He left me these books. Come, let us go out in the yard and have them burned."

"Are you sure this is a good idea, Daskale? I asked nervously as I leafed through the meticulously calligraphed texts. I knew they were full of secret unpublished information on the practice of magic in Moslem cultures. Perhaps they contained priceless anthropological material. I was certain that those who wrote them must have spent years if not decades of magical practice and writing. I implored Daskalos to reconsider his decision to burn the manuscripts.

"I am telling you, Kyriaco," Daskalos said impatiently, "these materials are not Socratic dialogues but evil stuff that must be burned. A lot of people suffered as a result of what is in these books." Daskalos explained that they were magic formulas on how to make invocations of demons and evil spirits, which was why he was so determined to proceed with their destruction.

He asked me to take three of the four books out into the yard while he searched for gasoline and matches. The fourth book lying at the bottom of the pile was not for burning, he instructed me. That was the Koran.

"Can you imagine how many thousands of pounds some

people would have offered to get hold of such books?" Das-kalos lighted a match and set the gasoline-soaked manuscripts ablaze. He then stood and watched the books burn as he murmured some prayers and made with his hands symbolic gestures I could not understand. Later he explained to me that he was doing a form of exorcism. The fire and the praying were ways of burning the evil elementals attached to the magical texts. From Daskalos' point of view, what I witnessed was not book-burning but a purification ceremony for purposes of healing.

Daskalos was not a scholar in the sense of having as his primary concern the accumulation and publication of information about "knowledge," irrespective of consequences. He was first and foremost a healer concerned about the bodily, psychological, and spiritual well-being of his fellow human beings. For Daskalos the books were evil because they contained magic formulas on how to do sorcery for selfish, egotistical purposes. That is why such knowledge should not be disseminated. I, on the other hand, being schooled within a tradition that valued knowledge for knowledge's sake, irrespective of consequences and human cost, felt deeply uncomfortable watching the densely and carefully handwritten monographs engulfed in flames. With his provocative act Daskalos forced upon me a reevaluation of my long-cherished beliefs concerning the purpose of knowledge, its accumulation and dissemination. From the perspective of Daskalos' values, the accumulation of knowledge and the unlocking of Nature's secrets must parallel the spiritual growth of those who possess that knowledge so that it may not be used for destructive purposes.

Our modern quest for knowledge has disregarded this concern, for the most part. In our universities we have been relentlessly tapping the secrets of Nature without any provisions to ensure that the custodians of such knowledge be spiritually advanced beings. The scientists of Spaceship Earth in mindless pursuit of careers, money, and fame split the atom, brought to existence unimaginable varieties of deadly poisonous substances, and manufactured more than fifty thousand nuclear warheads ever ready to be unleashed for the incineration of Mother Earth at Armageddon. Should universities, I wondered, perhaps incorporate some of the qualities and practices that have historically been associated with ashrams, lamasaries, and spiritual retreats? Should the future men and women of knowledge be expected to explore and develop their inner realities as they are offered the opportunities to accumulate knowledge of the outer world? Should scientists be expected as they are initiated into the secrets of Nature to develop with appropriate meditation exercises and spiritual practices their capacities for compassion, detachment, and love? And, finally, could the human race survive its technology and accumulated scientific knowledge while matters continue as they do now? These were the thoughts and questions that crossed my mind as I watched Daskalos murmur prayers and incantations over the ashes of the Egyptian muezzin's magical texts.

Daskalos poured a bucket of water over the hot ashes. "Now it is time for some coffee," he said as he rubbed his hands. We went inside into the living room and Daskalos slowly gratified his great weakness for caffeine. Already there were several people in the hallway waiting for their turn to consult him.

6 Universal Memory

"Can evil acts generate a free-floating evil essence that may afflict innocent people?" I was reading from a list of questions a colleague from America had requested I ask Daskalos. I thought her question was relevant as a follow-up of what Daskalos had accomplished the day before with the black texts of the Egyptian hojah.

"Never," Daskalos replied categorically. "Yes, they can affect people with evil predispositions, but never the innocent. Now you may ask what an evil act is. To have an evil act you must have an evil thought and a corresponding emotional disposition. That means before you even carry out an evil act you have already created the evil. You have already created the vibrations that lead to evil acts. When you have an evil thought and evil disposition you generate the analogous vibrations and the corresponding form of the evil. So you have two conditions, the radiating energy of the evil and its form. The form is the elemental, which is charged with the intensity of the projected energy. This is what black sorcerers are doing, creating elementals having a particular shape and charging them with energy. But of course human beings with their hatreds and resentments create such negative elementals constantly. And they do so either consciously or subconsciously. Most people create these thought forms without knowing what they are creating. If you are a clairvoyant you can see these elementals coming out of people in the shape of animals like snakes of various sizes and colors, apes, bears, and so on that do not exist on the gross material level yet do exist within the psychonoetic dimensions. These elementals are harmful to human beings who vibrate on the same frequencies. Evil attracts evil in the same way that the good attracts the good. Innocent people have nothing to fear because their vibrations are on different frequencies than what your friend called the free-floating evil essence.

"Bear in mind that human beings create such elementals even while asleep, while dreaming."

"How so?" I asked.

"While you are dreaming your desires are much more forceful. They have greater power than during your waking hours, when you are preoccupied with daily matters. At night when you go to sleep your desires come to the surface and you as a present personality can dream in an evil way creating evil elementals. These can, for example, cause nightmares in children."

"Michael, the friend and colleague who designed the covers of my books, wondered whether books, movies, and art objects in general can create these kinds of elementals."

"Anything that may race in our thought, any mental picture or any desire, is creating an elemental. And elementals, I should point out, are created before you even put them down in books or create movies or pieces of art. It is your thoughts and your sentiments that create these elementals. Now, material things such as art pieces, jewelry, photographs, paintings, and so on can be magnetized consciously or unconsciously by these elementals. It is through this method in fact that we can construct talismans that can offer protection to people. It is done by imbuing something with benign thought-energy. So you can make a talisman that can radiate the essence of good. Likewise, negative sentiments of jealousy and hatred associated with the possession of an object like a precious stone may imbue that stone with elementals of such powerful destructive energy that it may cause trouble, or what people call bad luck, to its possessor. Material objects, you see, enslave in them elementals."

"Is this why it is possible to have phenomena of psychometry?"

"Precisely. An experienced master can attune his or her consciousness with any object and contact all the elementals that are attached to that object. It is for this reason," Daskalos explained, "that it is possible for an advanced mystic to concentrate, for example, on an ancient statue and uncover secrets associated with that statue, something that scholars working in libraries and laboratories for years and years may not be able to uncover."

"Based on these same principles," I added, "it is possible that certain places or localities may be energized with either positive or negative elementals."

"Correct. I have noticed, for example, that at certain places where there are frequent accidents there are elementals at work. One of our duties as Researchers of the Truth is to go to such places and dissolve these negative elementals. How, you may ask? By generating the energy opposite that of the elemental. Neutralized of its own energy, the form of the elemental will retire inside what we call Cosmic Consciousness or Universal Memory or what people sometimes call the Akashic Records. As I said before, once it is created an elemental can never be destroyed. When we dissolve such an elemental in reality we dissolve its energy. The form of the elemental will always remain inactive though, within Universal Memory."

"When you visit such places to dissolve the energy of these elementals don't you run the risk of being attacked?" I asked.

"Naturally I do. But can they do me any harm? No. Not at all. Of course this kind of work is not pleasurable. But these elementals will cause me harm only when I have hatred or even complaints and bad feelings against someone. Therefore Researchers of the Truth must be very careful to cleanse and purify their subconscious of any negative feelings and thoughts. Otherwise the negative energy of the elementals inside them will attract those evil elementals outside that they are trying to dissolve. I always make certain that before I do such work I and my co-workers have no traces of negative feelings inside us. Again, you see, people who are pure at heart do not have to worry about black magic, evil spells, evil influences, and the like."

"But how many people are really so pure as to be totally protected from evil elementals created by crimes and historical causes? Can such elementals attack an ordinary human being who may not be evil but who may not be so pure either? You may live, for example, in what people would call a haunted house and suffer as a result of whatever accumulated negative energies reside there."

"That is right. But whatever suffering you will experience will depend on the amount and strength of the negative energy that you have built up within you. Let me give you an example. I have noticed that some shepherds who for a long time have had fights with one another, cursing one another, had created with their thoughts and actions a 'free-floating evil essence,' to use your friend's words. At certain hours of the day the magnetism in the area where they waged their fights was such that it facilitated the expression and activation of those elementals. Suppose now that another fellow passing through that spot had had within him negative emotions against someone. Then the elementals created by these shepherds could attack him and make him suffer. But again, suffer to what extent? Bodily pain, weakness, nervousness, headaches, and the like. Now, such elementals do exist everywhere and it is the duty of the Researchers of the Truth and invisible helpers to go to such places and dissolve them—that is, dissolve the energy of these elementals and banish them from the scene. And we do that all the time through exomatosis, by traveling to these spots with our psychonoetic bodies. It is easier and cheaper to do it that way." Daskalos chuckled. "It is also more effective to work from the other side."

"Why is it easier?" I wondered.

"Because when you are working outside your material body you can muster a greater force and energy to dissolve the energy of these elementals.

"Let us move on to the next question," Daskalos said after waiting for me to go over my list.

"This one," I said, "is about prophecy. My friend asks whether it is possible to foretell the future, and if so whether human freedom is possible."

Daskalos smiled and proceeded to answer. "On the basis of our personal experiences as Researchers of the Truth we have concluded that nothing is predetermined. We have said this many times. Foreseeing the future means nothing more than foreseeing probabilities. Something may or may not happen. It works in the same way as when scientists can make reasonable forecasts about the future based on present facts and trends." Then he said what I had heard him and Kostas repeat many times, that at every single moment human beings rewrite the history of the future. The future is an open question. It is so because human beings have the freedom to create the elementals of their choice, which in turn will shape the nature of the future. Therefore whenever someone prophesies what will happen in the future what he or she does, in reality, is 'see' the unfolding of events based on the present arrangement of hitherto created elementals. But human beings are free to create new elementals in such a way as to nullify the prophecies.

"I personally do not believe that karma can be accurately predicted beyond the time span of two to three days at the most."

"Why is that so?" I asked.

"During such brief periods the karmic forces may have matured to such an extent that for all practical purposes nothing could be done to change the course of events."

"Can you please make this more concrete?" I asked. "Can you give me a specific example from personal experience?"

Daskalos reflected for a few seconds and then said "One day many years ago I woke up and got ready to go to work. It was about six-thirty in the morning. I put on my socks and sat in bed for a few moments. I was fully awake. Suddenly I saw the following vision. I found myself near the place where I worked as a linotypist at the government printing office. I got off my bicycle right where the city clock is. I was getting ready to walk the rest of the way through the eucalyptus forest where the government buildings were. At that point I saw a man pushing a cart. I saw him very clearly. In fact I noticed that he had a scar on his face. His cart had a glass cover and he was selling *koulouria* [pastries like pretzels] and cheese. The moment he arrived under the clock he began advertising his wares very loudly: 'I have fresh, warm *koulouria* . . .' Then I noticed another man coming on his bicycle from the opposite direction. He approached the other fellow, dismounted, and started screaming at him: 'Finally I found you, you son-of-a-bitch!' 'You are the son-of-a-bitch' the other shouted back, and a brawl began. The man with the bicycle kicked the cart and turned it sideways. The glass broke into hundreds of pieces and the *koulouria* and the cheese were all over the asphalt. In a rage the vendor grabbed a large kitchen knife and was ready to assault the other. A government employee who was near the scene rushed and held the arm of the vendor firmly, shouting at him 'For God's sake, are you mad? Do you want to kill him?' 'Let me slaughter the son-of-a-bitch,' the other screamed. 'Look what he has done to me.' Then the other got on his bicycle and rode off in a hurry. At that point my vision ended. I shook my head and laughed. I just couldn't figure out why such a scene would come to me while dressing at six-thirty in the morning.

"In about twenty minutes I got on my bicycle and started for work. As soon as I reached the spot where I saw the vision I got off my bicycle and saw the events unfolding in real life exactly as I experienced them half an hour earlier. I saw the man with the cart, the scar on his face, heard his hoarse voice shouting about his warm *koulouria*, and so on. And then I saw the man on the bicycle, wearing exactly the same clothes I had seen in the vision and making exactly the same movements. As I watched I knew precisely what was about to happen next. I was able to do that because the karmic forces had matured to such a degree that it was virtually impossible to change anything. As I watched the scene I wondered who the fellow was that intervened and grabbed the hand of the vendor. You see, in my vision I failed to notice that detail. As I watched it happen I discovered that it was a colleague I knew. 'Oh,' I said to myself, 'so it was Constantinides who did that.' Of course, had I focused in my vision on that detail I would have identified the man. Then the police came and I went on to my office."

"Were you in full consciousness when you saw that vision?" I asked.

"Of course," Daskalos replied. "As I told you, I was putting on my socks."

"Since human beings have the capacity to foresee events that could take place within one or two hours, could they not also prophesy what will happen, let us say, a century ahead?" I asked.

"It cannot be done," Daskalos insisted.

"Therefore all these prophecies such as those of Nostradamus that so many books have been written about must not be taken as literal predictions of the future."

"As I said, on the basis of my personal experience I discovered that beyond three days ahead the future is nothing more than a probability."

"What about John's Apocalypse?"

"These are all probabilities," Daskalos repeated. "These things will happen *if*. . . . There is this *if*. Human beings have free will. It is free will that creates karma. Therefore its intervention at any moment can change the direction of karma. So-called prophecies may work and they may not work."

"Is it possible," I asked further, "that this principle is valid for individuals but not for entire societies and historical conditions? Human beings may have free will but the structure of historical conditions may not operate under the same principles and laws."

"When a large number of individuals change their consciousness then their national or collective karma can also change," Daskalos responded.

"Of course, there are probabilities and probabilities. If a prophet can see, based on present karmic conditions, a future event that has a ninety-percent chance of taking place, it is much different if that probability is only ten percent."

"All right," Daskalos agreed.

"What determines the degree of probability that a prophesied event is likely to take place?"

"The strength, energy, and force of the elementals related to that event. The greater the energy of elementals the greater the probability that an event will take place.

"I am personally against any foretelling of the future, particularly of horrible events that supposedly will take place," Daskalos said, raising his right hand to emphasize his opposition to fortune-telling.

"Why?" I asked.

"Because," he went on, "by foretelling the future you infuse energy into the elementals that will make these events more likely. Even an originally false prophecy may create new elementals with such power and energy that they may bring about what had originally been falsely prophesied."

"In other words, a prophecy becomes self-fulfilling."

"Right. And this happens when people begin to believe in the prophecies and implant within their subconscious the elementals of the prophecy."

"This phenomenon has been recognized by sociology," I pointed out. "But sociologists don't talk about elementals. For example, W. I. Thomas, an American sociologist, pointed out that an originally false definition of reality becomes real in its consequences."

Daskalos nodded. "Right. It is an elemental that is being energized once people believe in it. The more energy is infused into such an elemental the more likely that it will happen.

"Do keep in mind," he said, "that we are talking about probabilities, not certainties, and that karma, both individual and collective, can change at any moment. This is the essence of human freedom."

Daskalos then reminded me of a case in the Old Testament that he had pointed out earlier, when Jonah prophesied that Nineveh was going to be destroyed by God because of the accumulated sins of its inhabitants. But the people of Nineveh repented and the city was spared. They changed their consciousness at the last moment and their city was not destroyed. "It was not God," Daskalos said, "that changed His mind. It was the people themselves who collectively changed their karma by changing their awareness. That was the reason Nineveh was not destroyed."

"But Jonah's vision was real," I ventured.

"Of course it was."

"I mean, had they not changed their collective consciousness Nineveh would have been destroyed."

"Naturally," Daskalos replied. "But they had the freedom to change and they did. With new causes you have new effects."

"In reference to your own vision, Daskale, where you

foresaw what was about to happen in half an hour, could we not also conclude that at least theoretically karma could change, even at the last moment?"

"But when I saw that vision," Daskalos responded, laughing, "the first man had already started pushing his cart and the other man was already on his bicycle. The karmic forces had matured to such a degree that I don't believe anything could have changed it."

"What do you suppose made you enter into such a state that you could experience that vision?" I asked.

"But who can really know the reason? Did I perhaps foresee it because I was about to experience it in this dimension a short while later? Or was it perhaps a lesson I was being offered by the higher powers?"

"Was the experience you had," I asked, "a form of exomatosis?"

"No, I was not out of my body. My consciousness was right there at my bed. I was putting on my socks and was getting ready for work. It was, rather, a form of projection. During the vision my consciousness was both at my bed and near the city clock.

"You see, once you develop your clairvoyant sight you have experiences of this type constantly."

After a few moments' pause Daskalos narrated another personal account of foreseeing future events.

"One day, many years ago—at the beginning of the Second World War—my uncle invited my family to spend the evening with them and listen on the radio to Verdi's *Aïda*. My uncle sent me a special message. 'Spyro, I know you are very interested in this program. Make sure that you come.' I was really looking forward to listening to that opera. I had listened to Verdi's *Aïda* once before and I was literally enchanted by it.

"I remember it was the second day after Christmas and it was raining. My uncle's home was near Bayractares on the outside of the city walls. The moment we sat down and were getting settled to listen to the program I heard a voice inside me, 'Stand up, go!' 'But go where?' I asked. 'Go!' I heard the voice again. I stood up, put my raincoat on, and got ready to leave. 'Where are you going in this rain?' my aunt asked, puzzled. I heard the voice again: 'Go!' 'But aren't you going to hear *Aïda*? Why are you leaving?' my uncle asked from the other side of the room. 'I don't know, Uncle,' I replied. 'I don't feel well.' Mind you, in reality I was not feeling well. Then right in the middle of the rain I started to walk home. At the time we lived at Pantheon street. But the voice was urging me to follow a way that was a detour of more than a mile extra. I walked down the steps into the moat. Then I climbed up the steps to go on the other side of the walls inside the old city. From a logical point of view the way I followed to go home was irrational, particularly since it was raining. *'Kyrie Eleison,'* I muttered to myself. 'I don't understand this.' I was young and relatively inexperienced at the time. But I followed the instructions of the voice in spite of the fact that the instructions made no sense to me whatsoever.

"As I was walking," Daskalos went on, "not far from the mayor's office I saw a drunk Englishman, a military person, lying on the asphalt in a pool of water." Daskalos mimicked the sounds the drunk soldier was making.

" 'Pull him to the pavement,' I heard the voice commanding me. I bent over him and I tried as hard as I could to pull him. 'Fuck off,' the drunk moaned and tried to give me a punch as his fist and face dropped on the wet asphalt. It was impossible to get him on his feet. Then I heard the voice again, urging me to pull him quickly to the pavement. With a lot of effort I managed to pull him away from the street and onto the sidewalk. It was still raining. The Englishman was soaked and I was beginning to feel wet. The rain began to penetrate my raincoat. The moment I pulled him off the road a military truck zoomed by us. Then I said to myself 'Now I understand.' The truck would have certainly smashed him to death had he remained lying in the street. It was a sharp turn and there was no way the driver could have seen in time a man lying on the asphalt during that dark rainy night in December.

"The driver's eye," Daskalos went on, "caught us as he drove by. He stopped abruptly, put the truck in reverse, and pulled up next to us. The driver got out and approached us. He apparently recognized the drunk and began shouting at him as he tried in vain to get him on his feet. He asked me who I was and what had happened. The driver looked very sad. 'Give me your address, Sir,' he asked me in English. I gave it to him. Two others got off the truck and helped load the drunk. 'Alas for him, poor fellow,' I thought to myself. I was certain he was going to be court-martialed.

"Four days later, during the night," Daskalos continued, "I heard knocks on the door. I opened and I saw the driver, accompanied by the man I had pulled off the road; the fellow I rescued looked haggard and his head was bowed. He was depressed and unhappy. 'Sir,' the driver said to me, 'I want to thank you for saving his life. He is my friend. A bomb fell in London and his mother, father, and wife have been killed. That was why he was in that condition that night. Only his child was saved; it was with his sister in another town.'

"Had I not listened to the voice inside me and instead listened to Verdi's *Aïda*, that Englishman would have been squashed to death by his friend. Providence works in mysterious ways."

Daskalos was silent for a few seconds. "I have had many such experiences in my life," he went on. "A voice would guide me to a place so that I could be of service." Then he told me about one more case. While in his home on Pantheon Street he heard a voice commanding him to go to the area of the Pancyprian Gymnasium and the Archbishopric.

"Again that seemed irrational. Why, when I was sitting so comfortably in my study, should I begin walking without any apparent reason toward the gymnasium?"

This was during the 1950s, at the height of the anticolonial troubles. The students of the gymnasium were rioting and clashing with British soldiers. The voice guided Daskalos to a side street, where he found a teenager lying on the ground, bleeding and unconscious. With the help of a passer-by Daskalos pulled him inside a nearby house away from the clashes, offered him first aid, and brought him to consciousness. That teenager eventually became one of the most prominent British-trained lawyers on Cyprus.

"Who do you suppose had given you such instructions to go places and be of service?"

"I don't know. There are spirits, mind you, that from another dimension can foresee things that are about to happen. Then, assuming that karma would allow it, they would try to find someone with the analogous irradiance and vibrations with whom they can communicate and pass on a particular message. This was apparently what must have happened to me in the cases I have just described to you."

After leaving Daskalos' home I went for a long walk toward the old city inside the Venetian walls. I enjoyed strolling through the narrow streets of Old Nicosia, with its small shops, medieval churches, and historical sites. Unlike the rest of the city, where development proceeded unplanned and unchecked, Old Nicosia was preserved in its precapitalist phase. That was possible because of regulations imposed promptly and because of the ethnic strife between the Greeks and the Turks that kept developers away from the Green Line. The character and authenticity of the old city had ironically been preserved thanks to the tragic state of intercommunal relations.

As I walked through the narrow streets enjoying the relative quiet from the absence of traffic and listening to the sounds coming from the small shops of smiths and carpenters, I reflected on my conversations with Daskalos about the nature of time, prophecies, and karma. Daskalos, based on his own experiential investigations, has come up with an explanation on the nature of what scientific investigators call precognition. It has been shown in laboratory research that some psychics have in fact the capacity to "predict" future events. For example, the physicists Russel Targ and Harold Puthoff have shown that the psychics they studied could foresee the location one of the experimenters was about to go after the latter randomly selected the place in an aimless drive through town. A major issue that preoccupied and challenged these and other researchers was the question of free will. If the future could be predicted, then how can human beings be considered accountable in terms of their choices? How can we speak of human freedom if the future is already predetermined?

Daskalos had a rational answer grounded within the framework of his worldview and springing from within his own experience. That is, that the future can be predicted only within very short spans of time, when karma has 'matured' but cannot be predicted over the long run. Human beings can create with time elementals that can change the prophesied unfolding of events. That is, human beings are ultimately free to shape their own destiny. All experimental laboratory research on precognition has been based on predictions of events that were about to take place within a range of a few minutes or hours. Never over months or years, let alone centuries.

The last piece of the puzzle in Yohannan's system of prophecy and foretelling the future fell into place during a discussion Kostas engaged in at a meeting he held in Limassol with his own students and followers.

It was a Monday afternoon, a week since I had last seen Daskalos. I drove to Limassol to attend Kostas' weekly sessions with his own students and followers. I usually first drove to his house for a chat, but that day he was busy with the case of a man who apparently experienced severe psychological problems. He was not a member of The Erevna but had just joined a group where, without proper guidance, he engaged in what Kostas considered dangerous meditation practices. The result, Kostas claimed, was that this man's chakra at the solar plexus "opened up" without him having mastery over the situation. His kundalini energy began moving up and down his spine in an uncontrollable way. This government employee, who until that time had been considered an average, normally functioning fellow, began to hallucinate, lost his ability to concentrate, and faced the prospect of losing his job and entering the asylum.

Kostas' explanation was that when the chakra of the solar plexus opened up, lower-level demonic elementals found an opening to attack and take possession of it.

It is this type of case that has prompted Kostas repeatedly to caution his students not to experiment with their sub-conscious for the acquisition of psychic powers. Rather, he stressed the importance of cleansing the subconscious of negative elementals and the development of spiritual awareness. Psychic powers, he said repeatedly, must de-velop parallel to the development of awareness. They must develop at a point when the Researcher of Truth will be in a position to have mastery over such powers and utilize them for the sole purpose of healing.

The subject of Kostas' talk this Monday was Universal Memory. He said that anything we can possibly think or do is recorded within this Universal Memory or universal sub-conscious, and that what we consider our own subcon-scious in reality is part of this nexus of Universal Memory. Therefore, discovery of anything is really bringing forward knowledge that is already "discovered" within eternity.

Once the formal presentation of about twenty minutes was over and after practicing several concentration exer-cises Kostas opened the floor for discussion.

In response to a question Kostas said that "had the indi-vidual's awareness been able not to interfere with whatever springs from within his subconscious as imagination, this imagination would have been in every detail the expression of a reality.

"We are entering deep waters." He smiled as he noticed the inquisitive eyes of the fifty or so of his disciples who were in attendance.

"I am telling you," he repeated, "that had the present state of awareness of the individual not interfered with, and therefore distorted, that which springs from the subconscious as fantasy or imagination then what the individual would have been able to express would have been authentic reality. And when I say 'reality,' I mean with its most minute details."

"Can you offer us an example of what you mean?" a thirty-five-year-old woman asked.

"Let us take the work of authors who write science fiction. In general terms what they write about as fantasy is the product of a hidden reality. It springs from the subconscious of the one who has created it, but it filters through his consciousness and state of awareness."

"The state of consciousness of the writer," I volunteered, "is the mirror that distorts that which as authentic reality springs from his or her subconscious."

"Exactly," Kostas responded. "And it is here that one who knows can detect these interferences. But remember that behind these interferences there is a cause which is grounded upon the real. Believe me, nothing can be created from nothing."

Kostas then argued that we come closer to reality on the basis of our ability to penetrate into our subconscious, which is itself enmeshed within the universal subconscious. "In reality," he said, "there is no 'my subconscious' and 'your subconscious.' This is so because the universal subconscious resides inside every particle, every cell, and every atom of matter of all the universes, of all the worlds and of all the dimensions of creation. Consequently it is not necessary that a motion or an act within time and space take place within a particular planet in order for that motion, or the result of that motion, to spring up from within the subconscious of a person living on that planet.

"Let me make it more concrete," Kostas continued, sensing that some members of his audience were having difficulty following his abstract statements. "During the last century the science fiction writer Jules Verne wrote novels about humans landing on the moon and traveling with submarines to the depths of the oceans. During that time people read all that as just novels of fantasy, as fairy tales. In truth Jules Verne brought to the surface a reality from within Universal Memory."

"But Jules Verne," someone pointed out, "sat down and wrote what he wrote. His work did not spring up by itself. He thought about those things before he could write them down."

"Naturally. It was his awareness, his state of consciousness filtering that which was springing from within his subconscious. There is a reality behind whatever is expressed as fantasy or imagination by any human being, including children. The degree to which this reality is distorted in its expression will depend on the level of consciousness and awareness of the one who taps into that pool of Universal Memory where everything is imprinted."

"Kosta, can you please define for us what you really mean by Universal Memory?" an elderly woman asked.

"Universal Memory is that base upon which everything is recorded. It is that storehouse within which every single motion within the universes is imprinted."

"From which Universal Memory did Jules Verne, for example, bring forward his scientific fantasies?" she asked again.

"Not from 'which one,' " Kostas corrected her. "There is only one Universal Memory."

"Did he bring forward that knowledge from a previous life of his own?" she asked once more.

"No. That was not necessary. We have said that from the very moment a specific motion takes place within time and space it gets registered upon every particle, every cell, and every atom of Mind inside the entire creation. This is Universal Memory." Kostas then argued that "Something which has taken place within the 'universes' a million, a billion, or an infinite number of times is recorded within Universal Memory. It is there always."

"This is what gives meaning to the notion of the Eternal Present," I remarked.

"In other words, Kosta," someone else added, "every invention, such as the laser, for example, has always existed and it is already discovered right there within Universal Memory. What then actually happens during a particular discovery or an invention is that someone taps into Universal Memory and discovers something which is already present within eternity."

"Exactly! There is nothing which is not already discovered within the universes. Perfection has always been within the static condition eternally. There has never been, in other words, an imperfect beginning for there has never been an epoch when the Absolute, or God, has not been meditating within Itself.

"It is within this context," Kostas continued, "that we must understand the arrival of the Christ Logos on our planet." He then went on to first ask and then answer the rhetorical question, When do you think the Christ Logos expressed Itself on our planet? "The expression of the Logos within the universes is within the static condition of the Absolute. The Logos expresses Itself within a civilization, within a planet, at the point when human consciousness has reached such a level that makes the manifestation of the Logos possible and meaningful."

Kostas continued that Jesus Christ appeared on our planet at the midway point between our beastly unconscious past and the superconscious state of Theosis or God-realization. The latter is the inevitable end stage and destiny of every Spirit-ego or Pneuma that has passed through the Human Idea as it embarked on the cyclical spiral of incarnations.

"Suppose that someone, centuries before the birth of Jesus, had been able to penetrate into this static condition within Universal Memory. Then he or she would have been able to foresee the manifestation of Christ at the historical juncture that it took place on our planet," Kostas added.

"Was there ever such a person?" I wondered aloud.

"Of course," Kostas replied. "The Buddha. Even though he himself had not attained the highest states of Theosis so that he would be able to express this reality to its fullest, he did attain great heights of perfection and was therefore in a position to express this truth."

I asked Kostas how he learned that the Buddha actually made such a prophecy. Although I am not an expert on Buddhism, I have never heard of such a claim before. Kostas replied that the source of this information was not any written record but higher masters who passed on this knowledge to him and Daskalos.

"The Buddha prophesied," Kostas said with authority, "that within about five hundred years the Logos Itself would descend and incarnate within a human body. In other words, Buddha recognized that the average state of consciousness on our planet had reached such a level that at that point it made possible and inevitable the logoic expression. The Buddha had reached the heights of the 'Third Heaven,' the point where he was beginning to transcend his human form. The Buddha was not an incidental self-consciousness. After entering that state he was able to foresee what was about to happen and instructed his disciples on the matter. It was that prophecy that alerted the three Magi from the East to travel to Bethlehem in order to pay homage to the newborn Godman.

"The Christ Logos," Kostas said further, "is born and crucified eternally within the static condition of the Absolute. And this static condition expresses itself within time and space according to the level of consciousness reached by entities that passed through the Human Idea.

"Do you understand what is happening?" Kostas asked, smiling, and glanced with his piercing eyes at his attentive disciples. "All of these realities," he spread his hands around in the room, "are recorded within the universal subconscious. They are inside the static condition. And they come to the surface when humans of a particular planet have reached as collective awareness that point which permits the expression or the reexpression, if you will, of this particular motion within the static state.

"Whatever we do now, at this very moment, like this movement," he moved a pencil from one corner of the table in front of him to the other, "is imprinted within the static condition of Universal Memory."

"The question that many would ask, Kosta," I pointed out, "is this: Is it possible then that everything is preplanned? Once you enter into the static condition you can foresee, like the Buddha, for example, what will happen centuries ahead. Is this not prophecy? And how did the Buddha's prediction differ from any other prophecy that we have been told can be considered only as probability that may or may not happen?

"What the Buddha said was not a prophecy in the sense of just foreseeing events that were about to happen within time and space. He foresaw a structural turning point in the evolution of humanity. It is possible for an advanced master to declare with mathematical precision what stages humanity will have to follow in its evolution toward perfection. It is the stages that are already predetermined. It is the blueprint within which events will unfold within time and space."

"Is this valid for other planets also?" asked someone from the back of the room.

"But of course. There are other planets where human beings do not move about the same way we do here. They travel, for example, on donkeys. Their technology is still primitive and their collective awareness is not as developed as ours. There are others who have yet to discover the wheel and there are humans on planets that are further ahead of us on their evolutionary path. Sometimes it is not very wise to make revelations about the future stages of the planet, in terms of its technological development, for ex-

ample, because human beings even at the stage of consciousness that they are at now may be able to use such
knowledge prematurely and lead themselves to self-
destruction. Of course, let us not forget that there is divine
protection, an expression of Divine Mercy."

"These stages in the development of human consciousness form the archetypal skeleton of evolution which is
found within the static condition. These are everywhere
the same," someone pointed out.

"Precisely. This is the Divine Plan," Kostas replied.

"An advanced master," I went on as I probed Kostas to
clarify this point, "can predict with mathematical accuracy
the stages of human evolution all the way to Theosis but
cannot predict the historical *details* that will unfold from
one stage to the next. This is the space within which
human freedom can unfold."

"Very good."

"And you are saying," I said further, "that the incarnation of the Christ Logos in the body of Jesus of Nazareth
was not just a historical incident within the time-space
confines of this planet but a structural turning point in the
evolution of human consciousness here on this earth. You
are saying that the Christ inevitably *had* to be born in a
human form, given the collective maturity attained on this
planet by the human race."

"Exactly. The descent of the Christ into human form was
not just a historical detail within the unfoldment of phenomena. It is a stage that is inevitably reached on any
planet upon which human evolution unfolds. As I said before, it is part of the static condition within the Absolute,
eternally. The incarnation of the God-Logos is offered to
humanity at that level of collective spiritual development
to help humans realize that their destiny is to become gods
themselves."

There were further questions from the audience on this
topic, and the lively session did not finish until 11:00 P.M.

I entered my car, tuned the radio to some classical music,

and began the hour's drive back to Nicosia. At that late hour there was hardly any traffic. I let my mind wander and reflected on the lesson just given and the exchanges I had the day before with Daskalos.

Kostas' assertions on the significance of Christ's incarnation reminded me what the German scientist and clairvoyant Rudolf Steiner had to say in his *Christianity as a Mystical Fact*. I was quite certain that neither Kostas nor Daskalos had ever read or knew about Steiner. Therefore, as far as my own skepticism was concerned I knew that their argument on the *structural* significance of Christ for the evolution of human consciousness was not the product of book-learning. What was most significant was that such an assertion fit logically with the overall cosmological scheme of Yohannan's teachings as presented by these two masters. Specifically, it clarified for me the apparent contradiction that on the one hand the future is only a probability and, on the other hand, as both the Buddha as well as John the Baptist prophesied with authoritativeness and precision, the coming of the Logos is a certainty.

The resolution of this paradox lies in the distinction between prophecy as probability of unfolding events that may or may not take place and prophecy resulting from the entrance of the master into the static condition of Universal Memory, where one can attain perfect knowledge of the archetypal stages that lie ahead on the path of evolution. Such a stage was the incarnation of the Christ-Logos into a human form.

7   Awakening of a Master

At the end of August 1987 I returned to Maine to resume my teaching and start working on the field material that I had gathered during the summer months. At Christmas I returned to Cyprus for a more prolonged stay, having secured a leave of absence from my university for the spring semester of 1988. This arrangement offered Emily, the children, and me the luxury of staying on the island for the following eight months. It was a great opportunity to delve further into the world of Daskalos and Kostas.

We returned to the island during times of great upheaval. By January 1988 political fever had reached its highest peak as presidential elections were only weeks away. Christmas decorations were replaced by political banners, posters, and painted slogans advertising the favorite candidates. The indigenous masters were not exempt from the political excitement around them. Much of our conversations during that period revolved not around the attributes of the Abso-

lute but around the qualities of the candidates and the passions aroused by the virulent campaigns.

It was five o'clock in that February morning when I woke
up. I opened the front door to get fresh air, gaze at the
Pendadaktylos range in the north, and watch the sun rise.
As I breathed deeply I noticed on the front porch a leaflet
lying there. I picked it up. "For How Many More Years Are
We Going to Live Under the Damoclean Sword?" read the
title. I read further:

> It is a bitter experience and a tragedy to be a Cypriot
> today. Over our heads there hangs from a thin thread
> the sword of Damocles. And each morning that we
> awaken we wonder: 'What if that thread is cut today?'
>
> Fellow countrymen, we live on borrowed time. At
> this very moment, when other civilized peoples are
> carving wide avenues of a brilliant and secure future,
> we the Cypriots live in a constant state of insecurity
> and uncertainty. Within our own territory there lurks
> mute and lies in wait the Turkish invader. Time
> works for him and we do not know what else he is
> preparing for us. . . .
>
> For how long, fellow Cypriots, are we going to live
> under this terrible threat? For how long are we going
> to be drowned within this asphyxiating impasse? . . .
> For how long are we going to pseudo-live within this
> superficial tranquility, within this calmness before
> the hurricane? For how long are we going to live under
> conditions that poison our aspirations, that destroy
> our plans and visions, that drown with an insufferable
> feeling of futility every effort and every hope for the
> future?

The proclamation was issued by one of the leading opposi-
tion parties vying to unseat the incumbent government.
They waged an effective campaign, attacking the regime of
President Kyprianou for gross incompetence in handling

the "national problem" during the past ten years and for apathy in the search for a peaceful and speedy solution to the Cyprus problem. It was universally felt by Greek Cypriots that time was running short for them and that the threat posed by Turkey with its massive military buildup in the occupied section of the island increased by the day. It was feared that Turkey's ultimate design was to conquer the entire island.

Anxieties about the future originated with the establishment of the Republic of Cyprus in 1960 after five years of a blood-stained underground rebellion against the British colonial government that had ruled the island for the previous eighty-two years. Independence was a compromise, since the aim of the revolt was to unite the island with Greece. But because of the violent opposition of the Turks, who constituted about 18 percent of the slightly over half-million population, the nationalist aspirations of the Greek Cypriot majority were frustrated.

The deep mistrust and hatred between the two ethnic groups rendered the complicated constitutional setup unworkable and communal strife erupted again during Christmas of 1963. By 1974 Turkey, which lies only forty miles from the north coast of Cyprus, invaded the island under the pretext of protecting the Turkish Cypriot minority. This devastating experience for Greek Cypriots happened only a few days after a murderous coup, instigated by the military dictatorship then ruling Greece, overthrew the government of Archbishop Makarios III. It was after that fateful and cataclysmic event, when Turkey captured about 40 percent of the island and when almost two hundred thousand people became refugees that I first met Daskalos and Kostas and began my research and apprenticeship with them.

Politics was the centerpiece of conversation of any gathering—including assemblies of mystics, occultists, and metaphysicians. The Turks lost no opportunity to trumpet their mighty presence and therefore intensify the paranoia among the Greeks. On the slopes of Mount Pendadaktylos facing the Greek side the Turkish Cypriots carved a huge flag of their unilaterally declared state (the pseudo-state, according to the Greeks) and over it wrote in gigantic letters that could be seen clearly over a ten-mile distance the defiant and provocative Turkish epigram NE MUTLU TÜRKÜM DIYENE [It is great to be Turkish].

Daskalos loved the Turkish Cypriots and lost no opportunity to express his affection for them. The invasion by Turkey, he claimed, was not "accidental." From his point of view it was the paying off of national karma. "In reality," he said many times, "the enemy is not the Turks or the Turkish Cypriots but us. That is where we must work."

The Turkish Cypriots reciprocated Daskalos' affection for them. I was able, much to my amazement, to verify this on several occasions. The latest story I heard was from a United Nations diplomat, a good friend who served on Cyprus for several years. In a social gathering on the Turkish side he asked one of the Turkish politicians whether they had heard of "that man Daskalos." This United Nations diplomat told me "he [the Turkish-Cypriot politician] remained silent. Then I asked him 'Are you perhaps against what this man is doing?' 'No, no,' he replied. 'On the contrary. This man saved the life of a relative of mine. Thirty years ago my cousin was pronounced terminally ill with a few weeks to live. He was taken to Daskalos and he cured him. My relative is still alive. What a remarkable man!' " In fact, the same Turkish-Cypriot politician, considered one of the archenemies of the Greeks, told my friend at the end of their conversation "Daskalos is one of the few truly compassionate beings on this island."

Daskalos' explanation of the Turks' affection for him was simple. "When you genuinely love people it is natural to be loved by them." The Greek Cypriots, he often remarked, would solve their problems only when they learn how to truly love their Turkish compatriots. And that, he would add, applies also for the Turks. Otherwise karma will bring them time and again into similar situations so that they might learn how to love those who from the vantage point of their ignorance they have thought of as their mortal enemies. This is how karma works. The passions of hatred will repeatedly bring together those who have generated them into analogous historical situations so that the former enemies transform themselves into loving friends. Such historical situations can be truly transcended only when this psychological transformation takes place within human consciousness. Therefore, he would teach, the tragedies and calamities brought on by the Turkish invasion have simultaneously created great opportunities for spiritual growth and transformation for human beings currently expressing themselves as Greek and Turkish Cypriots.

By six in the morning I was on my way to Limassol to meet Kostas and join him on an all-day excursion to the Kokkinochoria region. He was to visit several villages in that potato-growing area of the island for a routine settling of some business accounts. I thought it would be an excellent opportunity to be with him all day long, keep him company during the trip, and chat about subjects related to The Erevna. Antonis, a friend and a new member of Kostas' Limassol circles, joined us for the same reason. A forty-five-year-old successful architect with a sharp, no-nonsense intellect, Antonis was an avid reader of philosophical and scientific books. He had, like Kostas, trained in England and was himself a refugee from Famagusta. Antonis became interested in Kostas' and Daskalos' teachings after his sister, an old student of Kostas', exposed him to the philosophy of The Erevna.

Antonis took the day off from his busy schedule to be with us and enjoy what he and I expected to be a prolonged and gratifying conversation. We left Limassol about seven-thirty in the morning. Kostas sat next to Antonis, who volunteered to drive. I sat in the back seat enjoying the brilliance of the morning sun and the deep blue of the Mediterranean. It had rained the day before and the earth emanated exquisite freshness.

We chatted for a while about the local political developments and expressed our speculations on who the likely winner at the upcoming elections would be. Then, sensing that the relaxed and informal nature of the situation would smooth the way to an insightful discussion, I asked some personal questions of Kostas.

"How did you become a member of Daskalos' circles, Kosta, and how did you develop your healing and psychonoetic abilities?" I asked as soon as we were outside Limassol, cruising on the new highway linking Limassol with the other cities of the island. Somehow I had the feeling that Kostas expected my question and without surprise or reservations he proceeded to tell us more about himself than at any other time during the ten or so years I had known him.

"Look, Kyriaco," Kostas began, "I have been interested in these matters ever since I was a child. I remember when I was still in elementary school, some books that dealt, among other things, with hypnosis fell into my hands. I could hardly understand them and yet I was drawn to them and I struggled to practice some of the exercises and experiments the authors of these books suggested. For example, they instructed the reader to concentrate on a particular object. I did so with regularity for hours on end."

"You used to do that as a child?" Antonis asked with surprise.

"Yes, Antoni. I was a pupil in elementary school. In fact, one day my mother entered the room and saw me sitting on my bed staring at the corner of the wall. She looked at me time and again, came close to me, and when she discovered that I had in front of me a certain book she gave me several slaps on my behind and warned me never to touch them again," Kostas said with a chuckle.

Daskalos had told me some time in the past that both of Kostas' parents had been members of his Famagusta circles and that he used to hold Kostas on his lap as a child. When Daskalos heard of the slapping that Kostas suffered at the hands of his concerned mother Daskalos raised his eyebrows and said to the woman "Don't you realize, my dear, that you are spanking a master?"

"Anyway," Kostas continued as Antonis and I listened with great interest, "my dreams were like a second life for me. In reality I had no idea what was happening to me. I thought everybody was having the same experiences as myself.

"In elementary school I discovered that I could move various things by sheer thought. I used to hang objects from a thread and with my mind I would move them left and right like a pendulum. I used to think that it was perfectly natural to do all that. I would also move empty matchboxes by concentrating on the tips of my hand. My hand would become like a magnet pulling the matchbox. Of course now such phenomena are not allowed."

"Why not?" Antonis asked.

"Because they scandalize and provoke people."

"What if you do them in private, by yourself?" Antonis asked.

"But why bother, since I know I can do them? Why waste precious energy that must be used for healing purposes? Besides, healing requires much greater abilities than moving objects hanging from a thread. I used to do such things in my youth at a time when I was not conscious of what I was doing."

Kostas told us briefly about his life. He was brought up in Famagusta, then the major port of the island. Had it not been for the Turkish invasion Kostas estimated that he would have been a multimillionaire by now, since his family had substantial landholdings in the then most touristed part of Cyprus. Kostas grew up wealthy and his engineering studies in England were a preparation for taking over his father's transportation-related business. But his karma turned him into a penniless refugee struggling to survive economically in the highly competitive Levantine world of Cypriot business. Kostas, like all the other thousands of refugees hoped, and dreamed of his eventual return to his home town.

"I knew of Daskalos early in my life," Kostas said, "because my parents were very close to him and belonged to the circles of the Research of Truth. Whatever problems my family had—I mean various illnesses—they would first consult with Daskalos. When, however I completed high school and went to the university in England I was no longer interested in these matters. It was later on—in 1972, several years after my return from England—that I first got interested in spiritual matters again and attended one of Daskalos' meetings. That year Daskalos reopened his circles after seven years of inactivity. Yohannan had given instructions to Daskalos to close the circles for the duration of those seven years because of some problems.

"The first time I attended his gatherings I came home and sat in an armchair in our living room. My wife and son were asleep. I watched television for a while, but there was nothing of interest and I turned it off. I sat there pondering Daskalos' lesson. I suddenly entered another plane of existence in full consciousness. The television in front of me disappeared. The walls vanished and I entered inside a radiant, starry, brilliant light. What a light! It was not of this world. You cannot experience such a light here within this dimension. The euphoria I felt was beyond anything imaginable. There are no words to describe what I felt."

"How long did you stay in that ecstatic condition?" I asked.

"I don't remember exactly, but I must have remained in that state for quite some time. Then gradually—not abruptly, mind you, but gradually—I began to descend into this dimension. I saw how matter was slowly becoming solidified within the vibrations of the three dimensions. I began to see the wall acquiring form and concreteness. The same with the furniture, the television, and everything else in the room. Slowly, slowly I landed within my body. But I must say that I as self-consciousness had not moved into some other location. Everything took place within the same space. This experience took place the first day that I attended Daskalos' meetings, when I began to ponder and meditate over the lesson he had just given us."

"When did you reach the point when you could enter into those ecstatic states at will?" I asked.

"These abilities developed slowly within the span of a few months," Kostas replied. "I could then enter into those vibrations any time I wished. However, I must say that I began experimenting right the next day. I waited for my family to sleep and then I went into the living room and sat in the same armchair. Then I tried to enter into that ecstatic state. It worked!" Kostas said triumphantly.

"How did you do it?" I asked.

"There is really no way that I could tell you." Kostas smiled.

"Did Daskalos perhaps give you a secret meditation exercise that put you into that ecstasy?"

"No, nothing like that at those early stages. Let us say it just happened by itself."

"What else was happening to you during those initial stages?" Antonis asked with animated interest.

"My dream life was becoming a greater, more substantive reality for me. Of course, as I told you, I had always had vivid experiences with dreams and other strange phenomena. But in the past I had no explanation for them. For me it was routine, and so I did not take much notice. My dreams, for example, were so alive it was as if I were living a parallel existence. I often could not separate happenings within my dreams and in my daily life. I used to think that such experiences were ordinary for everyone. Later on, through my involvement with The Erevna, I could make sense of most of the things I was experiencing while dreaming."

"When you say you lived within your dreams, what did you actually do?" I asked.

"I was fully conscious within my dreams and I could do whatever I wished. In other words, I was a fully rational entity within my dream life. If I wished to go somewhere I could. Yet there was continuity and coherence in my dreams. I was not jumping from one totally unrelated dream event to another as most people do. I have come to realize in studying people and human nature that most people jump from one incoherent episode to another in their dream life. They are being swept in their dreams by what we call the psychonoetic winds."

"Why so?" Antonis asked as he stopped the car for a flock of sheep to clear the road.

"Because movement within those vibrations is the product of thought. When you are incapable of mastering your thoughts you are literally at their mercy."

"Did you develop your dream life and become conscious within your dreams as a result of the exercises Daskalos was assigning to you?"

"No," Kostas said decisively. "Those were experiences I have always had."

"So you brought these abilities from previous lives," Antonis remarked.

"Of course. These experiences sprang from within me. They were not the product of external training within this incarnation. In fact, as knowledge was coming forward from within me Daskalos himself was actually trying to hold me back. You can ask him about that," Kostas said, laughing, and turned back toward me.

"Why would he hold you back?" I was somewhat puzzled.

"Because at first he was concerned that I might not be able to cope with the knowledge and memories that were rushing forward. When I would mention to him, for example, that 'you know, I have met So-and-So'—that is, someone who did not live within this dimension—he would react with astonishment. 'Where did you meet him?' he would ask."

"How come Daskalos knew that person?" I asked.

"Well, he happened to know him too," Kostas replied and chuckled. "One day I told him 'I am beginning to live the life of such-and-such a person.' 'Holy Virgin!' he said. I began to enter my previous lives. On this score Daskalos really did not help me at all. But things were happening by themselves."

"Are you saying that Daskalos did not help you in your development?" I asked.

"Of course he helped me. What he was teaching me," Kostas explained, "allowed the knowledge that was already within me to come forward."

"So Daskalos' teachings served like a catalyst for you," I ventured.

"Exactly. Knowledge was coming forward much more easily. But the experiential knowledge was already within my subconscious. At the stage where I am now I could simply turn the switch on and knowledge would come forward like a torrent."

"How so?" I asked.

"Because, Kyriaco," Kostas continued, turning around to face me again, "the knowledge I have assimilated and expressed in previous lives I am yet to express in this present life. It is there, however, within my subconscious." Kostas pointed to his chest.

"Why don't you turn that switch on?"

"Because I don't want to," Kostas replied, smiling.

"But why not?" I persisted.

"Because it will interfere with my social responsibilities in this life, my wife, my children, my family. I have to think of them. Do you follow me?"

(Daskalos had an additional explanation. He mentioned once that Kostas often "held himself back" because he did not wish Daskalos to leave this world. "He is the one who keeps me a prisoner in this sack," Daskalos said as he pointed to his aging body. "He just wants me around here.")

"In several incarnations we had in Peru, for example," Kostas went on, "we expressed tremendous power. I am telling you that inside those mountains [the Andes] there are huge undiscovered monuments, including pyramids." He spoke with certainty. "They have been engraved in granite in such a way that would have been impossible to reproduce with today's technological sophistication and power. Believe me, they were not carved with material tools and technology," Kostas said with an ironic intonation. He then spoke of the region and cultures of what is today Peru and pointed out that among all the other regions of the planet that was the area where he had undergone a large number of his incarnations. "The knowledge of Peru," he said half-jokingly and with a broad smile, "is now in Cyprus. The only difference in my present life from those Peruvian incarnations is that today we express knowledge through the lenses of Christianity. This is what is added to me in my present life. But when it comes to general knowledge and power, we knew more then—or, to be more precise, we manifested more, than we do now."

"So your mission in this life," Antonis remarked, "is to bring this knowledge to Christianity."

"Precisely. This is what Daskalos has been doing and this is the responsibility I have on my own shoulders."

"I suppose you would say, Kosta," I added, "that you and Daskalos are expressing greater wisdom-knowledge today than you did during the Peruvian lives."

"Oh, absolutely, absolutely," Kostas replied, turning back toward me. "We may not manifest the technical knowledge of mind that we expressed then, but now we operate from a higher spiritual platform and state of awareness. Oh, yes. Every incarnation is better than any previous one. Whatever knowledge we express now is through the lenses and filters of Christianity. This is the great difference."

"I suppose this filter prescribes that power must be employed only for service and healing," I said.

"Exactly. This is the big difference." Kostas repeated that the knowledge he teaches is not something that he learned in his present incarnation. Rather "It comes by itself from the source of knowledge." He said further that he and Daskalos are totally attuned, and what one teaches and knows the other also knows.

"When you give a lesson, Kosta, are you in full awareness of what you are saying or is the knowledge simply leaving your mouth without you being aware of what you are saying?" Antonis asked.

"Look. I must say that quite often many of the things that have come out of my mouth in my present incarnation I have learned and heard for the first time. This has happened to me several times. It usually happens when certain issues have not preoccupied my awareness until someone asks a question. Then the answer would simply emerge."

We gazed at the road ahead and at the passing hills covered with olive trees. After a few moments of silence I asked, "What other stages did you go through to reach your present state of awareness?"

"To reach the stage," Kostas replied, "where I could leave my body at will."

"Did you have a specific experience at first which shook you up, so to speak?" I asked again.

"One of my earliest experiences was to penetrate inside time and experience our planet in its fiery state."

"Were you in full consciousness when you were undergoing that experience?" Antonis asked.

"There are no words to describe that state. It was not only a matter of full consciousness but something far superior. I was in a state of superconsciousness."

"Did you actually go back in time? Was it a memory or an illusion?" Antonis, somewhat puzzled, asked with his characteristic skepticism. "That was a billion years ago," he added.

"You simply penetrate into your subconscious," Kostas said slowly and emphatically. "It is there."

"Are you saying that you existed during or prior to the fiery planet?" Antonis asked again.

"It does not matter whether I did or not. But I can tell you that later on I did verify for myself that I actually did live even at that time. But again it is not necessary to have been in existence at that period in order to penetrate back into time."

"How is that done?" Antonis asked, not quite knowing how to take what Kostas was claiming.

"You just penetrate within the subconscious of the planet," Kostas replied with a wide smile. "Everything is within you and you are within everything."

"But how could you have existed during the fiery state of our planet?" Antonis asked and shook his head, smiling in disbelief.

"Look, Antoni," Kostas elaborated his seemingly incongruous statement. "As we have said in previous lessons, planet earth was much bigger than it is today. The original planet was called Maartouk."

"In what language?" Antonis asked with a touch of sarcasm.

"This name is the literal sounds of the vibrations of that original planet. It is not a question of language but vibrational sounds."

"I see."

"The human entities who lived on Maartouk, as we said, acquired power in their hands by unlocking the secrets of Nature. They had developed awesome psychic abilities but hadn't developed their spiritual side, their awareness. As a result they managed to explode that planet and the earth became a smaller and fiery celestial body."

"What happened to the rest of Maartouk?" asked Antonis.

"It became the asteroids that are circling our solar system."

Kostas said that many of the people who live on planet earth today are reincarnated entities who had experiences on planet Maartouk. And contrary to everything that science tells us about the past, Kostas claimed, organized human life existed on planet earth after the explosion of Maartouk. Human life developed at a certain point later, while the fiery lavas were flowing all over the planet. Human life existed then on solid oases. He claimed to remember, or more precisely vividly relive, this state of the planet, once his past incarnations were rushing forward in his consciousness. "In reality," he said with light laughter, "we are all Maartoukians."

"Can you tell us about some of your past lives?" Antonis asked.

Kostas smiled. "Allow me to duck that question." In fact Kostas did tell me in earlier encounters some of the vividly remembered periods in which he lived—without revealing details of who he actually was. For example, he mentioned to me once that he, like Daskalos, was a painter in Italy during the Renaissance. In his present life, he said, he could not even "draw a line." He did not dare pick up a brush now because his mission was different and he did not wish to "reawaken the painter" within him.

"Kosta, why are you so much against helping someone recover memories of past incarnations?" Antonis asked and thereby broached a touchy subject. This was an issue that Kostas felt very deeply about and had a definite stand on. In fact, more than once he sharply criticized Daskalos himself for giving hints to people about their previous lives. "This is not allowed," Kostas told his master with severity. Daskalos would not argue the point, admitting that it was perhaps a mistake. But, alas, Daskalos was as addicted to this habit as he was to caffeine. He could hardly control his enthusiasm when he met someone he claimed was close to him in another life, another country, another time. Kostas told me once that talk about past lives simply stimulates egotism.

Antonis described a "strange" feeling he had experienced when he visited an Indian exhibition in Europe and wondered whether it had something to do with a previous incarnation. He asked whether Kostas could give him some clues.

"No, I cannot do that" was Kostas' predictable answer.
"If I tell you about such matters, memories may come to
the surface of your subconscious and you may adopt all the
feelings related to the state of awareness at your previous
incarnation.

"You see, my dear Antoni"—Kostas gently tapped his
friend on the shoulder—"one must go back in time only
when one is ready. It will happen naturally. Don't be in a
hurry."

"Come on, Kosta, do tell me," Antonis replied playfully.
"I do want to find out why I had experienced those feelings."

"You see, my friend," Kostas replied, "every new incarnation is better than any other in the past. When we go
back in time we go back to a lower level of consciousness
and awareness. Therefore, before we develop such psychic
abilities we must first work on the chakras of awareness.
To prematurely energize centers of psychic abilities can
wreak havoc on the present personality."

"Why?"

"Because the laws created by the Absolute prevent us
from remembering. And that is for our own good." Kostas
argued that Divine Mercy has shut the doors of perception
and memories of previous lives to allow for our spiritual
growth unencumbered by troubling memories of the past.
To artificially bring forward these memories would be tantamount to tampering with the law, the law of oblivion.
Elementals of past lives that have become inactive may be
revived again with greater energy and may come forward to
haunt the present incarnation. When a certain level of spiritual evolution has been reached, recovery of past memories would not have any negative effects on the present life.
The elementals of the past no longer pose any potential
threats to the present. The individual has deenergized them
by paying off karma.

"Past-life regression is fashionable in Europe and America," I pointed out.

"This can be dangerous," Kostas said thoughtfully.

"Thank God there are the invisible helpers that intervene and prevent a lot of bad things from happening to people. You will never hear me tell you exactly who you were in a past life. If I do that I break the law. And who am I to break the law? I am nothing in front of the law. If you succeed in recovering your memory by your own spiritual struggles and growth, then fine. But suppose I tell you that you were such-and-such a person in a specific past life. Do you know what could happen? Believe me, you will most probably adopt the mannerisms and the behavior of that person. Imagine if that personality that I would mention was someone famous. Then what you may do is get some books and read about that person. Before you know it you will end up behaving like that personality. Just remember," Kostas continued after a moment of pensive silence, "no personality of a previous incarnation was on a higher level of consciousness than the one you are now on."

"There is purpose behind every incarnation we have. Right?" Antonis gave a sideways look at Kostas.

"Right."

"If for some reason you failed to learn the lesson you were supposed to learn then perhaps going back to a previous life may be a way to find out where you went wrong," Antonis pointed out.

Kostas laughed. "Believe me, there is no way of escaping pain and karmic debts if you have failed to learn the lessons you were supposed to learn. You don't have to go back into past lives for that! You will pay in the future. Unless, of course, you transform your awareness. When you change the vibrations of your awareness past elementals that bound you within, karma cannot affect you any more. This is how it works. This is what we are trying to do as Researchers of the Truth. Once you raise the vibrations of your awareness, then memories of past lives will not affect your present incarnation. You are then liberated of the law that holds you within different experiences."

We were so engrossed in our conversation that before we

knew it we found ourselves driving past the ruins of the Roman aqueducts lying at the outskirts of Larnaca. Kostas had some business to take care of in town and Antonis and I waited for him at a seaside café.

(Before the Turkish invasion of the island in 1974 Kostas had been the sales representative of the Shell oil company in the Famagusta district. After the Turkish army took over Famagusta Kostas lost all his revenues and property, including his commissions for providing fuel to the Shell gasoline stations of the district. Only a few villages within the Famagusta area were spared the invasion. Kostas continued to represent the company for the few remaining gasoline stations that were left outside the occupied area. He told me, however, that it was an economic burden on him to continue serving these stations. Not only did he not make any profit, but quite often he would be in the red. Nevertheless, he kept the exclusive right for distributing fuel to these stations with the hope that eventually Famagusta would be returned to its rightful citizens. When I mentioned to him that perhaps the invasion may have accelerated his spiritual development he disagreed. He said that his gradual awakening began prior to the Turkish invasion and that had he been economically secure he would have devoted his entire time fully to The Erevna and would have committed most of his wealth to it. "But," he sighed with a bitter smile, "it was not to be. I had to undergo this karmic experience.")

After about an hour, in which I had a pleasant and philosophical chat with Antonis, Kostas arrived and once more we were on our way to visit some of the coastal villages of the unoccupied Famagusta region, known as the Kokkinochoria ("red villages"), named after their fertile red soil.

We drove north of Larnaca with the sea on our right. We crossed the British base at Dekelia and followed the road dividing the Turkish-controlled area from the rest of the island. We were driving right on the Green Line. On our left there were Turkish flags and soldiers at the observation posts and on the right of the road the Greek and Cypriot flags, Greek Cypriot soldiers manning the outposts. Driving on that road, which I had not traveled since the time of the invasion, was an eerie feeling. We were silent most of the way, each of us reflecting the tragic events in 1974 that brought about that depressing state of affairs. We finally turned right toward the village of Liopetri, away from the barricades.

In an effort to reopen our discussion on Kostas' awakening as a master I asked whether he had had any other experiences during his early involvement with The Erevna and Daskalos that could be called turning points in his spiritual development. After a brief pause Kostas described what happened to him one day as he lay in bed fully conscious and alert.

"Suddenly one part of myself was a little above my body and another one was near the ceiling. All of them were fully developed bodies in the same shape as my gross material body. Then, another body of mine was half below the roof and the other half above it. And I could really see the view over my house. Another part of myself was inside the wall. I was seeing and observing simultaneously with all of these bodies, including my gross material body.

"Conventional psychologists," I said lightly, "could have attached to you all kinds of psychopathic labels had you described such an experience to them."

"Nonsense," Kostas said, scoffing at conventional psychological thinking."These are experiences of superconscious self-awareness. There are many forms of superconsciousness. This type is one of them."

"All of the experiences that you have mentioned, Kosta," I pointed out, "such as ecstasies, remembrance of past lives, entrance into the subconscious of the planet and witnessing its fiery state, out-of-body travel as well as being in more than one spot at the same time, and so on, have remained with you as psychic abilities. Correct?"

"Yes, but at first these experiences just happened without my having any conscious control over them. Gradually, and with much practice, I developed mastery over these and many other psychonoetic states of consciousness. For example, at first I had no control over my exomatoses. I would just find myself outside my body looking down upon it from the ceiling. When you are a beginner, being close to your body makes it very difficult to keep out of it."

"I listened," I said, "to Daskalos give instructions to a new member of the inner circle to make certain not to run far away from her body at first. Why?"

"Because there are dangers, that's why," Kostas replied turning toward me and smiling. "When you are a novice you do not have the familiarity needed for your well-being and that of others. You are not used to the radically different laws that operate within these other vibrations."

"You mean, of course, the laws of the various psychonoetic dimensions," I said.

"Yes, but primarily those vibrations that are very close to the gross material level. Let me give you an example from my personal experience. When I first experimented with conscious exomatosis I encountered some difficulties. I mistakenly thought that my psychonoetic body was bound by the laws of gross matter. But of course it is not so. The psychonoetic body is less dense and can penetrate and go through the gross material world. I got out of my body one night and looked at it sleeping next to my wife. I then decided to leave the room. The door was closed. At that moment I forgot that I could go through the walls and I tried to open the door. By the sheer force of my will I lowered the vibrations of my psychonoetic body to the point where I really opened the door. Somebody awake in the room at that moment would have seen a door opening by itself. It would have been a very frightening experience. When I finally realized what I was doing I shut the door. It closed with such a bang that I worried I might have awakened my wife."

"What would have happened, Kosta, had Lenia tried to wake you up at that moment?" Antonis asked.

"I just would have shot back into my body. Nothing else would have happened."

"And I presume she would not have realized anything about your exomatosis."

"Right. She would not have."

"Then what dangers do you face once you move away from your body?" Antonis asked further.

Kostas smiled and paused for a few moments. "When you are out of your body on a mission of service you run the risk of being attacked by other humans who, unlike yourself, are bound to the opposite side of the good. When they notice that the self-consciousness that normally resides in that body has left it they may try to attack."

"You are really putting frightful ideas into my head," Antonis complained.

"Oh no. Don't have any fears. I myself have never been frightened. Just know what you are doing." Kostas explained how one can protect oneself during exomatosis. "Before you leave your body," he said, "you must remember to create an elemental of protection over your gross material body. You do that through strong autosuggestions, saying to yourself, for example, 'Nothing will happen to my body during my absence.'

"On long journeys, where you go for substantial service, it is advisable to go with at least one other person. I usually go with Daskalos. Of course, it is not necessary that the other person is of this dimension. In the event that upon coming out of your body you confront threatening elementals you feel you cannot handle, your last refuge is your body. Just shoot back into it. There you will be safe."

"Do you know what I have discovered, Antoni?" I interjected as I leaned forward from my back seat. "The more I become familiar with these teachings the less frightened I have become with circumstances that normally would have caused panic in me." I then described a lucid dream I had had several nights earlier. "I became conscious that I was in a dream and that I could affect situations within my dream. Like other similar experiences I was fully conscious of the fact that I was outside my body. But it was unplanned and deeply pleasurable." Those kinds of experiences, I told them, appear in my consciousness as more deeply real than the three-dimensional existence. "Suddenly a very ugly and threatening elemental appeared in front of me. It had all the characteristics that we normally associate with demons. Now, in previous years such an encounter—and I had some —would have terrified me. My heart would have accelerated, I would start swimming in a pool of sweat, and my body would have pumped up all the adrenalin it possessed. Instead of all that happening I started laughing. I said to the demon 'You cannot frighten me. Not any more. Daskalos taught me how to deal with the likes of you.' Then I pointed my finger at the demon and with an extraordinary coolness that surprised even me I said 'In the name of Jesus Christ I order you to transform yourself from a negative energy into a positive one.' "

"What happened then?" Antonis asked, chuckling along with Kostas.

"The demon," I said, "began melting away and in his place there blossomed a most beautiful flower."

After we spent some time talking about our dream life, Antonis asked Kostas what methods he used to develop his psychonoetic abilities.

"The method is knowledge itself that springs from within you," Kostas replied cryptically and smiled. "Of course I had help not only from Daskalos but also from masters who do not live within the gross material universe."

"Who are these people? Can you tell us?" Antonis asked, his curiosity getting the better of him.

"One of them, as you know, is Yohannan. He is the one who oversees The Erevna and presides over the circles of the Research for Truth. He is the one who guides us and always stands by our side."

(Kostas claimed repeatedly that the knowledge that pours

out of himself as well as out of Daskalos was knowledge offered by John the Beloved or Yohannan. Like Daskalos, Kostas had reached the state in his spiritual evolution that he too had become a vehicle through which Yohannan's mystical wisdom was disseminated to the world. It was for this reason that Kostas had been anointed equal and successor to Daskalos as a master of The Erevna.)

"Of course," Kostas continued, "Yohannan was not a human being."

"What was he?" Antonis asked, his eyebrows raised to reveal his disbelief.

"In reality he was an archangel who took human form in order to facilitate the manifestation of the Logos on our planet." Kostas explained that Yohannan was not an ordinary human being in the sense that he did not, like all humans, embark on a series of incarnations for the attainment of spiritual perfection. He was already perfected in his first ascent into matter. When Antonis asked Kostas to elaborate on this point, Kostas replied that that was a question we were to explore in greater depth at some future point. He proceeded instead to talk about other human masters and invisible helpers he had encountered once his chakras began to open up and he consequently was able to live fully conscious within the other dimensions of existence.

"One of the first masters I encountered on the other side," Kostas said, "was Brother Immanuel. When I first met him he introduced himself with these exact words 'I am Master Immanuel.' Later on I discovered that I had a prior relationship with Immanuel. This man lived as a Catholic priest during the Venetian period (sixteenth century) in Famagusta. The Greeks at the time called him Manos. Since then he has never reincarnated and has been serving human beings from the other side."

"How does he look now?" Antonis asked.

"He looks exactly the way he used to look in his last incarnation as a Catholic priest. In fact, he is still wearing his brown robe. That is how I saw him the first time and that is how he appears to me whenever we meet. If you ask him now about his occupation he will reply 'I am a Catholic priest.' "

"Whom does he serve, one person or many?" Antonis asked.

"No, my dear. He is serving the entire planet. He is serving human beings for their spiritual development."

"Where is he now?"

"He is everywhere. Whenever you speak and think of him he is present."

Kostas then spoke of other masters who are both serving humanity and guiding him on his path. He mentioned the name of another Catholic priest, Father Dominico, whom he had been meeting regularly and who had also been one of Daskalos' spiritual guides.

"Our discussion was interrupted when we reached the village of Liopetri, where Kostas had business. After Liopetri we stopped at several other Kokkinochoria villages, including the tourist spots of Ayia Napa and Paralimni. I hadn't been to that part of the island for several years and was horrified with the unrestrained construction that was turning picturesque fishing villages into concrete, noise, and discos. In spite of the political tensions both on the island and in the region of the Middle East the Nordic tourists kept coming to lie lazily on the sunny, sandy beaches of the unoccupied southern part of the island. The need for quick economic development and the understandable local obsession with the presence of the Turkish army created a consciousness vacuum over issues related to the long-term ecological survival and viability of the island. Every inch of coastal shore was rapidly becoming prime target for development.

We managed to discover a quiet spot near the village of Paralimni, where we had lunch. It was February and the tourist season had barely begun. The beaches were relatively free of umbrellas and plastic mattresses. After lunch we took a short stroll by the beach near Fig-tree Bay.

On our way back to Larnaca, after Kostas completed another business transaction at Ayia Napa, Antonis brought the conversation around to Kostas' experiences with exomatosis. You can leave your body, for example, Kostas claimed, and visit another part of the gross material planet and see what is happening there. Or you can leave your body and visit other dimensions of existence lying at higher vibrational frequencies than the gross material level.

Antonis asked: "How can you verify that what you experience is a real existent world and not your imagination, fantasy, or sheer hallucination?"

Kostas replied that when you are truly into those vibrations you just know. "It is like asking me now whether you and I and Kyriacos are real people talking to one another at this place at this very moment. When you know you know. Besides, I have been continuously cross-checking my experiences with Daskalos so that there is not a trace of doubt in my mind about the authenticity of my experiences."

"Can you tell us of a recent experience when you have done just that?" I asked as we saw Larnaca in the distance.

"You know," Kostas said, turning toward me, "this is the first time I have talked so much about myself."

"Marvelous," I exclaimed and tapped him on the shoulders. Antonis enthusiastically joined me in urging Kostas to describe further the exotic world within which he lived. Kostas smiled and after a short pause proceeded to narrate an experience he had had with Daskalos when the two of them left their bodies to visit a town in Turkey.

"We were searching for the whereabouts of a missing Greek Cypriot. He had been lost since the time of the Turkish invasion and there were suspicions that he might still be alive somewhere in Turkey. When his father brought the picture of his son to us we detected from his aura that in fact he was alive. We decided one night to leave our bodies and gather more information about him. It was amazing. We found him married in Turkey to the sister of a Turkish officer who took part in the invasion."

"Are you certain about this, Kosta?" I asked, incredulous.

(The issue of the approximately two thousand missing is of paramount importance to Greek Cypriots. In fact, one of my close relatives has been missing. The last information we had about him was that he was arrested by the Turkish troops in the town of Kyrenia. All indications suggested that the missing were probably dead. They were killed either during the early days of the invasion or executed after their arrest. The Turkish government had repeatedly claimed that there were no Greek Cypriots living in Turkish prisons and the missing had simply died in the heat of the battle during what the Turkish government officially labeled the "Peace Operation." The government of the Republic of Cyprus, based on what it considered documented evidence, insisted that at least some of these people might still be alive somewhere in Turkey after they were shipped there as prisoners of war. Kostas claimed that that was one of those rare cases.)

"Yes," Kostas insisted. "I have seen it with my own eyes. This man literally became a Turk. He is content and has no desire to return to his father, with whom he was not getting along.

"When we visited them it was summertime and they were eating outside on their large veranda. It was a huge house—in fact, it was a villa. His wife came from a very wealthy family."

"You don't have any doubts that that experience may have been something that was simply springing from within your subconscious?" I questioned.

"No, my dear, no. They were eating on their veranda," Kostas stated emphatically. Then in a light tone he went on to describe what happened to Daskalos during their nocturnal journey to Turkey.

"In front of the house he saw some beautiful rose bushes in full bloom. You know Daskalos' great weakness for flowers. In spite of my protests he went ahead and got entangled in the bushes." Kostas laughed. "He just can't change, even in exomatosis. In order to experience the pleasure of the smell of the roses he foolishly lowered his vibrations and came close to the vibrations of the roses. But it was time to return back to our bodies. Instead of elevating his vibrations first and then coming out of the bushes he rushed out while he was almost semimaterialized there."

"What happened?" Antonis asked, momentarily turning toward Kostas with an incredulous look in his face.

"When he returned to his body he was full of scratches," Kostas said, laughing.

"Were you with Daskalos that night or were you in Limassol and he in Nicosia?" I asked.

"No. I was with him in Nicosia that night."

"So you checked your experiences against his and they were identical?" I added.

"But of course."

"And you did see with your material eyes the scratches on Daskalos' body?" Antonis added.

"That is what I have just told you." Kostas said that it was this type of cross-checking he had been doing with Daskalos continuously so there was no trace of doubt in their minds of the authenticity of their nonordinary experiences. Kostas said further that such an experience was a routine matter for him by then and that he could leave his body and visit other planes and other vibrational spaces at will.

"Even now as I am talking to you—at this very moment —I could also be somewhere else and be fully conscious there as well," he claimed.

"Are you saying that at this very moment you can go, visit, and enter inside Apostolos Andreas and see what is happening there?" Antonis asked.

(The monastery of Apostolos Andreas, located at the easternmost tip of the Karpasia Peninsula, has great symbolic significance for Cypriots. The local lore is filled with stories of extraordinary miracles and healing phenomena attributed to the saint's icon. Both Greek and Turkish Cypriots are said to have been healed by the miraculous powers of the island's saint. More important, Apostolos Andreas symbolizes for Greek Cypriots the totality and integrity of Cyprus as a unified whole and a promise for the most important miracle of all, the departure of the Turkish troops and the freedom of the refugees to return to their ancestral homes and villages. The monastery and all of the magnificent Karpasia Peninsula was overrun by the Turkish army during the invasion and most of its Greek inhabitants fled to the southern part of the island. For me Karpasia was a great loss since some of my sweetest memories belonged in that region. Being unspoiled and undeveloped, of unmatched natural beauty, the long Karpasia Peninsula was my favorite area for snorkeling, spear-fishing, and hiking. Above all it was a region whose inhabitants, including some close, personal friends, lived a life of laughter and joy, so much so that I often compared them to Colin Turnbull's Forest People.)

"My dear Antoni," Kostas chuckled "I can go wherever I wish on this planet."

"You mean that in a couple of minutes you can be at Apostolos Andreas?" Antonis asked again. It was hard for him, a thorough rationalist and still new to The Erevna, to digest what Kostas was saying.

"What two minutes?" Kostas scoffed. "When you know how, you can be there in a split second. There is no time as such."

"Have you not been curious to visit Famagusta and see your home?" I asked him.

"Unfortunately, I have done so."

"Why unfortunately?" I pried.

"It is not allowed. It is one thing to go there in order to be of service and it is another to do so because of personal reasons and curiosity."

"In what way would it be different had you simply found a way to visit Famagusta in your gross material existence and learn what is happening?" I asked again.

"My dear Kyriaco," Kostas replied with a smile, "when

you express yourself primarily within the three-dimensional world you must, as a Researcher of Truth, assist and serve the laws of the dimension within which you find yourself. The only legitimate way to use power that you derive from a mastery of a higher dimension is for purposes of healing and service. Otherwise it is abuse of power."

"But in your case," I said, "out-of-body travel has become second nature. It happens effortlessly and automatically. In such a case who would be harmed by your visiting Famagusta to quench your yearning to discover what is happening within your own home, a place to which you have no access in an ordinary way. Okay, it may simply be to satisfy a personal curiosity. But I don't see who would be harmed by this type of curiosity."

"Fine. You don't bother anyone, but you do utilize etheric energy that is not yours in reality," Kostas replied. "This etheric vitality belongs to the Logos and the Logos is the 'Bearer of the sins of the world.' Am I to borrow from the Logos so that I may satisfy my curiosity? I admit, and I regret, that I have done so. It was a human weakness of mine. But I would not do it at this point since I now know better. I was pulled by Famagusta like a magnet. Actually, I used to roam around all over the occupied area. And let me confess to you another mistake I made during those early years. I worked very hard over Famagusta."

"What do you mean?"

"Many times I would go in a state of exomatosis over the city and with my mind I would create a powerful protective umbrella. I used to inject that elemental with energy so that no one would settle into the city."

"Well, you have certainly done a great job," I quipped. (Out of the entire Turkish-occupied territory Famagusta was left relatively intact. Whereas in every other town and village the Turkish administration had brought and settled into the abandoned Greek homes either Turkish Cypriots or Anatolian Turks, Famagusta remained a ghost town. It remained without inhabitants or life other than Turkish military patrols and light contingents of the United Nations Force in Cyprus. It was taken for granted among diplomatic circles that if there were to be a solution to the Cyprus problem Famagusta must be returned to its Greek Cypriot inhabitants. It is for this reason that the Turkish government, bowing to international pressure stopped short of proceeding to populate the emptied city in spite of repeated threats to the contrary. For this reason Kostas and all the other Famagustian refugees kept high hopes of eventual return.)

Kostas was not a mystic unaffected and unmindful of the political turmoil surrounding him. Neither he nor Daskalos was the type of contemplative who removed themselves from the passions and concerns of ordinary citizens. On the contrary. Both of them plunged into the mad fury of the nationalist upheavals and worked from their own vantage point, from their own platform and state of awareness. In fact, after the island assumed its independence in 1960 Kostas, fresh from his engineering studies in England, played a leading role in the organization of civil defense of the villages in the Karpasia Peninsula at a time when there was no national guard and there were routine threats of a Turkish invasion. When the invasion did come, Kostas was among the last to flee as the Turkish tanks rolled into town. During those tragic hours Kostas had undergone an experience which remained a mystery to him. It was at a point when Turkish planes were bombarding the city, causing the collapse of several seaside hotels.

"I was next to a wall by the beach," he told us, "when a plane came from the side of the sea spraying bullets. Had I stayed there I would have been killed for certain. There was nowhere for me to run and save myself except on the other side of the wall. But it was too high and physically impossible for me to jump over it. In my despair I tried to do just that. It was amazing!" Kostas marveled as he described this episode to us. "Some force pushed me over and I found myself safe on the other side at the moment when bullets were raining all around." He said that at the time he could not make any sense of his miraculous rescue, since the experience took place a few years prior to his full awakening as a master. "In retrospect, I must have been rescued that day by higher forces," and Kostas mentioned the names of the various masters and guides that have been with him all his life.

As we continued on our journey home Kostas told us that during his early years of awakening he carried out various psychonoetic experiments as a means of verifying to himself the validity of the teachings and the worlds into which his awareness was unfolding. "For an entire year," he said, "I hardly ate anything. I nourished my body directly with light."

Kostas claimed that he performed this experiment just after he fled from Famagusta. "During that period my father-in-law, a medical doctor, lived with us. He just would not believe that I could go on living without food. I barely ate anything. I would occasionally eat some watermelon. According to his medical understanding, I should have died a long time ago."

"Did you tell him what you were doing?" I asked.

"No. I kept my involvement with Daskalos and The Erevna a secret. Only my wife knew what I was up to. My father-in-law simply shrugged it off and assumed that I was engaged into some kind of farce, that I was eating secretly either at home or in restaurants."

Kostas argued good naturedly that it is possible for human beings to live with hardly any food assuming that they know how to energize their etheric double with special meditations. "Let me add," he emphasized, "that during that long period of almost total fasting I had not lost a single ounce of weight. In fact, I was heavier then than I am now." Such feats, he said, have been performed throughout the centuries by yogis, Christian ascetics, and mystics. It is a question of psychonoetic training and discipline, of will over matter.

Kostas' story brought to my mind a question I once raised with Daskalos concerning whether the evolutionary thrust of humanity would eventually lead to a universal vegetarian diet. "No," he had replied. "Our evolutionary destiny is to become 'light-eaters.' Instead of consuming light via the medium of vegetables or even more remotely through the consumption of animal flesh, human beings will eventually sustain their bodies by means of direct absorption of life-giving etheric energy."

"What stopped you from continuing your fasting?" Antonis asked.

"I discovered that it was not the right thing to do," Kostas replied. "First it was upsetting the people I lived with, like my father-in-law. It created unnecessary problems and suspicions. And of course in the meantime I had become aware through The Erevna that psychic abilities must be used only for healing—period. Never for the sake of curiosity or for impressing others. Second, I was beginning to face serious problems in my everyday existence. I could not stay put within my body."

"What do you mean?" Antonis asked.

"I just found myself too often outside of my body and I faced serious risks. One day, for example, I was driving on the Nicosia–Limassol road. Suddenly I found myself floating above the car while my body, like a robot, was driving inside. I was not able to control the situation. I could have had an accident. Then I realized that I had to stop the experiment. You see, this kind of life-style and these experiments are carried out by ascetics and yogis living in isolated hideouts. They don't live in the midst of the modern world, where they have to drive cars, handle power tools, and so on. From that day on I started to eat regularly. I said to myself 'Enough is enough.' "

Kostas then stated, with a hint of playful irony in his voice, that he not only ate regularly but also periodically smoked his pipe to burn some of the excess energy in his body, which created problems for him. After reaching a certain level excess etheric energy kept him outside his body for longer periods than he cared to be. "Smoking," he asserted, "is a bad habit because it burns your vital energy. In my case it is a way for grounding myself. I would periodically smoke a pipe over short periods until I felt that I had total control over my exomatoses."

Daskalos had a different explanation. He told me confidentially that Kostas' periodic indulgence in pipe-smoking was a leftover habit from his Native American incarnations. "Look at his face," he told me once in a lighthearted tone in front of Kostas, "doesn't he look like an Apache?"

I noticed that Kostas would start smoking his pipe profusely over a period of a month or so. Then he would quit and not touch a pipe for a year or two. Then I would see him smoke again for a short period; then he quit with the same predictable ease as before. He reassured us that it was not an addiction on his part but a purposeful policy to make certain that he was well grounded within the three-dimensional world. He certainly did not recommend it to anyone and urged his students to avoid tobacco if they wished to become masters of etheric vitality.

I remember one day that Kostas came to my house in Nicosia early in the morning before a scheduled meeting of the inner circle. He confided that the day before he had had an experience that shook him up, as he put it. "I was in the kitchen when I suddenly found myself on the other side. It was not a voluntary entrance into those worlds, and that's where the problem was. I had a hard time returning to my body. I moved about mechanically into the next room where my wife and daughter were watching television. I sat down, pretending that I was also watching the program. In reality I was desperately struggling to return to my body. I finally succeeded." What bothered Kostas was the involuntary nature of his exomatosis. When I asked him what he thought were the causes of that experience he replied that probably his three bodies, tired and overworked, were out of alignment, and that he needed physical, mental, and emotional rest. Kostas mentioned to me that day that had this happened to someone untrained and unschooled in esoteric practices, philosophy, and research it could have led to a schizophrenic breakdown. That is why, he said, he always cautioned against amateur experimentation with psychic matters.

"Oh my poor father-in-law," Kostas chuckled as he reminisced about what he had done in one of his early yogic experimentations. "He once bought a very expensive machine to measure the heart performance of his patients. He asked me whether I would be willing to let him test the instrument on me first. I said fine. He wired me up and turned it on. I decided to play a joke on him and I made my heart behave irregularly. At one point I stopped my heartbeat completely, then I made it go very fast, then slow. The poor man looked so worried that they had shipped him a defective instrument," Kostas said, laughing. "He would tap it; he would look under it to check whether all the wires were in place; he would shake his head with annoyance and sigh. At that point I realized that I had gone too far and I quit the joke. I let my heart beat normally and that put my father-in-law's heart at ease. His machine worked all right and he sighed with relief. Of course, I never revealed to him what I had done."

Kostas reassured us once more that these kinds of practical jokes and psychonoetic experimentation on his part belong to his past and that once his awareness developed he had been thenceforth employing psychic power only for healing.

It was close to four-thirty in the afternoon when we made a brief stop at Larnaca to pay a visit to two other members of Daskalos' inner circle: Sister Maro, a longtime close friend of Daskalos, and sister Chariklia, a forty-year-old newcomer to the inner circle. We were generously treated to refreshments in Chariklia's home, which was near the Saint Lazarus church. Before we departed for Limassol we walked there and lit candles. Vespers had just began. There were several aged worshipers, and tourist onlookers admired the architectural and artistic magnificence of this extraordinary shrine built by a Russian prince about the ninth century in honor of Lazarus. It is said that after he was resurrected by Jesus, Lazarus was persecuted by the Pharisees, who sought to destroy all evidence of Jesus' miraculous powers. Lazarus managed to escape to Cyprus, where he spent his remaining years. According to legend Lazarus was very solemn and serious during his life in Cyprus because, having died and resurrected, he was deeply conscious of his mortality. He allegedly laughed only once, when he saw a man stealing a pot. Asked why he was laughing, Lazarus replied that he could not help doing so after seeing clay stealing clay. The saint was buried for the second and last time at Larnaca at the spot over which the Russian nobleman built his church.

When we got back to the car for the last leg of our trip the sun had already set. Antonis, a classical-music lover, played for us on his stereo cassette some pieces from Vivaldi and Mozart while we chitchatted for a while. Absorbed by the music and the colors of the twilight we soon fell silent. I then lay comfortably on the back seat listening to the music. But my mind could not rest. Kostas' experiences as a novice of awakening were spinning in my mind.

I had no doubts that Kostas' descriptions of his personal experiences were genuine. I had known him too many years to question his authenticity. I had also over the years experienced the power of his energy and his ability to transfer it to others for healing. Many people, myself included, had felt the incredible torrent of energy flooding our entire bodies whenever Kostas would lightly touch our heads. And I knew that those experiences and many others could not be explained away by simplistic and conventional psychological and psychoanalytic arguments. Kostas, I reasoned, began his journey of awakening by involuntary and brief glimpses into superrational states of awareness. As I sat there I thought that his early experiences were similar to what Abraham Maslow had called peak experiences. But

Kostas—with the help of Daskalos and, as he claimed, invisible guides—was able to develop mastery over these higher states and able to enter there at will. This is how he became a master himself and the designated successor to Daskalos.

The idea of superrational realms of knowledge is very old. Throughout the centuries sages, particularly Indians and Tibetans, have identified with great precision and detail various stages of awareness that they have discovered in their meditative practices. These states of awareness were seen by these practitioners of esotericism as being far superior and more expansive of the knowledge of reality than the rational states, in the same way that the latter levels are far superior to the less rational modes of consciousness. The Canadian doctor Richard Maurice Bucke, during the heyday of scientific materialism, in 1901, published his bold work *Cosmic Consciousness*, thereby injecting into the mainstream of the Western intellectual tradition this revolutionary and yet very ancient idea. Mainstream psychology, the social sciences in general, and particularly my own discipline—sociology—enchanted with mechanistic notions of reality, either ignored or downgraded the insights of thinkers like Bucke. Among the great sociologists only the Russian Pitirim A. Sorokin, founder of the Harvard sociology department, was aware of and sensitive to the reality of what he called the "supraconscious levels" of awareness. Reflecting on the topic of creativity, Sorokin once wrote:

Side by side with the subconscious (or unconscious) and conscious levels in human personality, a third stratum—the supraconscious—is gaining increasing recognition. It is not the subconscious or unconscious, but the supraconscious energies that are beginning to be considered as the real source of all great human creations, discoveries and inventions in all fields of culture—science, philosophy, law, ethics,

181

fine arts, technology, politics and economics. . . . Such
phenomena as extrasensory perception and
psychokinesis; as the supraconscious religious
experience of the great mystics; as precognition; as
the so-called "calculating boys" or "arithmetical
prodigies"; as the state of samadhi of the yogi, or
satori of the Zen Buddhists; as cognitive and creative
intuition are neither subconscious nor unconscious,
but supraconscious, and, as such are not reducible to
the lower forms of vital and mental energy. [In
Harman and Rheingold, *Higher Creativity*.]

Thinkers like Bucke, Sorokin, Tielhard de Chardin, and
contemporaries like Ken Wilber have proposed that eventually all of humanity will reach the level of illumination
and higher awareness that mystics and avatars have been
teaching throughout the centuries. At first, as Wilber argued in his *A Sociable God*, people will get momentary
glimpses into those higher supraconscious states in the way
Kostas described to Antonis and me. These are the 'tastes
of paradise' to propel humanity to employ its faculties for
a permanent illumination at the higher levels of conscious
existence. I thought that if such arguments were valid, then
surely Kostas and Daskalos had already reached the state
where those earlier peak experiences had become part of
their ordinary routine consciousness. This was in fact what
they claimed about themselves.

I had been so engrossed in those thoughts that I was star-
tled to see we had already reached the coastal road at the
outskirts of Limassol. I sat straight up in my seat, opened
the window halfway, and filled my lungs with the breezes
coming from the sea. I then mentioned to Kostas what I
had been thinking. He smiled and nodded in agreement.
Then I mentioned that many people ignorant of these
super-rational states confuse experiences like those he described to us with madness and the "irrational."

"When you reach those levels of awareness," Kostas said,

"you do not abandon your reason. On the contrary, you experience an expansion of your rational faculties. But you must develop your reason first before you go beyond it. Otherwise, there are grave dangers."

It is partially for this reason that Kostas had been extremely cautious in exposing people to the secrets of esoteric knowledge. When I asked him once whether he instructed his eighteen-year-old son in the wisdom of The Erevna his reply was that it would have been premature to do so. "First," he said, "let him ground himself within the three-dimensional world into which he would have to live and function. Once he does that he will be in a position to reach for higher knowledge without creating a disturbance in his present personality."

Following the same logic, Kostas once advised a member of his circles not to push her twelve-year-old child to flirt with mystical ideas and practices because the boy, who showed signs of clairvoyance and other pananormal abilities, needed a solid grounding within this world first. Otherwise a premature preoccupation with psychic matters might create gaps in his development. As one of the members of the inner circle had said to me once, "Mysticism and the pursuit of esoteric knowledge must never be allowed to become a license for insanity."

8   Discoveries

The afternoon lesson in the Stoa was over and Daskalos, as was customary, gathered with some of his close associates for small talk and funny tales. While Aspasia and Chariklia, members of the inner circle, prepared coffee and pastries, Kostas placed his hands on Daskalos' head. With closed eyes and intense concentration Kostas breathed deeply and "flooded" Daskalos with etheric vitality to refill his depleted reservoir. "The lesson was too intense," Kostas explained after the ten-minute treatment.

I have seen both Kostas and Aspasia do that on occasion. It relaxed Daskalos and with a few deep breaths of his own he quickly regained his energy. There were no longer any signs of fatigue on his face.

For the next forty-five minutes Daskalos told jokes, "read" the dried leftovers of Liza's (another member of the circles) coffee cup, and analyzed with zest the local and international situation. Then suddenly he mentioned excitedly an experience he had the day before. His tone became serious and he began to share it with us.

"We have been teaching," he said, "that the psychic worlds are made up of seven major planes and that each plane has within it seven subplanes. And we know that the three lowest planes are what we would ordinarily call the 'hells.' Then the plane just above these three lowest planes is what the Catholics would call purgatory, a psychic space for the convalescence of troubled souls, so to speak. Beyond this plane with its corresponding subplanes there are what we could call the relative paradises. This is what we have been teaching.

"The other day," Daskalos went on, "I found myself working with invisible helpers belonging to circles other than our own. For a while I could not tell where I was. It was not clear to me at which subplane we were working. I was able to observe the characteristics of neighboring subplanes, but where I was specifically I had no idea. I asked this invisible helper, who could not have been human (he must have been from the class of the archangels, servants of mercy), 'Please tell me inside which subplane are we now.' 'Well, which one do you suppose?' he answered back. The conversation, of course, was being carried on mentally. 'We must be,' I replied, 'in one of the subplanes next to purgatory.' 'Yes,' he replied, 'but within which of these subplanes are we? You shall learn something today that so far you have not noticed. You have been working within these subplanes but you have not noticed their finer differences.' 'What differences?' I asked, puzzled. 'All these subplanes,' he said, 'that you are now working are very much alike, with only slight differences one from the other. Therefore, you have not yet paid attention to the fact that each of the subplanes is made up of seven other sub-subplanes.' 'What?' 'My dear, you must realize,' he said, 'that the total number of planes and subplanes of the psychic world is not forty-nine. They are much more than you imagine. You have just not noticed them in their finer subdivisions even though you come and go in here and you work with the greatest of ease. Each subplane is also made up of seven other sub-subplanes.' 'Why,' I asked, 'are the seven subplanes of each level further classified into another seven sub-subplanes and not a different number?' 'This is a law,' he replied. 'It is always seven. You will find the number seven even in the lower world, where you have, for example, seven colors, seven musical notes, and so on.' "

"Has this experience, Daskale," I asked, "led you to revise your teachings about the planes and subplanes of the psychic dimensions?"

"No. The forty-nine planes and subplanes that we have been teaching are real. 'In the psychic world,' this archangelic entity told me clearly, '*there are* seven major planes, which you know very well.' He also told me clearly that each of these major planes does have a subdivision of seven subplanes 'which,' he said to me, 'you also know since you work there. But,' he said, 'the seven subplanes have their own subdivision, which you know subconsciously since you work there.'

"What this invisible helper taught me is to pay greater attention to finer subdivisions. It is as if you are aware that in a building there are so many floors, so many apartments. But you are not aware exactly how many rooms each apartment has."

"So now you have made a psychic discovery and you are certain," I added, "that every subplane has its own seven sub-subplanes?"

"Yes, but who knows? Perhaps there are more subdivisions than I have been able to identify yet.

"I asked this invisible helper," Daskalos continued, "whether we could escort the person we were trying to help move to a higher plane so he could join up with someone he loved and find peace. 'No,' he said, 'this is impossible.' 'However,' he went on, 'the beloved one who is more spiritually advanced and who lives within the higher plane can visit the other at the lower plane any time she wishes.'

Then I asked him the following question: 'Up to and within which planes could a person travel, and what kinds of limitations are there for the average person to move through the various levels?' 'Limitations?' he said. 'There are no such things. There is no god who placed guards preventing people to move from one plane to another. It is the quality of their psychonoetic body which determines where they can and will go. Is there a guard over the surface of the sea which will prevent the fish from flying out?' he asked. 'Why not? Because it is their nature to be inside the water. If you take people from lower psychic levels and place them at higher levels they will not feel well. They will not feel comfortable. Their vibrations will not match the vibrations of that level. Therefore, there are really no outside limitations and obstacles. It is a matter of ability and the maturity of one's consciousness. All the planes and subplanes of all the worlds,' he went on, 'are open to all human beings. The limitations lie on the level of their maturity. It is not possible to grab people from one plane and place them at a higher level. They will not fit there. They will move down again automatically. It is a form of gravity and coordination that will bring them to the plane or subplane into which they belong and in which they will feel most comfortable. It is gravity that will bring them where they could be in complete attunement with the vibrations of that environment. And when they develop the desire to climb higher all the opportunities will be open to them. There is no one there who will block the passage of human souls to higher levels. But it is they themselves who must wish it and who must coordinate themselves with the higher vibrations in order to move up. I repeat,' the angel said to me, 'those who are presently in the most horrible of hells have open in front of them the option and the freedom to ascend to the highest and most numinous paradises. And they *will* be able to do that one day. No one gets lost, no one has ever been lost, and no one will ever be lost as an ego-soul.'

"Now that was great news to me, that no ego-soul can

ever be lost," Daskalos said with excitement and satisfaction.

"But how could it be news to you since this is what you have been teaching us?" I looked at the others, who seemed to share my confusion.

"Yes. You are right. But I feared that egos of the likes of Hitler, of Napoleon, of Stalin may get dissolved within the holyspiritual condition. Fortunately he put my fears and doubts to rest. This invisible helper reaffirmed for me that no human being could ever be lost, no matter how evil he or she may be as a present personality. In fact, I did ask him specifically about Hitler and about the others. 'Their ego,' he said, 'will not be dissolved. They will simply be put to sleep for a very long time and when their time comes to awaken they will move one step upward, but only one. Their ascent, or if you wish to call it their maturation, will be gradual and very tiring. You, for example,' he said, 'do not get tired. You know how to fly. But for one who does not know how to fly and must walk step after step and feel the heaviness of his body, ascent is very onerous. It will be very exhausting for him to reach the second step and then the third and then the fourth and so on.' "

"Could we assume, Daskale," I asked, "that people like Hitler who played such a dominant and destructive role in history are in fact developed old souls who somehow got on the wrong turn in their spiritual evolution?"

"I cannot answer this question because I have not studied it. I do not like to speculate. Unless I verify something on the basis of my personal experience and am certain about it I prefer to remain silent. And even then, after a lot of study and observation there is a chance that I could still be wrong because, as in the case we have just discussed, I may not have noticed some finer details. It was really a surprise for me to discover that there are more subdivisions within the physical dimension."

Loizos, a young medical doctor and member of Daskalos' inner circle, hypothesized "Perhaps there are as many subplanes, Daskale, as there are human beings so that each one will go exactly where he or she belongs."

"My dear Loizo," Daskalos snapped, "we must not jump to conclusions. A master must explore something, test it with his experience, study it, and then arrive at conclusions. We need to study this further." Then, with a light-hearted tone Daskalos repeated the Socratic aphorism "I know one thing, that I know nothing."

As Daskalos completed his sentence the telephone rang. I picked it up. It was Theophanis calling from Paphos. In a trembling voice he asked for Daskalos.

"But what have we been teaching all these years, Theophani?" Daskalos said loudly as he tried to offer comfort to his gentle seventy-year-old friend and long-time collaborator. "Remember, my dear Theophani, that there is no death. No need to cry, please. Go into the next room and lie down on the sofa where I usually rest whenever I visit you there. I will try to help you calm down. Okay?"

As he put down the receiver, Daskalos informed us of what had happened. Theophanis had just arrived in Paphos, the southwestern port town, to find his seventy-three-year-old sister dead.

"We tried to warn him this morning during the meeting of the inner circle," Kostas recalled. "In fact, instead of the regular lesson we spent the time trying to prepare Theophanis for what he was about to discover on his return home."

Kostas told us that he and Daskalos knew what was about to happen but that it was difficult for Theophanis to get the message and the clues directed at him because he was too fond of his sister. Daskalos, in fact, did tell Theophanis that his sister was not feeling well that day. The unsuspecting Theophanis understood what Daskalos meant after the three-hour return trip to Paphos.

Daskalos did not seem to be distressed at all, in spite of the fact that he was himself close to Dora, Theophanis' deceased sister. Instead, he philosophized on the illusory nature of death and stressed that it was simply natural for old people to die.

"I better go and see what's happening," Daskalos said abruptly and with a touch of concern in his voice. "Dora may need help."

We remained silent as Daskalos closed his eyes, leaned his head backward to a comfortable position, and folded his arms. The five of us who were present—including Theano, Kostas, and Aspasia, all members of the inner circle—fixed our eyes on Daskalos' face as he entered into what I thought was a deep trance. We remained silent for about ten minutes. Daskalos' mouth was half open and I could hardly notice any breathing. Everybody understood that Daskalos was out of his body visiting Paphos to be of assistance to Dora. Suddenly he opened his eyes, straightened his back, and began reporting on his experience.

"She is doing fine," Daskalos said with his usual authoritative tone. "She was not aware of her situation. 'Daskale,' she said, 'I haven't seen you for such a long time. How did you appear so suddenly?' Then she told me that all day long she was not feeling well but that now she was fine. 'Come, my dear,' I said, 'it is time for you to go to sleep and rest for a while. You are tired.' I escorted her," Daskalos continued, "to a psychonoetic space away from her body and her house because the wailing of the relatives created tension within her consciousness."

The screaming and hysterical crying of the living, Daskalos said, often create confusion for those recently departed. It is for this reason that he had to completely cut the connection between Dora and the gross material level so that she could find peace.

Half an hour later Theophanis called again to thank Daskalos. He had rested as Daskalos prescribed and felt much better.

The case of Dora offered an opportunity for me to discuss with Daskalos the after-death state in greater detail. I mentioned that I was reading a book by the German mystic and scientist Rudolf Steiner and that I was impressed with the similarities that I found in Steiner's writings and what Daskalos had been teaching us. In fact, a chapter of the book I was reading was related to the after-death state, or *Kamaloka* in the Sanskrit terminology. Daskalos expressed admiration for Steiner, but when he began describing Steiner I realized that he confused the German sage with some healer in a wheelchair. Steiner was not known for being a healer and was certainly not an invalid.

I decided to quickly drive home and fetch Steiner's book so that I could discuss this issue with Daskalos. I was back in half an hour hoping that Daskalos would continue to be available for a discussion on the matter.

When I entered his home I discovered that the others had already left. Daskalos was lying on the couch listening with eyes closed to Russian Gregorian chants on his portable stereo cassette recorder. The music was so loud that he apparently did not notice my presence as I entered and sat in an armchair at the other corner of the living room facing him.

Daskalos seemed to be deeply engrossed in his meditation. As I gazed at him the thought crossed my mind that he was perhaps back to his beloved Russia. Although born a Greek Cypriot of half-Scottish parents (both his grandfathers were Scottish expatriates who married local Greek women), he had a special identification with and love for Russia. His small library in the Stoa had several dusty old Russian monographs. He confided to me once that in his immediately previous life he was a Russian writer and that his memories of that life's intense experiences were still too vivid in his consciousness. It was not difficult for me to fantasize Daskalos as a bearded nineteenth-century Russian novelist living in the midst of historical turmoil and passionately delving with his quill pen into the great mysteries of existence.

In about twenty minutes the Russian Orthodox liturgy ended and the tape recorder clicked off. Moments later Daskalos opened his eyes and, after straightening his body on the couch, noticed my presence. It was unusually quiet. There were no distracting visitors, and as it was late afternoon there wasn't the usual construction pandemonium from the lot nearby. To my great relief the telephone was silent. Daskalos was rested and in the mood for conversation. I resumed our earlier discussion by summarizing some key ideas taught by Steiner on the after-death state. "Steiner claimed," I said, "that when one enters purgatory or Kamaloka one will undergo a process of reevaluation of the life just lived. The ego, says Steiner, will remain in Kamaloka for a time equivalent to a period lasting one third of the life just ended. During that period the ego will suffer from all the unfulfilled desires and lusts that it still contains. At the end of this trial the astral body will dissolve after going through this process of purification. In Kamaloka, says Steiner, we experience everything we have done to others from the vantage point of the other. For example, a killer will experience what he or she had done from the point of view of the victim."

"Exactly." Daskalos nodded.

"After Kamaloka," I continued, "Steiner claims that the ego moves to the spirit realms and can choose the next life to pay back karmic debts and rectify any wrongdoings. Steiner argues that we choose the environment that we shall enter into, including that of our own parents."

"Not exactly," Daskalos responded. "It is not the present personality that will choose where it will incarnate but the ego as inner self. Our ego-soul will accompany us into the world of matter along with our guardian angel that the Absolute assigns to us from the moment of our first incarnation until our liberation. And we feel this angel, as we said before, as ourself. It is the mirror which offers us the possibility to observe all the phases of our conscience so that we may be able to become aware of what we are doing. It is a mirror which we cannot break or put aside. Whether we like it or not, this mirror will always be there and we cannot avoid seeing reflected in it our thoughts, our feelings, and our actions. So you have killed? You shall be a witness to your own death. The moment you have killed someone, you have already signed a contract for your own killing. Steiner is right. If you live by the sword you shall die by the sword. The law applies both in gross matter and within the psychonoetic dimensions. Do you understand? The moment you have disturbed the laws within the psychic worlds you will pay within the psychic worlds, and the moment you have violated the laws on the gross material level you will settle your accounts on the gross material level as well."

"So you are saying, then," I responded, "that after you enter the psychic world you can still create karma."

"Of course."

"And it is within the psychic world that you will have to pay and not within gross matter?"

"That is correct." Daskalos nodded and explained. "If your thoughts and emotions led to action within the gross material world it is within the gross material world that you will have to come and pay your debts. Everything is classified in accordance to its level of reality. Suppose, for example, that you pulled a knife to kill someone within the gross material plane but you were prevented from doing so or unable to. You have already committed your crime. 'Whoever lusts after a woman,' Jesus said, 'has already committed adultery within his own heart.' This is exactly the meaning of Christ's statement. You will confront such emotions and thoughts within the psychonoetic worlds. And just keep in mind that even if you do not kill someone, your hatred has generated the destructive elementals which can influence that person within the gross material world itself, assuming of course that the other person vibrates on the same frequency. Within the psychonoetic world you are in this case a murderer already, regardless of whether you actually had killed someone or not. 'Nothing,' Jesus said, 'will remain a secret.' You shall pay."

"In what way will you pay within the psychic world since your emotions have not materialized within gross matter?" I asked.

"But they have materialized within the psychic dimensions, my dear," Daskalos replied earnestly. "The psychic world, as you know, is matter at different levels of vibrations."

"So you are saying that the elementals you created with your emotions and thoughts will come to haunt you within the psychic dimensions?"

"Yes. And who do you think will allow them to do that?" Daskalos asked, leaning his head forward as if he was about to reveal a great secret. "You yourself as an ego-soul." He pointed his forefinger at my heart. "Do you follow? It is not you as a present personality who will decide your future incarnation. We as human beings, as we have said many times, are made up of two parts, the present personality—which is sinful and irrational, so to speak, and which inflicts self-punishment on itself—and that part which is pure and all-wise, the inner self. The latter caresses the present personality and says 'You feel pain, my love, don't you? But what can I do? You ought to feel pain for your own good.' Your inner self as the ego also experiences sorrow resulting from the transgressions of the present personality."

"In the same way I suppose that Jesus experienced sorrow for the transgressions of humanity."

"Right. So it is your ego-soul in cooperation with the four great masters of the elements who will incarnate you within gross matter."

"You mean it is not just the inner self that decides?" I asked.

"Of course not. With what right could the ego-soul alone interfere within gross matter without prior cooperation with the masters of the elements? The elements that make up the worlds are not just thrown out there. They have their masters. It is the masters of the elements who will offer you a material body to express yourself. We call them *archangels*. They are the Gabriels, the Michaels, the Raphaels, and the Ouriels. The Indians gave them other names. When you advance in your evolution you will be able to contact these archangels and become one of them. It is only then that you will be able to have mastery over the elements yourself and learn how to carry out materialization and dematerialization. Because it is the elements that you will have to utilize in order to carry out such phenomena."

Daskalos remained silent for a few moments, then went on: "It is not easy for the present personality to come to its senses. It will have to be slapped repeatedly by the inner self before it begins to reason properly. The present personality tends to be like a cunning lawyer to itself rationalizing its own actions. And as long as this goes on, its spiritual evolution remains stagnant. Do you understand now why I place so much emphasis on self-analysis and self-mastery? That which you will have to do through compulsion you do now willingly and avoid the painful experiences of karma. The meditation exercises and self-analysis will accelerate your evolution."

"The moment you become aware and exposed to these realities you automatically begin to observe and scrutinize your thoughts and actions, and your capacity for a more objective evaluation of yourself expands," I reasoned. "You become a better human being."

"When the present personality will eventually come to a realization and say 'I admit my crimes, my mistakes—' "

"But it is not enough to say 'I admit,' " I interrupted.

"No. To reach that state it means 'I surrender' to my inner ego and recognize that 'you are right to discipline me.' But how is your inner self going to make you reach that state of awareness? It is when your inner self places you within the role of the person you have harmed or done an injustice to. It is through this method that your ego-soul will help you as present personality come to your senses and admit your crimes. Otherwise, as long as you see things from the vantage point of the egotism of the present personality you will never be able to understand and evolve as a spiritual being. Do you understand what is happening? It is not punishment as such that the inner self is employing against its lower part, the present personality. It is rather a method of awakening. The Most Merciful One does not allow for punishments. He allows only for lessons that will help us advance on the spiritual path."

"Could you describe to me a concrete case of how this reversal of roles takes place within the psychonoetic dimensions?" I asked.

"It is difficult to talk about these matters, which is the work of the invisible helpers. Within the psychic world we encounter such situations constantly. We meet someone, for example, who comes to us and asks for help because he feels someone is after him, trying to kill him. And we as invisible helpers realize that it was that person himself who earlier killed the one he feels is now haunting him. Now who is sending the elemental of the murdered to haunt the murderer?" Daskalos was silent for a few seconds. "The inner self of the murderer," he resumed in a soft voice, "that is himself. In such a situation the victim may be innocent and not the type who will avenge his death. Of course, there are situations where the victim may be vengeful and may project the elementals that haunt the killer. In most of the cases that I have studied, however, it is not the victim who projects those vengeful elementals. Rather it is the killer himself who sends them to himself."

"When you say the killer himself I presume you mean his inner self, the source of his conscience," I interjected.

"Of course. However, if the murderer learns his lesson and truly repents, he is freed from the burden of his karma and need not go through the suffering of his victim. This is an important detail to which we must pay attention. If you learned your lesson there is no need for you to be slaughtered because you slaughtered. At first, you see, I thought that the law of 'If you live by the sword you shall die by the sword' was an absolute and irrevocable law. But after further inquiry and experience within the psychonoetic dimensions I discovered that that was not necessarily the case. It does not mean, however, that the law does not apply or that it is false. It simply means that it can be transcended. You will die by the sword assuming that you have not learned your lesson, that you have not come to your senses. And it does not matter whether your victim is not the type who eventually will kill you with his own hands. If your victim has advanced spiritually and will not avenge his death and you yourself have not awakened to the reality of your actions you may die, for example, in the hands of a surgeon. But, again, this will happen assuming that you deserve that lesson for your spiritual growth.

"Suppose, however," Daskalos went on, "that you have reached a certain stage in the evolution of your consciousness, that you recognize the evilness of your past actions, that you have undergone a radical and genuine transformation of your consciousness. Then God lifts your burden and liberates you from memories of the details of your past actions, allowing only the essence of your experience to remain. Then in your next incarnation you may become a good surgeon—again you live by the sword—but in this next life you save lives. You use the sword in your hand to heal rather than to kill." Daskalos' raised fist held an imaginary sword.

"So you are suggesting in effect that the law of karma is not an absolute and irrevocable law but one that can be overcome?"

"That is correct. Let me explain. As we have said many times, karma is a natural law. But, just as with every other law, it can be transcended via a higher law. This is what Christ teaches. That is why He advocated repentance, et cetera. Had it not been so, had karma been a rigid and merciless law, then Christianity would have gone down the drain and the admonition 'Bear each other's burdens' would be meaningless.

"Karma is the law of cause and effect and we can observe

it within all the realms of creation, including the gross material. From the moment gross matter was created through the law of cohesion and love it became subordinated to its own form of karma."

"I am not certain I understand what you mean."

"Let us take for example the karma of a rock. The combination and synthesis of water, mud, and a certain temperature have created, let us say, this particular rock. The karma of this rock was the result of the karma of a certain amount of water, earth, fire, and so on. And from this vantage point we can foresee, based on certain mathematical calculations (the rotation of the earth around its axis, temperature, rain, et cetera), the future karma of this rock. That it will be dissolved within one hundred, two hundred, five hundred, or a thousand years."

"Are you saying that the physical laws are forms of karma?" I asked, somewhat surprised.

"For certain they are so," Daskalos replied emphatically. "However, there is another law, a higher law, that of mind, of the human mind. And although I can study the law of this rock and discover that it will be dissolved in a thousand years, if I take a stick of dynamite I can blow it up in a matter of seconds. The rock which by itself would have withered away in a thousand years is now dissolved in seconds as a result of the intervention of the human mind. The karma of a thousand years has been overcome in seconds. A radically new reality and a radically new karma is now created. This does not mean, of course, that I have abolished karma or the karma of all other myriads of rocks around me that will take a thousand years to dissolve. In the same way the human mind has invented the jet plane and temporarily overcomes the law of gravity so that in a matter of hours one can fly from Cyprus to London. But if the engines are shut off the plane will crash. The law of gravity can be transcended temporarily but cannot be nullified. It will always be there. The law of gravity, of karma, will remain.

"We have seen from these two examples that mind can affect and alter karma on the gross material level. In the same way mind in the form of human will can alter personal karma not only on the gross material plane but within the psychonoetic planes as well."

"Can you give me a concrete example of how that is done?" I asked.

Daskalos thought for a few seconds and straightened his back. "I will give you an example from my own investigation into this matter," he replied. "One of the best surgeons of Cyprus happened to be a student of mine, and a most dedicated one at that. He died several years ago but I am still in contact with him. In his previous life he was an Austrian politician of the nineteenth century. He was an enemy of the Greeks and of the Greek revolution against the Ottoman Empire. His hostility to the Greeks was such that he was instrumental in the arrest and execution of expatriate Greek revolutionaries. Now notice how karma worked in this case. In his next life he is born a Greek in Cyprus facing the Turks. His obsession was Germany and German culture. They used to call him 'the Germanophile.' He studied medicine in Germany and returned to Cyprus to practice as a surgeon. In spite of the fact that he was a Greek Cypriot he was appointed honorary consul to Cyprus.

"One day after a lesson we went together to a party in Limassol. It was at that party that I first met Makarios [archbishop and first president of Cyprus]. The surgeon was a friend of Makarios, and at some point during the evening he asked the archbishop whether he believed in reincarnation. The archbishop's answer was 'Allow me, my dear, not to answer your question.' Naturally he was careful. After all he was the archbishop. 'My dear Spyro,' the doctor said. 'Perhaps you can enlighten me about something. And to make it easier on you, let me tell you that I accept reincarnation as a fact of life. I have certain experiences that I want to verify. But before I tell you anything, let me go to the next room and write down these memories so that there is no chance that I will be influenced by whatever you may tell me.'

"He went to the next room and wrote down 'I was either a German or an Austrian. I was an enemy of the Greeks. I do not remember but I feel as if I have done a lot against them such as sending them to drown in the river. To be born a Greek in Cyprus is a punishment for me. Already I feel as if I have been going through some kind of expiation. I pray to God that He may spare me violent death. I just dread that.'

"Before he read me his statement I entered his subconscious and I saw that in his previous life he was Austrian. I said 'You were an enemy of the Greek revolution.' 'So far so good,' he replied. 'You were a Turkophile and you still are,' I said. 'What's wrong with that?' he asked. 'Nothing is wrong with that,' I replied, 'if by that you mean that you feel and consider the Turks as your brothers and sisters and not a Turkophile on political grounds. As human beings I love them as much as you do,' I said, 'and perhaps more so.' 'I accept that,' he replied. So we continued and I explained to him his situation. 'Now,' I said, 'you have become a surgeon. With your knife you save lives. You live by the sword. But it does not mean that you shall die by the sword. You are doing good in this life as a form of karmic expiation for what you did in your previous life.'

"It was the first time that I discovered that you can erase evil you have committed in the past by analogous positive good deeds. That you need not suffer the same evil, assuming again that you have learned your lesson."

"Was it you who first discovered this karmic law?" I asked.

"Others must have discovered it and others will discover this law in the future. It was the first time that I discovered it in my own experience. With further observations into the lives of other people, by studying their incarnations, I confirmed and reconfirmed this law for myself. Based on these experiences and observations, I am confident that it is true. Of course these things are not written anywhere, as far as I know. But to me it fits better the church hymn on the 'Most Merciful God, the Forgiver of sinners,' and so on.

"Therefore," Daskalos went on, "someone could pay back his or her debts through good deeds. And then I reasoned, that must be the purpose of metanoia [atonement] offered us by Christ. Otherwise what would have been the meaning of metanoia or repentance?

"Karma is such a complicated mechanism. And I repeat what I told you before, I hardly know anything about it. There is so much more that I need to study and learn!"

"Yet I am truly awed with what you have just explained to me about karma," I added.

"I am awed too, my dear. And let me tell you that the details of how karma really works are not known even to the angels. What we have been talking about is life itself and the organization around life. Do you understand?

"So this friend," Daskalos continued, "came seeking my advice. 'What do you suggest I do?' he asked. 'Whenever a poor person comes to you for surgery,' I replied, 'you shall operate free of charge.' So he promised and so it was done. In exchange he asked for my help whenever he faced difficult cases. He wanted me next to him right into the operating theater. I offered my help and was always next to him whenever he needed me. During his lifetime he was the leading surgeon on this island. He died of old age."

"You mean you were present next to him at the operating table with your gross material body?" I asked, just to set the record straight.

"Yes, of course. He was a good friend and whenever he would call me I would go to the hospital and stand by him. He expiated himself from his karmic debt," Daskalos stressed, "without having to experience a violent death. He was awakened to the nature of his past actions and therefore learned his lesson. There was no need for equal punishment."

201

"The question that comes to my mind is this," I said. "Why did this man pay off his karma in this positive way whereas others must suffer repeatedly before they can pay off their debt and come to their senses?"

"All human beings are given the option to choose. When you are in Kamaloka your inner self will come in conscious contact with the four great masters of the elements to offer you the opportunity to come down and pay back your karmic obligations. How you do it is your own choice. I accept what Rudolf Steiner says about your choosing to come down—that your inner self chooses. But when is that done? Only after you have studied your ledger of debits and credits, what you owe and what others owe you." Daskalos pretended to hold an imaginary ledger flipping the pages one by one with his finger.

"I have studied many other cases like the one of this doctor and I have reached the realization that all human beings are free to choose how their next life will unfold prior to the second death. They can choose before the second death and before their next incarnation how they are going to come down and deal with their karma. If you were a murderous wolf in your previous life and you remain a murderous wolf in Kamaloka, then you come down to be a wolf, to bite and be bitten over and over. On the other hand, when you come to your senses because in Kamaloka you have assimilated the lessons offered in the previous life and realized what you have done, then from a wild wolf you can be transformed into a wolf-dog who can protect and be of service. You now come down to serve rather than to kill. The chance is given to you. It is the great mercy of God at work."

"Several years ago, Daskale," I said, "you mentioned to me that once you have created karma you are held responsible for it regardless of the fact that you may have transcended the condition that led you to the creation of that karma and irrespective of the fact that you may have learned your lesson. You are bound, you said, to confront whatever elementals you have created, good or bad. Is this not contradictory to what you have told me today about transcending your karma and about God's Divine Mercy?"

"No, it is not contradictory. Let me explain. As we have said repeatedly, karma has to be paid off in one way or another. It is the law of cause and effect. Balance must be restored."

"If so," I countered, "then there is no way that one can transcend karma."

"Of course one can transcend it," Daskalos said forcefully. "You transcend it in the sense that you do not repeat the acts that have created it. You do not add to it. If you stop increasing your debt you will reach a point where you will be able to pay it off."

"In the case of your friend the surgeon you explained that he was spared the experience of having to die by the sword even though he had committed acts in a previous incarnation that normally would have led to his paying accordingly."

"But, as I said, he paid his debt with analogous good deeds. He was burdened with debts, yes. He had to pay in one way or another. Since he learned his lesson he erased his karmic obligation in a positive way rather than through the painful whip of karma. He balanced his balance sheet that way."

I nodded. "I see. You must pay your karma either through suffering or through altruistic deeds."

"Absolutely. Let me give you a simple example. Suppose I am a gambler and one night I lose two hundred pounds. So I write on a piece of paper an IOU. The next evening I gamble again and I lose another one hundred pounds. My debt has now increased to three hundred pounds. I then feel unhappy and gradually I begin to recognize that gambling is bad for me. The following night I restrain myself and stay home. I do not gamble. I gradually begin to show indifference to the temptation of gambling. This indifference, however, grows by stages. I am not strong enough, so on the fifth day I succumb again to the elementals of gambling and once more I experience the disastrous effects of my weakness. I lose another five hundred pounds. Now my debt reaches eight hundred pounds. The pain is too much for me. At last I learn my lesson. There and then I make an irrevocable promise to myself: no more gambling. But my debt is still standing. It is still mine and I must pay it somehow."

"In the same way," I interrupted, "you may have killed many people in past lives but after recognizing the criminality of your acts you may not suffer a similar fate but pay your debt by doing good and by saving lives, like your friend did."

"Right. You have learned your lesson."

"You said to me some time ago," I said, "that today's murderer is tomorrow's saint and master of enlightenment. But I wonder. How are those mass murderers in history ever going to pay their debts, even if we assume that they have reached a point in their evolution where they have learned their lesson and repented?"

"Then," Daskalos replied, "God's Divine Mercy intervenes. Remember, He is 'The Bearer of the sins of the world,' as the gospels tell us. This is the role of Jesus Christ the Logos." Daskalos' eyes shone as he pointed dynamically upward.

"At what point does the Logos enter to shoulder a person's karma? In your example you mentioned a total debt of eight hundred pounds, a manageable obligation. But what if the debt were five hundred million pounds? What then?" I said, smiling, uncertain whether my question was too simplistic.

"You shall pay in accordance to your capabilities. You will pay two thousand pounds," Daskalos responded. "The rest will be taken care of by the Logos—assuming again that you have learned your lesson.

"Remember what Christ said: 'You and I are one.' Do you understand now what is happening? He said 'Whatever you have done to my brother you have done it to me.' Therefore, whatever act you have committed, good or bad, it is He who is being charged, and according to our religion 'He who offers alms to the poor lends to God.'

"You as a human being," Daskalos pointed at me, "have certain birthrights. You will not be tempted or tormented beyond your capabilities for paying off for your weaknesses and so-called sins. The remaining obligation will be assumed by the Logos. This is what makes the message of Christ so compelling. He is indeed 'The Bearer of the sins of the world,' and this is what is symbolized, among other things, by the crucifixion."

"You have pointed out to us many times that the Logos is 'the true Light, which lighteth every human being that cometh into the world.' It is found in every one of us. Therefore the example of the Logos being crucified on the cross is in reality an injunction to bear in each other's karma."

"Exactly. But realize that when you bear somebody else's burden in reality it is always your own. When in your evolution you reach the stage of development of Christ-consciousness, then you will realize that the burden of the other is in fact yours. You are a human being having Christ inside and the other is a human being having Christ inside. Therefore we have a common destiny. We have common debts. Do you understand?"

Daskalos continued: "Even though one finds this reality within our Orthodox religion, the priests are totally ignorant of it. Of course, as I have said many times, no one can fully know how karma works. And do you know where most people stumble? On the reality of Divine Mercy."

I said, "I suppose Divine Mercy may perhaps be understood with the following metaphor: A loving mother may wish to train her child to develop certain important skills. To do that the mother allows the child substantial amounts of freedom to go about and explore. But the child in the meantime may fall down many times and get bruised repeatedly. The mother, however, is always watchful of what her child is doing. The moment the child is about to fall over a cliff she rushes and rescues it. That is when the Logos as Divine Mercy intervenes to lighten our burdens and rescue us from the precipice of our karmic debts."

"Exactly."

"And therefore," I added, "even the most notorious of mass criminals will eventually be redeemed and rescued from the abyss."

"Absolutely," Daskalos exclaimed. He then proceeded to recount certain experiences he had had at the age of fifteen, when he was beginning to struggle with this issue.

"At that time I wrote a poem that scandalized some people. I complained to God that while I was kneeling and praying to Him to save me from my burdens He was looking elsewhere, focusing His attention on a criminal. At the end of the poem Christ answers 'I love the sinner as much as I love you. He needs my help now. You, my love, you can wait.' "

"I suppose that was part of your early training to accept willingly the karma of others."

"That is so." Daskalos smiled. "First you learn how to assume the karma of those close to you and later on you learn how to bear the karma of those who are considered sinners and even your enemies."

"To be able to do that," I observed, "you must reach great heights of spiritual development."

"Yes, but this *is* The Way. This is the example that Christ set for us. Remember what He said while He was being crucified: 'Forgive them, Father, for they know not what they do.' "

Our conversation was interrupted when Myranda, a friend of Emily's, knocked at the door. She asked Daskalos to examine her six-year-old boy, who had been suffering with pains in the abdominal region for over a year. The doctors who had examined him could find nothing wrong. Myranda insisted that there was a problem and that her son had difficulty sleeping. Daskalos took the boy on his lap and tried to calm him down with child talk while he was stroking the boy's belly. Daskalos' diagnosis was quick and to the point.

"It is nothing to worry about," he said with authority. "The boy has parasites in his intestines." He then advised some nonprescription medicine and assured the mother that her son would soon get well. Myranda thanked Daskalos, took her son by the hand, and left. When I checked with her a month later she informed me that as soon as she left Daskalos' home she brought her son to her physician and asked him to conduct an analysis of the boy's feces. Indeed, the test supported Daskalos' diagnosis. With some medicine the boy was freed from the parasites and the pains were gone. This incident was part of the routine events that unfolded daily inside Daskalos' house.

When Myranda and her son left, I resumed my conversation with Daskalos. By then Emily joined us, sat next to Daskalos, and listened intently.

"Daskale, I would like to ask you a question about the notion of the 'second death,'" I began. "When you say 'second death' I suppose you mean the period between Kamaloka, or the lower levels of the psychic world, and the time that you are about to reincarnate."

"Some people hear about a second death and they are horrified," Daskalos replied. "They imagine something analogous to the earthly death. It is very different. The second death is the dissolving of the psychic body in Kamaloka. You don't even recognize it because it is a very gradual process. It is not something that happens suddenly. It is unlike the death of the gross material body which, after it dies—or, rather, after you drop it—you can see lying there. The second death is the gradual cleansing of the psychic body from its negative vibrations whereby the surrounding environment becomes increasingly numinous. It is something analogous to the illumination over a landscape as the sun rises. You may be in the dark, hardly able to see anything. Then you can begin to see a landscape with the light of, say, a full moon. It is the same landscape. Then you begin to see colors. You begin to feel better, to experience more light. It is now morning. The landscape is illuminated, and refreshing breezes begin to blow from the sea. The birds begin to sing their songs. The landscape comes to life with greater illumination as the sun begins to move toward midpoint, shedding abundant illumination over the landscape. The second death is something analogous to that.

"The psychic space," Daskalos continued, "is the one into which you must be. It is unique to you in accordance to your state of consciousness and spiritual development. And remember that the sun that rises and illuminates the landscape comes from within you. It is not some celestial body, as it is on the gross material level. The change emanates from within you. I am speaking now on the basis of experience. With the second death you will feel that the dark, heavy and confusing world that you were in before gradually becomes lighter, more numinous and that your capacity for understanding has expanded."

"When you die, Daskale, and enter into a psychic dimension it does not necessarily mean that you enter into a dark landscape," I suggested.

"That would depend on the amount of light you bring along with you. You are the sun that illuminates the landscape. As I have told you many times, even the darkest hell is beautiful as objective space. Inside God, inside the Absolute, everything is beautiful, assuming that you are in a position to perceive that beauty. You will be able to see the beauty only through the beauty that you have within you.

"What I am talking about is quite strange, isn't it?" Daskalos said, looking at us both with a wide smile. "But it is the truth. The second death is nothing that you should be afraid of but rather something that you should pursue. Again, the second death is a process toward higher levels of awareness and illumination."

"Do all human beings go through this experience?" I asked.

"All human beings have the potential of having this experience. They will have it, assuming they have come to their senses and assimilated the lessons of the life just lived. Otherwise the masters of karma will put the ego as present personality to sleep. That is, the psychic body will dissolve instantly, will pass momentarily through the noetic dimension and descend down to the gross material level in a new incarnation. In such a case the individual will not experience or have consciousness of the noetic body. It is a very complicated process. Steiner, by the way, got it wrong when he said that the individual will stay in Kamaloka for a period equivalent to one third of the life just lived. The time span in this purgatory varies from individual to individual. In order to synthesize, study, and absorb the lessons of a past incarnation it may take one, for example, a hundred or two hundred years or a few months. It depends. If, for example, someone lived a very tragic and intense life which generated turmoil and violent vibrations within the psychic body, then a longer residence in Kamaloka may be necessary in order to allow for these violent vibrations to quiet down. So, you see, it is an individual matter of how long you stay within the psychic dimensions and not a fixed mathematical formula—which is the same for everyone.

"In studying my own incarnations I have discovered that I usually spend only one or two earthly years before I descend down again to work. And that is part of the reason why I can remember so much of my previous lives."

"Gaining and experiencing the second death," I said after a pause, "that is, remaining in full consciousness as you transcend the psychic body and enter into the noetic body, presupposes a certain spiritual evolution. It is, let us say, your reward for your spiritual struggles. And this reward is to attain consciousness rather than remain a hypnotized present personality—"

"This is it," Daskalos said, clapping his hands. "After all, what is it really that you own in this life as truly yours? Is it your bodies or your consciousness? What do you truly have as life within The Life, whether it is within the lower world of gross matter or the psychic world or the noetic or even beyond, which you can call 'mine' other than your consciousness? Look at your material body. Can you call it yours? Suppose I inject your body with an anesthetic and it lies right there. How can you then call it 'my body'? The I Am which is both the present personality and the inner self does not gain anything without self-consciousness."

"What do you mean by that?"

"Let me pose this question," Daskalos responded. "Does the present personality have self-consciousness? The answer is no. It has an impoverished form of subconsciousness. And it brags that 'I Am and I Am and I Am.' And as long as it is in that state it is entrapped within an overnourished egotism around the present personality. And it pretends that it knows about things. But what does it know in reality? At night this ordinary self-consciousness gets narcotized with sleep and remembers nothing upon reentering the gross material plane. Or it is tormented by nightmares of its own creation, the result of unbridled desires? This is the unfortunate lot of the great majority of humanity until the time of awakening."

(Daskalos repeatedly stated that the way the average person lives is an impoverished state and that part of the spiritual evolution of the individual is the parallel development of psychonoetic abilities. The gross material body, Daskalos teaches, is in a very real sense the prison-house of the ego-soul and a central part of human growth is to transcend its limitations. This includes the capacity to maintain full consciousness while the gross material body is asleep.)

After a half-hour break during which Daskalos attended to visitors with personal problems Emily said "I would like to hear more on what it means to experience the second death and what type of awareness one has there."

"You may reach a point during the second death," Daskalos explained, "whereby emotion, and a very base emotion at that, is no longer the dominant force within you but thought."

"How can we distinguish that from intellectuality?" I asked. "When you say 'thought' do you mean the absence of the sentiment of love?"

"Love is not a sentiment. It is the very nature of the Absolute. We must distinguish love from *Love*. We must distinguish the candle, the burning wood from the sun. The world of ordinary human sentiments, even those considered most noble, appear from a higher level of awareness as nothing more than burning wood providing us with very dim luminosity. You cannot compare a bonfire with the sun."

"But, Daskale," Emily asked, "when you say that during the second death you enter into the world of thought, do you mean that we abandon sentiment and emotion? Don't we need it there?"

"Again, we must distinguish emotion as essence from the phenomenon of emotion. In the higher noetic world you become love, you are love. It is not like in the lower spheres, where you love another basically as a reflection of your own egotistical self-love. In the lower levels you think you love but in reality it is yourself you are enamored with. This is what I mean here by emotion. On this planet few people know how to truly love."

"Well, it is a matter of degree," I said.

"Right. So when you enter the noetic worlds, what kind of emotions do you want to have?"

"You said it is the world of thought," I answered.

"But what kind of thought? Have you separated the meaning of thought from that of emotion?" Daskalos said. After a few moments' pause he smiled and in a hushed tone proceeded to warn us "We are entering deep waters."

"Let me ask you a question," Daskalos continued and leaned back after folding his arms. "What is thought in the higher noetic planes?"

Like a good pupil, I tried to offer a reasonable answer consistent with my schoolmaster's expectations. "Well," I said, "it is the formation and shaping of Mind."

"But is it formation and shaping of Mind about objects out there or do you yourself become the objects out there?" Daskalos stretched his hand toward imaginary objects lying in front of us. "At the higher noetic spheres you do not learn about things outside yourself. You become those things. This is what we mean by *at-onement*. At the higher noetic spheres you do not shape mind as thought forms in order to understand reality outside yourself. You become the reality outside yourself. And when you reach the higher noetic worlds you can consciously acquire any form you like and yet still be you.

"My difficulty," Daskalos went on, "is to convey these experiences with words. Sometimes I am forced to invent new words to convey the essence of an experiential reality that cannot be communicated with language. For example, in Greek we have the word *antilepsis* [perception, awareness]. The other day I introduced to the members of the inner circle the term *synantilepsis* [co-perception, co-awareness]. To my knowledge there is no such word. Yet there is an experiential reality out there."

"What is synantilepsis?" I asked.

"It means for two or more people to absorb a lesson or assimilate an object within their consciousness in exactly the same way."

"If I understand you correctly," I went on, "it is a state where everybody perceives something the same way."

"No. Synantilepsis means to become that something. And in order for synantilepsis to take place, at-onement must precede it. We use such words, but how many people really can understand them?"

"So at the higher noetic spheres, as you define them," Emily interjected, "you enter into the nature of things, into reality itself. You become the reality. This is what you mean by 'thought' at these levels and this is what you could gain during the second death if you are an advanced being."

"Fine. Thought at these levels is yourself. It is your nature. It is not something external to you which will excite or disappoint you. Thought there is love itself. To reach the highest stages it means that you truly understand and live by Christ's admonition of loving your enemies. You reach a point where it is your nature to consider even the murderer as yourself."

"To understand truth. This is the nature of thought in the higher noetic spheres," I added.

"No. To become the Truth," Daskalos corrected me. "What did Christ say? 'I Am the Way and the Truth and the Life.' *I Am.*"

"You reach a point," I went on, "when you abandon the vicious circle of sentiments and assimilate truth and reality."

"Good. Now what do you suppose is sentiment inside the higher noetic worlds? Does it get dissolved? No. It gets cleansed from the accumulated impurities. It is as if you have a pile of stinking mud in your palm—out of which, after subjecting it to fire, you are capable of separating the earth from the water so that you now have two purified elements. Our sentiments are like mud, emotions mixed up with temporal passions of hatreds, resentments, likes, dislikes, sympathies, antipathies, and so on. The earth element in its pure form is good. It is mother earth. The stinking mud in its pure form is earth and water. It does not mean that I should destroy the mud. It does not mean that emotion is destroyed. No. Through a higher agent I purify the mud into earth and water. The earth is pure and sacred, and so is water. And you have honored this earth element by using it to express yourself within the three dimensions. Do you understand what is happening? When you reach a certain level of awareness you realize that inside the Absolute nothing is ugly. What is ugly is a meaning given within the worlds of separateness and the degree to which you express it.

"When I reach the higher levels of the noetic world do I abandon love? Do I abandon the love for my friends, the love for my grandchildren? Do I abandon sentiment? It is here that you will be able to understand the words of Christ. The answer is no. You shall love everyone the same way. Do you understand?"

"You add to love," I commented, "you do not subtract."

"This is it. Some rebel when they hear such ideas. Is it possible, they ask in protest, to love your grandson the same way you love a tramp? Yes, it is possible and I must try. My grandson will lose nothing if I offer love to the other as well.

"What am I driving at now?" Daskalos asked. "Today's sentiment, which is nothing more than the satisfaction of an overdeveloped egotism, must be replaced with the true expression of love. With this you are sacrificing nothing. Rather, you have much to gain. Many would argue, saying that after Kamaloka sentiment has no value, that they will be deprived of an emotional life. Yes, sentiment as it is expressed today has absolutely no value. Water and earth that are mixed in a way that generates noxious smells have no value. Purify them and realize that both water and earth are good and benign. Use a higher agent, that of fire, to bring about their separation and purification. Become yourself Mind, purified Mind."

"You mean thought?"

"No, not thought. *Mind.* To provide a rough analogy, let us assume that mind is the light that hits an object. Then an image of that object is placed on our eye and becomes an irritation upon the optical nerve that transfers the image to your brain and then you say 'I see this object.' This, let us say, is ordinary thought. Then a sentiment develops. Do I like it or do I not? Do I want it or do I not? In this situation you have the 'I' which observes and the object out there being observed by the 'I.' And then you judge accordingly. But what I am talking about is something else. I am not waiting for the light as an outside condition to offer me this or that situation that I can observe, I the observer as something outside the thing I observe. No. I dress myself with

Mind Itself because I discover that me as 'I' has mind as its very essence, which is the essence of the Absolute Itself. It is a different condition than using Mind as an external reality to myself that I utilize to construct noetic images in order to observe objects outside myself. Rather, I fuse my consciousness with the object outside myself and become one with it. And when I become that I do not need to understand it. I know it. I become it."

Emily, like myself, was listening attentively and struggling to understand Daskalos' argument. She brought up the German poet Rainer Maria Rilke, who uses an argument similar to Daskalos' when he writes about the nature of poetry in reference to objects: "Rilke claims that in poetry the only way to understand an object is to become one with the object."

"Now just a minute," Daskalos retorted. "Does Rilke become one with the object or one with the surface of the object, with its image? Because at-onement is a scale made up of many steps."

"Let me give you an example," Emily said. "In one of his poems he describes a panther in a cage. The poet seeing the panther inside the cage gives a description from the outside. Rilke claims that this method is false. A poet can legitimately write about a panther only when he or she becomes the panther inside the cage."

"But how? How?" Daskalos asked. "It is not enough to say it. He must tell us how."

"Through his *Dingedichte* (Oneness with objects) you can get the feeling of what it means to be one with things, to be, for example, a caged panther," Emily explained. "The rhythm of the poem is perfect. You really come to live the experience of the panther imprisoned in his cage feeling entrapped and in despair."

"But he did not become the panther," Daskalos responded with a touch of irony.

"He created this feeling through his imagination," I volunteered.

"Rilke simply rendered the inner reality of things as he experienced it, the *Innerlichkeit der Dinge,*" (The inner reality of things) Emily insisted.

"Fine. But he did not become the panther. At-onement means whatever the panther is you become yourself, beyond time and space. And not to just observe the panther and empathetically imagine how it must feel to be caged in. His approach is a step in the direction of at-onement but it is not at-onement."

"How can you work so that you can reach that stage?" asked Emily.

"By developing your power of concentration and meditation. You may reach such levels of awareness whereby in an instant you can know things about an object which for a scientist may take years and decades of study. A botanist, for example, may spend years and years of study to accumulate knowledge about a species of a rose bush. This, in reality, is a very poor form of consciousness and knowledge. This is what we have down here in the gross material level. But if you can penetrate the higher noetic worlds then you can become the rose bush and you can know in an instant everything about that rose bush. I can know instantly everything associated with that rose bush from the time it was a seed until the time that it would dissolve within time and space. And I can do that because I become the rose bush."

"This is what you said to me once, that it is a form of *rush of understanding,*" I said.

"This at-onement is the most difficult thing to understand, even for the members of the inner circle. You go beyond time and space and become yourself the essence of things. You enter into the world of ideas and not of the concrete forms on the march of evolution. When I spread my consciousness in this state of at-onement what is outside becomes inside. Through at-onement I become one with creation and become aware of the role the archangels play and the Christ Logos, the giver of life. What do you gain? You enter inside the first principles, inside everything. You may ask 'When you reach such a stage do you undervalue things that are not at that level?' No. Because in reality there is no higher and lower.

"I must also add that our desire to know things outside ourselves can never be satisfied. Our thirst for that kind of knowledge can never be quenched. We can never find rest that way. As long as there is a separation between myself and that which I wish to know there will be dissatisfaction. Fulfillment and satisfaction come only when you become that which you wish to know."

Daskalos stopped for a moment, bent forward, and placed his hands over his head as his elbows rested on his knees. "It is not easy to discuss these issues," he said and shook his head. "Had it not been for Father Yohannan I could not have told you a word about the things we have been discussing today. Whenever I lose the coordination I stumble. Don't you feel it? This arteriosclerotic skull of an old man —Daskalos knocked at his head—"could not possibly hold all this material on its own. Don't you see that it is not me who is giving these lessons but Father Yohannan?" Daskalos' eyes shone with intensity as he looked at us.

Stranded as I was within my academic three-dimensional consciousness, I was perplexed. Lacking clairvoyant vision, I was unable to detect and experience in concrete form the presence of Father Yohannan. As we looked at each other I could see that Emily felt the same discomfort and frustration.

9 Cosmos and Mind

Daskalos was sitting on his front porch surrounded by jasmine bushes and a variety of potted plants and cacti when Stephanos and I paid him a visit. Wearing a light brown sweater, eyes closed and hands folded in front of him, he blissfully absorbed the warmth of the April sun. We walked up the steps and greeted him as he opened his eyes. Daskalos was particularly fond of Stephanos. Now in his early fifties, Stephanos repeatedly joined Emily and me for long talks and discussions with Daskalos. At one point Daskalos told me that Stephanos was a real "angel." Even though Stephanos was himself involved with the school of practical philosophy and had circles of his own, he was considered by Daskalos as some sort of a student of his as well. Daskalos thought that Stephanos was doing a great job as teacher even if he was not officially a member of his circles.

Several days earlier Stephanos told me that some of his own students had visited him and announced that he had healed them, although he himself didn't have the vaguest notion how he had done it. He wished to see Daskalos with the hope that he could offer some explanations about what was going on.

"I have a feeling," Stephanos said to Daskalos after we moved into the living room, "that I often have concrete contact with you. Your physiognomy comes to my mind in a real positive sense and offers what is necessary at the moment. And things just happen. I am not certain"—Stephanos paused—"whether I am fantasizing all that."

"No you are not. It is real," Daskalos reassured him with a smile. "I am always with you."

"All right." Stephanos nodded, then said that during the last three years many people have been healed through the school of practical philosophy. "I talk to a lot of people, trying to help them with their problems. I don't recall what I tell them because there are so many. Then they come and tell me that I healed them. The other day as we were meditating I noticed this young woman who suffered from acute arthritis. She was in severe pain. Suddenly I felt some mysterious force pulling me up and bringing me in front of her. Without thinking I touched her where she felt the pain."

"Very good!" Daskalos nodded.

"Her pain went away," Stephanos marveled. "I do this sort of thing and people tell me that I have healed them, but I do it in total ignorance. I really don't know what I am doing."

"But you *do* know what you are doing," Daskalos said, pleasure showing in his face.

"I feel at that moment," Stephanos said, "that I become some sort of a cable through which healing energy is transmitted to the other person."

"It is your inner self that does the healing. Remember, you are not only Stephanos. Stephanos is the temporal shadow of the real you," Daskalos said, pointing his finger at my friend.

"I see," Stephanos said softly.

"Your I-ness is something other than Stephanos," Daskalos repeated. "Stephanos is the costume of your ego-self, your Pneuma. It is your inner ego that does all that. At that moment your wish is to be of service. But who is the one who wishes?"

"It is not a matter of wishing. It is as if you are given a command to heal the other."

"It is because you wish it," Daskalos stressed. "It is you as an inner ego-self, not as just Stephanos, who acts at that moment. Karma uses Stephanos as an agent—subconsciously, though.

"These experiences," Daskalos continued after a pause, "are opportunities for you to reflect on the question of who you truly are. Ask yourself 'Who am I in reality and what is the nature of my projection within time and space?' It is not Stephanos who makes those decisions. Do you really think that it is I, myself, who does healing? I reassure you it is not myself as Spyros Sathi." Daskalos laughed. "You may say that it is the Holy Spirit. Yes, of course. But it is also I as an ego-self who is no longer Spyros Sathi. It is myself as Pneuma, as Spirit. It is that which attunes itself with whatever I focus on. In other words, at that moment you will feel that it is I who is carrying out the therapy because you are in reality in attunement with me. You feel that you and I are one.

"Kostas is fully aware of this condition." Daskalos turned toward me. "Sometimes people ask me whether I am Spyros Sathi or Yohannan when I do therapy or give a lesson. At that moment I am both. Do you understand what is happening? But later, when I am just Spyros Sathi, I know and I am fully aware that I am not Yohannan.

"Let me give you an example: Suppose I am a small candle with a feeble flame. Yohannan is a huge candle emanating a gigantic flame. These are two different flames. When I bring the smaller candle next to the larger one and merge their flames I will then have a single flame." With his hands Daskalos brought together two imaginary candles. "The smaller candle can now say 'I am the big flame.' But I am not only that. The moment I remove the smaller candle from the larger candle I will become again the small candle with the feeble flame. Notice that although the small flame can merge with the larger flame it does not lose its own identity as a small flame. It is, let us say, a state of attunement without annihilation. Do you follow me?

"Now"—Daskalos continued as he turned to Stephanos —"whenever you are about to carry on a therapy all you have to do is close your eyes and say 'Daskale, help me.' At that moment you and I will become one. And as one ego in attunement with me you shall be able to carry out the therapy assuming that karma will permit it. Do you understand what is happening?"

"What puzzles me," Stephanos said, "is that whenever I have a need you just come uninvited. In other words, I do not close my eyes to attune my consciousness with yours in order to ask for help. You just come and I feel at that moment a certain sweetness. I don't make any conscious effort to contact you."

"You don't need to."

"It is as if you are paying me a visit," Stephanos added.

"No, it is not a visit. I said something a while ago which you paid little attention to, that I am always with you," Daskalos said softly as he leaned toward Stephanos. "I shall always be with you inside the Eternal Present.

"In other words," Daskalos spoke aloud again and moved back in his armchair, "when I love certain persons and I have created a special bond with them, as in your cases, there emerges an elemental of myself created by you and by me. That elemental is always with you, within your aura. That elemental is myself. Well, it is and it isn't. Wherever I may be as an ego-self I will always be linked up with you since the elemental of myself will be always with you. Do you understand? It is not a matter of visiting you but a matter of being with you always. Therefore, whenever you need help either for yourself or for helping others, just close your eyes and call me. There is no need to visualize my image. All you have to do is call my name."

"But your image does come in the form of a general outline, without the details of your face. It is something like a soothing light."

"That is my ego as inner self, which is not confined to any particular place or time," Daskalos explained. Then after a pause he continued. "I know it is difficult for you to enter into the meanings of what I am saying. So, let me give you an example. With Kostas and Theophanis I am in continuous attunement. They hear whatever I wish to send them as a message. All I have to do is concentrate. They do know what I am asking them to do, and I do know what they are asking me to do. This is a form of attunement, not at-onement."

"I think I need more concrete training from you, Daskale," Stephanos said. "Sometimes I feel as if I need this physical contact, as we have at this moment, for a more conscious form of training."

"Fine. Any time you wish. In the meantime just practice."

"How?" Stephanos asked.

"If you wish, just isolate yourself for a while in a quiet space. Then close your eyes and bring the image of my face in front of you. Keep it for as long as you can and try to feel that there is that connection between us. Feel it consciously. This connection between you and me will no longer be something abstract and subconscious. It is Stephanos now and not the ego-self of Stephanos who is going to make this contact conscious on the lower level of your I-ness, the level of Stephanos as present personality. But I wonder, is it really necessary?"

"I don't know, I am just asking." Stephanos shrugged. "It will depend on whether you think I need to be educated by you in these matters. I feel as if I do things in a state of ignorance, a condition that I really cannot even explain."

"Things get done subconsciously," Daskalos pointed out.

"But Stephanos wants to become a conscious healer," I injected.

"Well, he is already advanced and can project energy. He is not as ignorant as he imagines. Daskalos smiled. "He does not really need any special training. All he needs is to attach himself to my image as I explained to him."

"Daskale," Stephanos asked after a pause, "what is the difference between attunement and at-onement?"

"The best way to make you understand," Daskalos replied, "is to give you an example from personal experience. As you know, for some time now Kostas has been conducting his Limassol circles in a factory room owned by one of his students. Everything was fine. One day as I was sitting here I saw a dark cloud moving and covering that room. There was nobody inside. Immediately someone's name flashed into my mind. I did not know anyone by that name. It was really very strange for me to see that vision. That day it happened that one of Kostas' students came here. I asked him whether there was anything wrong with the Stoa in Limassol. He said he did not know of any problems. I then decided to find out for myself. The moment I attuned myself with Kostas I saw the road leading to the new harbor. Then a two-story building flashed in my vision. On the second floor I saw Kostas setting up his Stoa. The first floor was a large shop for duty-free items. I was puzzled. Why did such an image come to my mind? The following day Kostas came to our meeting of the inner circle. 'Kosta,' I said, 'I saw this and that.' He started laughing. 'Why are you laughing?' I asked him. 'That's just the way it is,' he said. 'We shall have to vacate the room in the factory because the new owner needs it.' Then I mentioned to him the name that came into my mind. 'That's the new owner,' he said. Kostas described everything in great detail exactly the way I saw it in my vision. Then he informed me for the first time that he was planning to set up a duty-free shop outside of the Limassol harbor, right at the place where I saw it. On the second floor he was thinking of moving his Stoa. 'These are just thoughts of mine for the time being,' he informed me. I really did not know what Kostas was up to until I saw it in that vision.

"Now you may ask how come I could see all that? You see, Kostas and I are in continuous attunement with one another. Between beloved ones and advanced Researchers of Truth there are no secrets. Remember that. He has me next to him as an elemental continuously. He energizes that elemental from his side and I energize it from my side. Whatever he knows I know and whatever I know he knows. Subconsciously that is. Often this attunement becomes conscious either accidentally or when we wish it.

"This elemental of sympathy that you have towards me, which is energized by me, is affecting you subconsciously." Daskalos addressed Stephanos. "If you wish you can make our connection conscious from your own side. All it takes is some effort and training, nothing else.

"We call it elemental, but is it really an elemental? After all, it is a piece of myself. This is what I mean by attunement." He turned to me. "At-onement, on the other hand, is when you and the other become one. This state is at a much higher level. It is the state that I find myself in when I give a lesson. At that moment I and Yohannan become one in the way that I described to you before with the analogy of the candles."

Daskalos then explained that sometimes while giving a lesson in a state of at-onement the vibrations are so intense that Yohannan 'ejects him out' to protect his aging body. The higher master then takes over completely while Daskalos leaves his material body and with his etheric body listens to the talk like any other member in the audience.

"The other day at the end of a lesson of the inner circle Aspasia put her hand on my forehead and was shocked to realize how cold my body was. 'Of course it is cold,' Kostas told her, laughing. 'He was out of it all that time.'

"You see, our life is not limited within this dirt and flesh," Daskalos said earnestly and playfully tapped Stephanos' knee. "The greater portion of it is always outside. When people finally realize this they will understand the great wisdom in Christ's words that 'the flesh is of no use, it is the spirit that enlivens.' They will understand that there is no death—that is, there is no annihilation of the spirit-ego within."

Our conversation was interrupted by a group who sought Daskalos' help. He went out into the hallway to inquire about the problems of the visitors while Stephanos and I remained in the living room chatting and reflecting on a huge painting that Daskalos had just completed. The design of the painting was the Tree of Life and was similar to the drawings that I had seen in some books on the Jewish Cabala. Daskalos told me that the painting, although sharing certain similarities with the Cabala, was markedly unique. The Tree of Life he had painted on canvas with the guidance of Yohannan was the symbolic presentation, he told us, of the very structure of creation. "Only advanced Researchers of the Truth who have reached a certain level of development," he claimed, "could use it in order to penetrate deeper into the secrets of reality."

When Daskalos returned to the room where we were sitting he murmured "There are types of cancer that you can dissolve easily and there are others that you can do nothing about. Karma will not permit it." Then he sank into his armchair with a sigh. One of the visitors apparently suffered with the dreadful disease. Daskalos could do nothing in this case other than promise to help alleviate the pain.

"How can one protect oneself from cancer, Daskale?" I asked.

"Avoid the wrong way of living," Daskalos replied wearily.

"But what is the wrong way of living?"

"The absence of psychic tranquility. The etheric double is burned to the point that the material body becomes weak and cannot defend itself. The British have a phrase that embodies great wisdom, 'Take it easy.'

"Also make certain," he continued, "that your body gets

enough oxygen. The deoxygenation of the various parts of the body predisposes it to various diseases like cancer."

"Therefore," I suggested, "deep breathing exercises are helpful in keeping the body in good health."

"But obviously," Daskalos said and spread his hands out.

"I classify illness like cancer into two categories," he went on. "That which you as a healer can assume from others and you can do something about and the other, which is so serious that your intervention will cause no change whatsoever. That was, unfortunately, the case of the woman I have just seen. She has repeatedly come to me for help. But she would reject all the etheric energy I would flood her body with. It happened repeatedly. I then realized that karma would not allow healing and I had to prepare her to accept the inevitable. 'This body,' I just told her, 'is of no use to you any more. It is like an old suit that has worn out and cannot be mended. Prepare yourself to leave it.' "

"Is it possible to get such an illness that may not be due to karma?" Stephanos wondered.

"No, never. Everything is due to karma. But there are the serious and the not so serious cases. When the karma is light we often manage in such cases to burn the cancerous tumors. But when it is a serious karmic case I ordinarily warn them of the inevitable.

"Not long ago I had a case of someone with a tumor inside his head. I saw on one side of his brain a black spot the size of a large lentil. Usually what you must do in such cases is simultaneously to send ultraviolet and infrared light against the tumor. Through concentration you must create it in the form of a ball equal to the size of the head of a tiny pin. Then you must send it to penetrate the center of that tumor. You must not leave it there for more than fifteen seconds."

"Why?" I asked.

"Because it burns, that's why. I must warn you that you should follow this procedure with extreme caution and use

it only in very rare cases. I have practiced this method myself only for four or five cases so far."

Daskalos then told us that one of the cases he referred to
concerned a friend's son. "I accompanied the family to London where the operation was to take place. But the night
before I decided to practice this method. The doctors were
shocked when they discovered that there was no tumor
after all. The boy seemed to be okay. Keep in mind that
that lad could not even maintain his balance before my
intervention."

Daskalos' story reminded me of a similar episode. A few
years back I had met and become friends with Demetrios, a
Greek acupuncturist-healer practicing in New Bedford,
Massachusetts. Demetrios, whose authenticity I had a
chance to verify repeatedly, informed me of an extraordinary case. He once brought over from Greece Thomás, a
villager who in Demetrios' words was "another Edgar
Cayce." Demetrios humorously referred to Thomás as the
Apostolos (the Apostle). In a state of trance the Greek
psychic was transformed from a humble worker into a master of extraordinary knowledge and guided in that alternate
state by a spirit Demetrios baptized the ET (Extraterres-
trial). Thomás stayed with Demetrios for about a month
and together they carried out several healings. One day Jim,
a close friend of Demetrios, had a serious accident. He tried
to cross an intersection in downtown New Bedford and was
hit by a truck. Jim remained in a comatose state for several
hours and the doctors virtually gave up on him. His
chances of survival were slim. He was X-rayed and CT-
scanned, and they found that he had a large blood clot in
his brain. The doctors planned to operate, hoping that once
the blood clot was removed Jim might have a small chance
of survival. Demetrios was frantic when he learned of his
friend's accident. He rushed home to find Thomás. "Come
on," he told him, "we have work to do." Thomás was not
told what the problem was or that Jim, whom he had met,
was comatose. Once Thomás went into a deep trance my

227

acupuncturist friend asked him to bring within his vision Jim. The Greek psychic gasped. "Oh my God," he moaned, "what happened to him?" "What do you see, Thomá?" Demetrios asked. "I see a large black spot inside his brain." "Listen carefully," Demetrios instructed. "Create with your mind a violet ball equal to the size of that black spot. Okay? Now send it against that black spot in Jim's brain." Thomás followed the instructions and when he reported that the black spot had disappeared Demetrios asked him to proceed to destroy the violet ball. Then Thomás came out of his trance, excitedly asking questions about Jim's health. Demetrios rushed to the hospital and arrived there as the surgeons were entering the operating room. They were stunned when they discovered that there was no blood clot.

Jim had almost about fully recovered when I met and chatted with him three months later at a New Bedford restaurant owned by a Cretan friend of Demetrios. "The accident was the best thing that had ever happened to me," Jim said earnestly. "It opened my eyes to spiritual realities. In fact, I can now claim that even physically I am beginning to feel better than before the accident." Jim said that he felt no pain during the accident. "All I remember," he told me, "was that after I was hit I saw a soothing glowing blue light at the distance over the buildings. I later found out that at that point someone in the street took my pulse and pronounced me dead. The first thing that came to my mind when I regained consciousness several hours later was the blue light over the buildings."

There was more to this story in terms of coincidences and the twists of fate. The only surgeon who could have operated on Jim that day was planning to leave town for an important meeting in a nearby city. But at the outskirts of New Bedford he had a flat tire. He called his wife, who brought him their second car. Soon after he got into that car he had another flat. Disgusted, frustrated, and late for his appointment, he decided to return to the hospital for

Jim's operation after he received the urgent message on his beeper. When he arrived there Jim had already had the CT scan that showed the black spot in the brain. Jim was unconscious in the operating room as the other doctors waited for the arrival of this specialist surgeon. Jim said that his doctors later told him that his situation was so serious that they gave him only a five percent chance of survival. They also assumed that his chances of becoming mobile again were no more than two percent. He was defined as a high-risk case.

I asked Jim how the doctors reacted to his miraculous recovery. He said that they simply shrugged it off as something they could simply not explain, nor did they try to explain. "Such things happen all the time," they told him, and left it at that. The doctors said that their colleague did "a great job." Of course they were never told of the 'magical' actions of Demetrios and Thomás.

"I employed Thomás," Demetrios told me, "because he is such a great receiver and transmitter. I could not have done it alone, since I could not enter these other regions on my own. I knew what to do theoretically but I needed Thomás who has these abilities. I needed to have some sort of an agent to pass through on the other dimension and work from there. Thomás was that agent." Demetrios claimed that, given the nature of the accident, Jim should have been like a vegetable at the time I visited them in New Bedford. Normally he should not have been able either to walk or to talk. Demetrios told me that he learned how to work with colors as a result of many years of exploration and practice into the esoteric teachings on healing by relatively unknown masters of these arts.

I described this case to Daskalos, who had met Demetrios a couple of times, and asked whether he himself had burned the tumor of his friend's son in a similar way, with the power of focused visualization while in trance. "No," Daskalos replied. "In that case I employed projection. I left my body in exomatosis and entered inside the tumor." He then stated that he created the ultraviolet and infrared colors only after he entered inside the tumor.

"How do you do that?" Stephanos asked.

"In exactly the same way that we can cause the transmutation of metals," Daskalos replied and turned toward me. I nodded, signaling that I understood (to some extent) what he was talking about. Years earlier Daskalos had described to me how in his younger years he experimented with the transmutation of metals by turning silver into gold and gold into silver as well as olive leaves into brass. He entered, he said, inside the atomic composition of these substances and rearranged their molecular structures through the power of his will and concentration.

"I entered inside the tumor by miniaturizing myself," Daskalos explained to Stephanos. "I then worked from within by generating the two colors. Once I did that the tumor was eaten up. As I said, this procedure must not last for more than fifteen seconds."

"How can you determine time in such a state?" I asked.

"I can, I can," Daskalos reassured us, nodding several times. "I can determine time. In these matters I am very skillful. When you reach the point where you become master of time and space you can do all these things."

Daskalos said that although he 'annihilated' the tumor it reappeared nine months later and caused the death of his friend's son. Karma would not allow real healing to take place in this case. "When you do healing that contradicts the law of karma," Daskalos said with a bitter smile, "the disease will sooner or later return. But I must do whatever I have to do and let karma decide whether a healing will take place or not. I am not the one who is going to judge karma. It is possible that I as a human being can make mistakes. Therefore I must never judge. The higher masters have instructed us that we must always do our best and never be disappointed when we don't see the results we desire. Let me give you an example. Many years ago I worked on the case of a nephew of mine whom I was very fond of. A wound on his leg would not heal. I tried to cure him repeatedly, but to no avail. In spite of my efforts it took eight months for that boy to get well. One day during that same period while I was in the yard pumping water from my well, a Turkish woman arrived with her son. He had polio and his right leg was atrophied and shorter than the other. The boy was about thirteen years old. In no time that Turkish boy began walking straight without any support whatsoever."

"I have a question, Daskale," Stephanos interjected. "You have told us many times that healing takes place only when one has learned his or her lesson and only when the karmic debts have been paid."

"Right."

"Suppose someone learned his lesson but could not or did not meet someone like you who could cure him. Would it mean that such a person would miss the opportunity of being healed?"

"But there are the archangelic classes and the invisible helpers, my dear," Daskalos replied. "The healing would take place under unexplainable conditions, or so people would imagine."

"So you are saying, then," I added, "that when people's time has come for a healing, healing will take place regardless of any access that they may have to you or to someone like you?"

"Precisely. After all, I am only a conduit of the Divine Plan. Nothing else."

"But suppose the crippled Turkish boy had not come to you that day for healing. Would he still have been healed anyway?" I asked.

"He would not have been healed that day, perhaps. He would have been healed gradually, say in six months. So what? Besides, as I said, how many healings take place under mysterious conditions that orthodox science cannot explain?"

I stayed with Daskalos for a little longer; Stephanos left

to finish up some urgent errands. It was past midday and I was getting ready to walk the two miles between Daskalos's home in Strovolos and our apartment in Acropolis. As I was preparing to take my leave Kostas and Theophanis stepped into the house escorting Petrovna, a British medical scientist of Eastern European origin.

Daskalos was delighted to welcome them and signaled me to stay on. After the usual embraces we settled comfortably into the living room. Petrovna was beaming with happiness. It was her second trip to Cyprus for the purpose of meeting with Daskalos and members of his inner circle.

She was middle-aged, tall, distinguished-looking, and piercingly intelligent. For a long time she had been a well-established medical researcher and professor at an English university with an international reputation. But Petrovna was also psychic and clairvoyant. Because of her experiences she had come to realize, she told me, that conventional medicine was too narrow and restrictive, kind of groping in the dark, really. She felt that there was more to the health care of an individual than just examining, diagnosing, and treating only a small part of the human anatomy. Therefore she turned to the study of holistic medicine, the various forms of healing, and the ancient medical arts. To facilitate her search she left academe and embarked on an international quest for 'true knowledge and wisdom.' After her beloved physician husband passed away, leaving her with a measure of independence, Petrovna traveled the world meeting and studying with remarkable men and women reported to possess the hidden knowledge she was searching for. It was this search that brought her to Cyprus.

Kostas, who by temperament was sedate and cautious, was nonetheless exuberant with the appearance of Petrovna. He told me confidentially that she was highly evolved and had the potential, with some guidance, to develop into a foremost healer. Both Kostas and Daskalos spent much time with Petrovna coaching her in special meditation exercises reserved only for advanced adepts. "She needs," Kostas told me, "training on how to protect herself." When I asked why he replied that her chakras were already open. Kostas said that Petrovna was so willing to take on the pains of others that he had to make sure that she did not get crushed under the burden she put on herself. But Kostas' fascination was also based on his realization that Petrovna was for him an old and close acquaintance from his Peruvian, Mexican, and English incarnations.

Petrovna felt equally happy with her encounters with the Cypriot healers—Daskalos, Kostas, and Theophanis. "My Lord!" she marveled to me once, after she had met them for the first time. "These people have a direct access to the Logos," and she pointed her arms upward. I was not present when Petrovna first met the fragile and aging Theophanis. Yiannis, a close friend and member of Kostas' circles, drove her to Paphos to meet with him. He was sitting in a dark corner of his room when Petrovna appeared at the entrance, obstructing the sunlight that illumined a portion of the room. Without introductions Theophanis waved at her to move forward. "Come, my sister," he said in a trembling voice, and the two embraced. They had discovered at that moment that they had been brother and sister when Theophanis was an Egyptian pharaoh. "Theophanis' aura," Petrovna later told me with amazement, "is just brilliant."

Petrovna sat on the left of Daskalos, facing the large painting of the Tree of Life. Kostas and I sat on the couch with Theophanis on the right of his friend and master. After some of the small talk Daskalos always cherished Petrovna told us of a recurrent visionary experience she had had not long ago.

"I found myself," she said, "going upward with great speed. The light was becoming brighter and brighter. I then popped up like a cork held under water into the most brilliant light, where absolute peace prevailed and the colors were indescribably magnificent. I was among a group of beings, all dressed in white robes of very fine material."

Daskalos interrupted Petrovna and described to us with precision, she said, the quality and texture of the material. He told us also that it was a place in the noetic world.

"I could not distinguish," Petrovna continued, "whether they were men or women. They were in fact sexless. What amazed me was that I too looked and was dressed like them. It felt so right being with them. I experienced an ecstasy I have never felt before. It was as if they were my real family and more. I was truly one of them. What took place during these meetings were discussions of strategies for the future of the planet. Each one of us had a specific task. I was told that I had a mission to fulfill down on earth. My mission was to help develop the spiritual regeneration of the planet. Every time I came out of my vision I was profoundly moved. My life's purpose became crystal-clear." Petrovna waited for Daskalos' reaction and comments.

Daskalos grinned and looked at Kostas and Theophanis with a wily expression. "She has managed to put on the White Robe [become an initiate] on her own," he marveled, chuckling. Then he looked Petrovna in the eyes. "I want you to do something," he said seriously. "I want you to meditate on the Tree of Life."

"How?" Petrovna asked.

"I want you to concentrate on the chakra of the heart," Daskalos instructed and pointed at the center of the painting.

The symbol Daskalos was referring to in his painting was made up of a circle which included within it a six-pointed star that had a cross in the middle. The circumference of the circle was decorated with wavy red flames. Whoever mastered that chakra was at the doorstep of Theosis. We were also informed that that design was the symbol of Yohannan. It was the symbol that Daskalos and Kostas employed to construct talismans. The circle symbolized the infinity of the Absolute. The upward triangle symbolized the divine, logoic part within us and our ultimate destiny. The downward triangle symbolized the descent of the

Logos into gross matter as well as our lower self. The cross in the middle signified the four elements, mastery over the elements and service.

Petrovna followed Daskalos' instructions. She straightened her back, rested her hands on her knees, and with open eyes looked straight into the center of the painting. Nobody spoke. There was total silence except the ticktock of the antique clock in the hallway. Petrovna seemed tense and murmured that the monotonous sounds of the clock were distracting her concentration.

"The snakes of discontent are eating up your etheric," Daskalos whispered as he leaned toward her. "Concentrate and forget the clock," he said firmly.

Petrovna smiled and seemed relaxed. Apparently Daskalos' words had an effect on her. With a serene gaze she remained transfixed on the center of the painting. It seemed to me that Petrovna placed herself in some kind of trance. "You can come out of it now," Daskalos said softly after about fifteen minutes of total silence.

Petrovna took a deep breath and terminated her concentration. She then bent down and put her head in her hands. She remained in that position for a few seconds and then narrated her experience.

"The vibrations of the painting," she reported, "are very powerful."

It was the third time that I had heard psychics using those words to describe what they felt in front of The Tree of Life. "I traveled," Petrovna continued with emotion in her voice, "with almost unbearable speed, through a tunnel the entrance of which was the six-pointed star. The tunnel was lined with angels. At the end I came in front of a Christlike figure." After she described her mystical experience further and the features of the being she encountered on the other side of the tunnel Daskalos struck his knee exuberantly. He declared confidently that Petrovna had made conscious contact with Yohannan. "This is marvelous," he exclaimed, "just marvelous! An excellent omen."

From then on Petrovna was treated as if she were already a member of the inner circle. I sat there listening to the four of them as they reminisced of Egypt and Peru, mentioning names and places they said they recalled from those distant and colorful incarnations. Petrovna seemed to have remembered it all, nodding, affirming, and hinting of experiences that Kostas, Theophanis, and Daskalos had shared with her. I felt like an outsider. When I made a feeble complaint that I felt jealous of not remembering anything of any past life, they reassured me that when my time came I would also remember.

I stayed on and shared with Daskalos and his guests the quick and impromptu lunch we put together. Then the five of us walked to the Stoa, where Daskalos was to offer an afternoon lesson to members of his circles. Before the meeting, however, and before others arrived Daskalos wished to formally initiate Petrovna into the inner circle and dress her with the White Robe. He had just received an instruction from Yohannan, he said, to do so. Petrovna seemed perplexed and moved by this sudden development. She had told me earlier that she felt very comfortable with Daskalos' circles and the teachings of Yohannan. Her cultural background, she said, was more compatible with Daskalos' work than with the devotional pathways and methods of Oriental mysticism. The fact that Daskalos never tired of repeating that he opposed guru adulation and the personality cult with all its dangers and trappings pleased Petrovna's individualism and rational training as a Western scientist. "The Erevna is not me," Daskalos said many times. "I only belong to The Erevna."

An additional attraction of The Erevna for Petrovna was the fact that this school of esoteric knowledge sprang from within the Greek Orthodox tradition of mystical Christianity. Having herself been baptized and raised within the Eastern Orthodox church made it easier to accept the symbolism and participate in the activities of the inner circle.

Petrovna knelt and prayed in front of the icon of Christ

hanging over the altar inside the sanctum. Daskalos, Theophanis, and Kostas put on their white robes, lit the candles, and prepared the sweet wine for the *Koinonia tes Agapes* (communion of love). After Kostas 'energized' and blessed the communion cup, each one of us drank from it "in the name of the Father, of the Son, and of the Holy Spirit." Then Petrovna was asked by Daskalos to repeat after him the Seven Promises that every initiate must recite before being dressed in the White Robe.

"I promise to myself," Petrovna began, following Daskalos' lead, "to serve at all times and in all places the Absolute to which I wholeheartedly belong.

"To be ready at all times and in all places to serve the Divine Plan.

"To make good use of the divine gifts of thought and word at all times, in all places, and under all circumstances.

"To endure patiently without complaining all forms of trials and tribulations which the most wise divine law may bestow on me.

"To love and serve my fellow human beings sincerely from the depths of my heart and soul, no matter what their behavior may be toward me.

"To meditate and contemplate daily the Absolute with the objective of total coordination of my thoughts, desires, and actions with Its Divine Will.

"To investigate and check every night whether all my thoughts, desires, words, and actions are in absolute harmony with the Divine Law."

Theophanis and Kostas then helped Petrovna put on the White Robe. Daskalos placed the Unpointed Sword over her shoulders, recited a prayer, and with his right fingers made the sign of the Cross over her head and kissed Petrovna on the forehead. With that last gesture the brief ritual ended and she formally joined the others in Daskalos' innermost circle.

When we moved to the main hall of the Stoa most of the others had already arrived and were waiting for Daskalos to

begin the afternoon session. Everybody stood up when Daskalos began the lesson by first reciting the Lord's Prayer.
Kostas in the meantime prepared some incense, identical
to that used in the Greek churches, and placed the two large
white candles that were used for Petrovna's initiation on a
table in front of Daskalos. When the latter ended the prayer
we all sat down and the lesson began.

I was next to Petrovna and occasionally leaned to her ear,
whispering and translating from Greek to English the subject under discussion. Daskalos had instructed her earlier
to focus on the vibrations of his talk and to try as an exercise to assimilate the essence of the lesson psychically
rather than through my translations.

"Several times in the past we have discussed the nature
of the Absolute, what people commonly understand as
God," Daskalos began. "However, such terms as *God* and
Absolute cannot really lead us to a comprehensible, grasp-
able reality. Words and the meaning of words are too con-
fining for that purpose. Be that as it may, by using our
singularly inadequate tools of reason and language we may
indirectly draw a few tentative conclusions about some of
the more salient attributes of the Absolute.

"A basic characteristic of the Absolute is Its Autarchy,
its self-sufficiency, self-abundance. It has everything
within It and lacks nothing, and nothing is outside It. The
Absolute is Life Itself. In Its self abundance It simply *Is*,
unmanifest, unexpressed."

Had the Absolute been characterized only by self-abundance and Autarchy, Daskalos said, It would have not manifested Itself and creation would have been impossible.
Therefore, another attribute of the Absolute must be Its
propensity to express Itself. This he called Thia Evareskia,
Divine Self-expressiveness, meaning the love and adoration
of the Absolute for Itself and the manifestation of Itself by
Itself.

"Now, in order for Thia Evareskia to manifest Itself,"
Daskalos proceeded, "the Absolute created Mind. It is that

supersubstance, that infinite ocean of vibrations with which all the realms of creation, all the worlds are constructed. But again, do keep in mind that Mind is not the Absolute. It is only the means by which the unmanifest Absolute manifests Itself."

Daskalos argued, as he had done time and again, that the Absolute is characterized by total wisdom, total power, and total goodness. These three attributes express themselves through Mind as the Christ Logos and the Holy Spirit.

He clarified that the Logos is that part of the Absolute that makes possible the reality of self-consciousness; the capacity, for example, of human beings to say *I Am* and thus create the possibility for spiritual evolution, free will, individuality, and God-realization. The Holy Spirit (or the holyspiritual condition) is the dynamic part of the Absolute that makes possible creation itself.

"We distinguish these two conditions," he went on, "simply on the basis of their functions and the role they play within creation. In reality, within the phenomena of life we find the logoic and the holyspiritual expression working simultaneously. Nevertheless, we can distinguish the one from the other. The logoic offers us self-conscious intelligence in all its multifaceted expressions, from the ordinary human form of self-consciousness to the superconscious archangelic levels of self-realized awareness."

Daskalos mentioned once more that Jesus Christ represents the logoic part of the Absolute. He then elaborated that the holyspiritual condition has its own consciousness, which is beyond human comprehension: "A simple illustration to distinguish the two aspects of the Absolute is to study the basic difference between human beings and animals. The former are both logoic entities and holyspiritual. In other words, human beings possess self-consciousness; they are aware of their existence. This is strictly a logoic attribute. At the same time, human beings are holyspiritual since they do have bodies that are being kept alive by the omniscient power of the Holy Spirit. Animals are only holyspiritual in that they lack self-consciousness; that is, they lack the logoic.

"To repeat, the Absolute in Itself is self-sufficient life, complete, unmanifested, beyond time, space, and human comprehension.

"Now I ask you What are we as human beings? Are we life or the phenomenon of life? Obviously, as a living organism, as a body with a given present personality, we are the phenomenon of life, we are the holyspiritual phenomenon of life. Our material body is built by the Holy Spirit. Yet our I-ness, or *I Am*, whether it is in a state of undeveloped subconsciousness, consciousness, or superconsciousness is a logoic reality. We are logoic because, as I said, we possess the power of reasoning. More precisely, we possess the power to utilize this supersubstance we call Mind and to shape it into thoughts and sentiments. The inner core of us is life itself.

"As a Holy Monad we are one with the Absolute. When we project ourselves within our divine self we *are* life. We do not derive our life from somewhere else. We do not become enlivened from a source outside ourselves. Yes, as a body and as a present personality we do become enlivened. Our three bodies—the gross material, the psychic, and the noetic—are created, enlivened realities. But we, as a soul self-consciousness, as a Holy Monad, we simply Are. We are life itself."

Daskalos stopped a few moments for us to reflect on the material he was offering us. Then, after answering certain queries, he proceeded with the lesson.

"So, Life is the Absolute. It is the Absolute reality, the Truth. Now I would like to make an analogy. We know that hydrogen is the primary component of water, that hydrogen is necessary in order to have any amount of water, whether it be a drop of water, a glass of water, a lake, a river, or an ocean. All of these are children of hydrogen. As expressions of hydrogen they are all one reality, yet very different one from the other. They have their own individuality, so to speak. A glass of water is quantitatively different from a lake or an ocean. But the ocean and the glass of water are both water.

"In an analogous way, we have the Absolute as the underlying reality of all the logoic expressions. There is the Absolute, the primary Logos which has authority over all the other logoic manifestations, according to the church fathers. However, there are, like the manifestation of hydrogen, many logi, large and small, serving a particular purpose within the Divine Plan. Every archangel and every archangelic class is a logos. Human beings too are logi. They are logoic entities. But as a logoic expression an ordinary human being is of very low quantity and intensity. A glass of water is not the ocean, yet qualitatively they are both water, as we said. A little flame is not the sun, yet they are both fire. Where do I want to arrive at? The living universes are filled with various forms of logi expressing different levels of consciousness and awareness. There are ordinary human logi as well as archangelic logi, planetic logi, galactic logi, all the way to the Pan-Universal Logos.

"We have said that within the Absolute there is movement, vibration, pulsation without anyone or anything moving or vibrating. It is only through the creation of Mind that movement and vibration find expression. With Mind the Absolute begins to create the universes, the higher and lower noetic, the noetic, the psychic, the etheric universe, and finally at the lowest levels of the vibrations of Mind the gross material universe.

"Let us think for a moment. Within the infinity of space we can imagine an infinite amount of galaxies. We know now that the distance between one side of a galaxy to another is measured in millions and billions of light years. And that within a single galaxy there are myriads of solar systems. They are the theaters within which the phenomenon of life unfolds.

"We have said," Daskalos continued, "that the Absolute is life itself. And since It is everywhere, then life is everywhere. Therefore, do not imagine there is space without life. The universes are living realities. This supersubstance which we call Mind and through which the universes are constructed has its own self-sufficient life. Therefore it is endowed with the omniscience and wisdom of the Absolute.

"Mind is alive. Just as our material body is a living reality made up of various living organs, in the same way the universes are living entities. And just as the human personality is made up of a gross material body, a psychic body, and a noetic body there is also a gross material universe, a psychic universe, a noetic universe, a higher noetic universe and beyond. As with the microcosm so with the macrocosm. As above, so below.

"Consider it axiomatic," Daskalos continued, "that gross matter, with its solar systems and galaxies, represents only the most infinitesimal expression of the phenomenon of life. Infinitely more numerous are the psychic galaxies, the psychic centers of expression through which nothing has been expressed as a gross material universe. These unexpressed psychic universes, however, enclose their yet-unexpressed noetic counterparts. But there are also universes that are only noetic realities without so far having expressed themselves within a psychic dimension. Beyond these noetic universes there lies the interminable ocean of noetic substance within which noetic, psychic, and gross material universes are being born, maintained, and dissolved.

"Just make a note of the following point." Daskalos glanced at his attentive audience. "Before a gross material universe is born within the infinity of space, the growth of its psychic and noetic counterparts will precede it. The Christ Logos and the Holy Spirit through total power, wisdom, and goodness project, through Mind, the primary worlds of ideas through which a noetic universe is first constructed. After myriads of years and aeons, if we may in fact speak in terms of time, a psychic universe, the counterpart of the noetic, begins its expression. And again after the passage of thousands of years there begins the manifestation of a gross material universe, the counterpart of the preceding psychic and noetic.

"At this very moment, within infinity universes are being born and universes are being dissolved. Similarly, within a society some human beings are born, some carry on their lives at various stages of growth, and others die and depart. Likewise within the infinity of space, and at this very moment, myriads of universes, not just galaxies and solar systems, but universes, begin their genesis as others mature and dissolve.

"Pay attention," Daskalos said sharply. "There has never been a Pan-Universal Night because inside the Absolute, inside Its eternal creative condition, there has never been an epoch without the genesis, maturation, and dissolution of universes. Just so, there has never been an epoch within creation when there have not been human beings who were born in societies, matured, and departed. As it is in the macrocosm so it is in the microcosm. As above, so below.

"Some speak of cosmic nights and cosmic days. And that at this very moment there is at one place a cosmic night and at another a cosmic day. The divine drama, the divine symphony is eternally reenacted and there has never been and there can never be an epoch without creation. The Absolute eternally meditates within Itself and is joyous of Its expression; that is, the materialization through Mind of universes—noetic, psychic, etheric, and gross material.

"With today's lesson new horizons have opened up within your awareness. You need to sit down and meditate over the ideas that have just been presented so that you may proceed on the path toward reality and self-discovery."

With these last remarks Daskalos ended the lesson and waited for questions from his audience of about thirty people. But before any questions were asked Marios, his teenage grandson, entered the Stoa and whispered to Daskalos that he had visitors waiting for him. Daskalos stood up and left the room as Kostas continued the lesson by opening it up for discussion. Lydia, a practicing clinical psychologist who was also a member of Kostas' circle in Nicosia, asked the first question.

"You have repeatedly stated in the past that, with the exception of God, everything is Mind at various frequencies of vibrations, if I understood you correctly."

"Correct," Kostas responded. "Mind is a creation, it is not God. It is through Mind that God expresses Himself. Some mystery schools have confused Mind with the Holy Spirit. It is a mistake."

"If I understand correctly, Kosta," Lydia proceeded, "certain noetic worlds are Mind at more rarefied levels of vibrations and I have heard, I believe, about certain worlds that are beyond Mind. Or am I mistaken?"

"Now, look. We must distinguish between formed Mind and Mind as condition. The worlds of dichotomies and polar opposites are formed, shaped worlds. In other words, from the lower noetic worlds down we have worlds of form and shape. The higher noetic world is shaped to a lesser degree, but beyond that we become disentangled from the limitations and confines of shaped forms and we enter into Mind as condition. But it is still Mind—unshaped, though. Remember, within the realms of creation everything is Mind."

"We have said," Lydia continued, "that human beings are Mind, since they are made up of three bodies—."

"No, no," Kostas protested, interrupting her. "A human being is not Mind. Yes, it is through Mind that human beings express themselves. They do so the same way the Absolute expresses Itself through Mind. But human beings are not Mind."

"Then who is the one who becomes self-realized after returning to the original point of departure into the worlds of separateness, of Mind? Is it the human individual?" Lydia asked.

"No, my dear. It is not the individual as present personality that becomes self-realized at the end. It is the I-ness, the soul or spirit within, if you will, that becomes self-realized. It is that which has descended through the Human Idea into the worlds of polarity, of Mind, to acquire experiences in order to develop individuality, autonomy, and uniqueness. Because it is through this individuation that eventually our inner self will acquire its self-realization. It is the experiences within gross matter that will eventually make possible for a self-realized soul to say, upon its return into the autarchy and multidimensionality of the Absolute, *I Am I* and to differentiate itself from the All."

"Are you saying," Lydia persisted, "that these are not conditions of Mind?"

"No," Kostas said with emphasis. "It is beyond Mind. Everything is Mind within creation, not within Autarchy. Do you understand?"

"I need some clarification," asked Leandros, an accountant in his late twenties and a newcomer into the circles. "Autarchy equals—?"

"Autarchy equals God," Kostas replied.

"What about the rest? Is everything else outside God?"

"No, everything is within God. But not everything is God. Everything is Mind, through which God expresses Himself.

"Look," Kostas went on as he tried to clarify what must have appeared a paradoxical argument. "Consider for a moment the Absolute as vibration, as movement without anything or anyone vibrating or moving. There is, let us say, energy there without any effect. Creation is movement, vibration with *something* that moves and vibrates. In order to have that which vibrates there must be the cause behind it. These are the properties of the Absolute in its state of Autarchy or self-sufficiency. The property of vibration, of movement, must precede the phenomenon of that which vibrates and moves."

"At which point does the phenomenon of something vibrating make its appearance?" Leandros asked again.

"At the point of the creation of Mind. And as we said, even though Mind is not God it is nevertheless within God."

"What is the relationship between Logos and Mind?" asked someone from the back of the room.

"It is through the Logos that Mind has been created," Kostas said. "It is the cause for the existence of Mind. There are certain philosophical schools which consider the Holy Spirit and Mind as one and the same. They are totally unaware of the Logos as the cause of Mind. For them Mind is purely a holyspiritual expression. On the basis of our work and investigation, however, this is not so. Mind was created through the Logos and it is being utilized and shaped by the Holy Spirit for the creation of the worlds."

"I have a question," interjected Vladimiros, an architect and another newcomer into the circles. "Had we been Muslims, would we still be utilizing the same terminology— Christ Logos, Holy Spirit, and so on? Or would we be referring to the same truths through a different vocabulary?"

"But of course," Kostas responded. "Don't the Muslims also speak of God? We use the words *Logos* and *Holy Spirit* to identify and understand a certain reality. It does not matter how or with what language we approach that reality."

"But aren't we already influenced in a certain way by the meanings of such terms that we have formulated in our minds through our schools and churches?" Vladimiros persisted.

"Look! In our research, in the Research for Truth, we aim at approaching reality through direct experience. We do not accept blind faith, advocated by some priests as a virtue. We follow what the Christ Logos has taught Himself, the injunction 'Know the Truth and the Truth will set you free.' Do you understand? Whether one belongs to Islam, Hinduism, or any other religion is of no importance to us. All religions in fact to a degree and in accordance to a given level of collective awareness assist human beings to liberate themselves from ignorance."

"I would like to return to our discussion of Mind," another student, an artist, interjected. "I would have preferred a different term to identify the condition represented by that word. You see, in our culture we usually refer to mind when we mean the intellect. Is there any reason why we cannot use instead of *Mind* the word *Love?* In other words, rather than saying 'Everything is Mind' can't we say that 'everything is Love?' "

"No."

"I suppose Love is within Mind," the woman artist murmured.

"Love," Kostas said, "expresses itself through Mind within the worlds of creation. And within Mind there exists complete harmony, an expression of the total Love of the Absolute.

"Qualitatively, Mind is perfect. However, the way it is shaped and formed through human awareness expresses a certain disharmony. Make a note that this disharmony is not of the Mind in itself but the product of human awareness. Mind does not get soiled no matter how soiled and distorted human awareness is.

"Suppose right here we have a mirror and this mirror is our inner self," Kostas tried to explain the meaning of his words. "Whatever events, no matter how distorted they may be, no matter how deeply enmeshed in a cesspool they are, whenever they are reflected on this mirror they can never soil the mirror. The moment you remove these events in front of the mirror the mirror will appear perfectly clean. It is so with Mind. It cannot become soiled. It assists human beings to acquire experiences for their spiritual evolution. It is through Mind that we as human beings acquire experiences within time and space. Had Mind not existed we would not have been able to express ourselves in the various worlds of existence."

"If I understand you correctly," Lydia ventured, "you

speak of Mind as some kind of energy. I still wonder whether the love that Christ taught, not only the love between human beings, but love as power, as energy, can be considered as an integral part of Mind."

"But of course," Kostas exclaimed, spreading his arms. "Love, which is life itself, is in everything and everywhere. The harmony within creation I referred to earlier is the result of love. It is the product of pan-wisdom. In every expression and form of Mind there is, as we have said repeatedly, the total power, the total wisdom, and the total goodness of the Absolute."

"Let us proceed with our meditation exercises," Kostas said after answering further questions. Following his instructions, we spent ten minutes with the meditation for the replenishing of our etheric vitality. Then he guided us through another form of meditation he called meditation for service.

"This exercise is of great importance," he said as we were getting ready. "This circle has a responsibility to preoccupy itself with this exercise, which contributes to the alleviation of pain in the world. I urge you to practice this form of meditation daily because it is of vital importance. Let us begin.

"We start by entering again into a state of complete peace and tranquility. Expel any thought that preoccupies your present personality. Visualize yourself again radiating an all-white luminosity. You feel now, however, only vaguely the confinement of your form. You feel your weight diminishing. You feel light and you visualize that you are in an environment of abundant white-blue light.

"You are all-white, and the environment all around you is filled with abundant white-blue light. You reach a point now where you lose completely the sense of your weight. Gravity is no longer a restraint for you. Nothing can hold you on your seats.

"You now feel," Kostas continued, "the movement of your consciousness upward. You ascend and you proceed ever upward. Feel this motion of your consciousness.

"When you reach a certain great height, stop and be still right there. You look downward and you visualize that you are at a great height over Cyprus. You recognize it to be Cyprus because you know its shape. To your right you have the east, to your left the west. In front of you there is the north and behind you the south. From this position you suspend yourself over Cyprus.

"Now from your chest, from the center of your heart," Kostas instructed, "begin to energize your love's sun. White-rose light radiates in all directions. You are all white; the environment around you continues to be filled with abundant white-blue light. Concentrate now and focus the irradiance of your love's sun downward and illumine our island, including a portion of the sea around it. Fortify Cyprus with your love. This place needs a lot of love. Wish better days to be ahead for our island. Wish for right thinking of all the people on this place. May your love protect this place. Wherever there is love only love can grow.

"White-rose light on Cyprus," Kostas continued slowly in his firm voice. "Wish for mutual understanding and friendship between all peoples on this place irrespective of ethnicity, religion, ideology, or political affiliation. Better days for Cyprus.

"I want you now without abandoning your focus on Cyprus to feel again the movement of your consciousness upward. You ascend further and further all the way up. You reach much greater heights. Once you reach a very great height, become still at a certain spot having the same orientation as before. You look down now and you notice that the region of the planet that you can see widened to such a degree that in your vision you include in a circle the countries of Greece, Turkey, Syria, Iraq, Iran, Lebanon, Israel, Jordan, Saudi Arabia, Egypt, and Libya. Your center point is still Cyprus," Kostas said as we followed his instructions with eyes closed. "Spread out now the light of your love's sun on this entire region and wish for mutual understanding, trust, and good-neighborliness between all the peoples, nations, and states of this region. Wish for better days for all these peoples, that they solve their differences within the context of international laws and respect for human rights. Peace and tranquility may prevail in this region. May love prevail in this part of the world.

"Now I want you to focus your attention on another part of our planet. Bring to your mind the country of China." (This was during the days of the aftermath of the violent crackdown of the pro-democracy movement in China that shocked the world.)

"Embrace that country," Kostas said, "with the white-rose irradiance that pours out of your heart. May better days come for the people of China. Wish that the color of your love alleviate the pain of the Chinese people.

"Now bring also in front of you in the shape of a large balloon our planet as a whole. Cover our planet with the color of your love. Embrace the planet with the white-rose color of your heart. White-rose color covers Cyprus and all the countries of this region; white-rose color covers China and our entire planet. Better days for Cyprus, for the countries of this region, for China, and for the entire planet. Peace, well-being, love.

"May the love of the most Beloved One, of the great masters, and of your earthly masters be in your homes, with your loved ones, and with the whole world. We stand by the Lord with pure hearts, always. That will be all."

(Kostas had explained to me before that this meditation has as its objective the neutralization of negative vibrations through the conscious creation of positive vibrations. This type of meditation generates benign or angelic elementals that combat evil. He said that one can have as a vantage point for this visualization the country or place that one happens to find oneself in.)

10 Shaping the Psychonoetic Body

In the middle of June 1989 we had just returned to Cyprus for the summer. I was sitting in my father's backyard among the lemon and orange trees wearing my sunglasses, enjoying the morning and reading over my notes. I was to meet with Kostas and Petrovna at Daskalos' home later in the morning.

My peaceful interlude was interrupted by a knock at the front door. It was Anna, a friend of Emily. I invited her to stay and wait for Emily, who happened to be out of the house. As I boiled water for herbal tea I noticed that Anna was extremely depressed. It was impossible to extract a word out of her even though ordinarily she was very talkative. I asked her whether she was perhaps unhappy as a result of the political situation. (I knew that she was a strong backer of the former president, Kyprianou, who had been ousted the year before by George Vassiliou, a successful economist supported by liberal and leftist parties.) She indicated that her depression had nothing to do with the political developments, even though she was deeply unhappy with them. Anna simply would not talk. I knew her well and I felt at ease asking her personal questions in a futile effort to help her come out of what I thought was a serious form of depression. All my therapeutic and psychoanalytic interventions were futile. At that point I decided to follow a different strategy.

I went into the next room, shut the window, and pulled the drapes. Then on a small table I placed a white candle and lit it. Next to it I placed a glass of water and a small plate with a teaspoon of salt. "Come, Anna," I said and led her into the room. I asked her to sit on the chair and listen carefully to what I was about to tell her. "Concentrate on the candle," I whispered. "No thought should come into your mind. Just focus your attention on the flame. Do that for ten minutes," I told her as she followed my instructions without saying a word. "After ten minutes of concentration," I continued softly, "I want you to close your eyes but maintain the image of the flame mentally. Then make a very strong wish that whatever elementals are tormenting you at this moment be burned by this flame. Visualize these elementals being burned one by one. The flame will purify your subconscious from all the unhappiness you are experiencing now."

I left the room and shut the door behind me. I went back to my notes, waiting for her to finish. In about half an hour she emerged from the room, totally transformed. Her eyes were full of tears and she was smiling. At that point she found her "old self" and began describing excitedly how therapeutic that exercise was for her. "It was as if a huge burden got off my chest," she exclaimed. I asked her to drink the water and throw the salt into the yard. I explained to her that the glass of water was 'magnetized' with therapeutic elementals and that the salt symbolized the earth, the element with which the elementals must never come in contact. By the time the therapy was completed Emily returned and Anna, full of energy now, described the episode to her. I never found out about Anna's source of depression, nor did I care. What was important was her recovery from that morbid psychological state she had been in.

When, later on, I recounted the episode with Anna to Daskalos he chuckled and shook his head. "You are becoming," he said, "a master of suggestion."

"I am just imitating you," I replied in a similar tone.

Daskalos taught that the mental problems people suffer from are caused by elementals working within the subconscious. Therefore healing would imply the deenergizing of these elementals, rendering them harmless. This deenergizing can be accomplished through a variety of such means as meditation, self-analysis, suggestion, prayer, and the like. Sometimes probing the subconscious through conventional psychoanalysis may have deleterious consequences. The individual may reenergize elementals, or 'demons,' that have long been silently buried within the deepest recesses of the subconscious. A therapist unfamiliar with the law of elementals and employing psychoanalytic techniques may be unable to handle such elementals once they are unearthed and brought to the forefront of human consciousness. In such cases the elementals are recharged with energy, only to haunt the present personality.

After the meeting with Daskalos I spent the afternoon escorting Petrovna to the various religious shrines of the capital. The old walled city of Nicosia is full of ancient churches, some of them dating back to the Middle Ages. It was familiar cultural territory for Petrovna, who had grown up within the Eastern Orthodox tradition. We visited the churches of Faneromeni, Tripiotis, Ayios Kassianos, and the very old one next to the Archbishopric dedicated to Saint John the Evangelist, Daskalos' and Kostas' Yohannan.

Petrovna would stand at various parts of the church, sometimes in front of certain icons, sometimes under the dome of the church or in front of the altar, monitoring and relaying to me the degree and intensity of vibrations. It was as if she were holding some kind of an instrument checking the emanation of radioactive particles. Standing under the dome facing the altar, she informed me with excitement that the vibrations were "just overwhelming." Petrovna urged me to stand at the same spot and see whether I could also experience what she was feeling. "Try, just try," she urged and gently pulled me by the arm. I stood where she instructed, feeling awkward as I realized that the *kandila-naftes* (curator), dressed in black and nervously counting his worry beads, was watching us with intense and suspicious curiosity. "Do you feel anything?" Petrovna asked eagerly.

"Well," I mumbled, "I always feel good whenever I am in a church, particularly a Greek church." I then apologized for disappointing her, that I was not psychic enough (unlike herself) to feel anything that I would not normally feel whenever I found myself in the serene surroundings of an Orthodox church. Petrovna patted me on the back with understanding and with a sigh she urged me to "keep writing."

By six o'clock we drove to the house of Rea (one of Kosta's disciples), where Kostas was scheduled to offer his bimonthly lesson to his Nicosia circle. He was already there, as were most of his students, packing Rea's spacious and comfortable living room.

The students of Kostas' Nicosia circle included many members of the cultural elite of the island. They were primarily professional people, men and women in their thirties and forties who combined their social and cultural activism with a newfound interest in esoteric teachings. Most of them had higher degrees from foreign universities, both from the Western as well as the Eastern block. Among them there were graduates from British, American, French, and Russian universities. Coming of age in the booming sixties, these acolytes spent years studying abroad, importing into Cyprus a cornucopia of perspectives, ideologies,

254

and foreign manners. Cyprus lacked a university, a casualty of the chronically unsettled political situation. Consequently higher education had to be pursued overseas.

I had known many of Kostas' disciples from my pre-Daskalos years. Some of them were old friends, and discovering them in Kostas' circle truly astonished me. I had known them as agnostic secularists who scoffed at religion as fit primarily for the local peasants and their black-clad grandmothers. Among the women disciples there were in fact some radical feminists, critics of the local patriarchal church. When I first saw these people in Kostas' circles I knew that times were changing.

All political and social colorations were represented in Kostas' circles. A few of them had links, through birth or marriage, to the local Communist party. Others were active in conservative and right-of-center political alliances; and so on. There were disillusioned historical materialists, antibourgeois capitalists, conventional-looking and conservative Cypriots as well as shipwrecked veterans of the sexual revolution. These aspiring avatars were certainly not the stereotypical monkish mystics consuming their days in prayer, meditation, and introspection within the tranquility of a cloistered existence. Rea, a film director of the local television station and hostess for the meetings of the forty or so people, was a highly energetic and passionate nonpartisan activist who was one of the organizers of the Women March Home, a movement that aimed through nonviolent resistance to lead Cypriot women back to their ancestral homes in the occupied north.

These professional psychologists, sociologists, artists, physicians, businesspeople, and architects were attracted to Kostas' teachings and circles because of the rational principles upon which the teachings were founded. They were also attracted to these teachings because of the nondogmatic approach to spiritual questions and the ecumenicity, tolerance, and diversity of its central message. The absence of any cultish element in the circles was an additional attraction, not to mention the total freedom of exploration and "research" emphasized by Kostas and Daskalos. Most important, however, Kostas had recruited some of his followers after they had witnessed "miracle" cures he had performed in front of their eyes. Maria, for example, a clinical therapist and a graduate of Moscow University, told me that she became a student after she had witnessed Kostas' miraculous healing of a paralyzed air hostess.

Before Kostas began his lesson I took my turn and presented him with a pile of letters and pictures I had received from readers and acquaintances who sought Kostas' or Daskalos' help. Kostas went over the pictures one by one, feeling them with his fingers and with closed eyes, offering a diagnosis and a promise to do everything possible to help the patient.

"Kyriaco, we have examined this one before!" Kostas said, opening his eyes as he held one of the pictures in his hand.

I checked the photo carefully and I realized that indeed the picture, which Kostas had already examined several months earlier, was accidentally mixed up in the new pile. There was another photo that was also included from the earlier bunch and again Kostas reacted the same way. Now, I did not place those two photos into the new pile deliberately to check Kostas' clairvoyant sight. But to my amazement that was exactly what happened.

"How did you know, Kosta?" I asked. "You must have examined hundreds of pictures of strangers since the time you first checked these photos. How did you remember?"

"It is simple," Kostas replied. "The therapeutic elementals I created at that time for these people came to me the moment I touched and felt the pictures. It is the elementals that informed me of what happened."

There was a similar episode with Daskalos. A woman came to see him and showed him a picture of her three-year-old son, who had a serious illness. I was told by a witness that when Daskalos felt the picture he spontaneously exclaimed with excitement that the boy was a reincarnation of "one of the Bachs." The boy was cured, migrated to Europe with his family, and eventually became an internationally famous pianist. I was told that twenty-five years later someone brought a current picture of the same person, now a grown man, to Daskalos. Without being told who he was, Daskalos reacted in an identical manner the moment he closed his eyes, felt the photo, and took some deep breaths. When I asked Daskalos about that case he offered me an explanation identical to what Kostas told me, that it was the angelic elemental he created for the child of three that came and identified the man of twenty-eight. Those were the kinds of experiences that people who knew Daskalos and Kostas had constantly witnessed and thereby maintained their reputation as authentic healers and spiritual masters for so many years.

After everyone who wished to have a private audience with Kostas did so, he began the lesson. I sat next to Petrovna, whispering translations to keep her informed about the general topic of discussion.

"We have so far learned," Kostas began, "that every atom, every cell, and every particle of the gross material body has its etheric, psychic, and noetic counterpart. Therefore, parallel to the gross material body we also have a psychic and a noetic body that together serve as the womb within which our gross material body is built. And this is true of the entire gross matter of creation. For example, the gross material earth has behind it a psychic earth; that is, the earth that exists within the fourth dimension. And there is the noetic earth; that is, the earth that exists within the fifth dimension. It is the same with our own material body. This 'psychonoetic body,' as we said, is under the direct supervision of the Holy Spirit and has as its main function the maintenance of the gross material body."

Kostas taught that in addition to this holyspiritual psychonoetic body, which is perfect and matches cell by cell the shape of the gross material body, there are also two

257

other bodies, a psychic and a noetic, also called the "psycho-noetic body" for short, that has as its center the heart. This body is originally amorphous, and the aim of every human being is to "shape" it, to make it as perfect as the gross material body is with its psychic and noetic counterparts.

"This psycho-noetic body," Kostas argued, as he echoed what Daskalos had been saying, "is in the process of becoming formed and expresses the level of our awareness. *It is* the center of our awareness. The Researcher of Truth will gradually shape this amorphous body so that he or she may be able to use it and acquire knowledge and consciousness of the higher worlds and of other dimensions. Without shaping this body you cannot absorb objective knowledge of your existence within these other worlds and other vibrations."

"What about the other psychonoetic body that is already shaped?" I interjected. "What does that represent?"

"That psychonoetic body is the base and the center of your spirit and soul, of your self-consciousness. It is the center of your I-ness. It is that center which receives experiences and impressions. It is the unalterable *I Am*. There are no words to describe the radiant beauty of this psychonoetic body.

"At the moment," Kostas continued, "you do not have that body as the center of your awareness. Our purpose is to shape the amorphous psychonoetic body, the body of awareness, and fuse it with the perfect psychonoetic body, the body of our soul self-consciousness. It is within this context that we can understand Christ's words 'Blessed be the pure at heart, for they shall see God.' The center of the evolving psycho-noetic body is, as we said before, the heart. To be 'pure at heart,' literally means having a fully developed psycho-noetic body that becomes identical with our already perfect psychonoetic body."

"What you are saying then, Kosta," I tried to clarify, "is that our awareness which has as its base the amorphous psycho-noetic body becomes one with the perfect psycho-noetic body, the center of our I-ness, of our *I Am*."

"Precisely. The perfectly shaped psychonoetic body is, in terms of its quality, the same for all human beings just as it is with all the archangels. On the other hand, the psycho-noetic body that we must shape varies in quality, shape, and radiance from individual to individual. No two human beings have exactly the same psycho-noetic body. It is that body that makes possible human individuality. It is the body of our thoughts and our sentiments."

"Are you saying, then," my friend Neophytos asked, "that the purpose of fusing the two bodies is to obliterate the results of individual experience? Is it not due to experience that the two are different?"

Kostas repeated what he and Daskalos have said many times, that the aim of the cycles of incarnations is to develop individuality within the oneness of the Absolute and that this individuality is not lost once the amorphous psycho-noetic body develops and becomes one with the psychonoetic body of the inner self.

"As long as you exist within the cycles of phenomena your psycho-noetic body is basically not fully shaped," Kostas argued.

"Is it always like that?" Neophytos asked.

"No, not always. It is possible that after you have fully shaped your psycho-noetic body you may decide to return to the worlds of separateness and polarity in order to fulfill a particular task. Believe me, once you perfect your psycho-noetic body it is here that you shall be." Smiling, Kostas pointed at the ground. "It is here that you shall return to help others on their spiritual path."

"I am a bit confused," someone who listened quietly up to that point said with slight exasperation in his voice. "Which is the amorphous psycho-noetic body? Is the amorphous the perfect one?"

"The amorphous," Kostas repeated after the rest of us stopped laughing at his innocent tone, "is that which we try to shape. The characteristic of the perfect psychonoetic body is its indescribable radiant beauty. A god is enthroned there. On the other hand, the psycho-noetic body that we must shape looks literally like an amorphous mass around the region of the heart. When you look at a person within the lower psychonoetic worlds what you actually see is something like a sack, like a sack of potatoes, if you will. Such a person can be seen, by one who is advanced and can see, having neither hands nor feet. Such a person literally looks, from the vantage point of real seeing, like a sack.

"This is the truth," Kostas said earnestly, as the rest of us chuckled with his choice of words.

"Kosta," Neophytos asked, "if the amorphous psycho-noetic body looks like a sack, are you saying that the perfect one has the exact shape of the material body?"

"Of course."

"In other words," Neophytos went on, a puzzled look on his face, "you are not speaking metaphorically. In reality through the cycles of incarnations the amorphous tends to become shaped like the gross material body."

"Exactly. This is what I am saying. This is our objective. Why? So that we may be able to live fully conscious inside every cell and every particle of our three bodies, the gross material, psychic, and noetic. That is how we become masters of our three bodies."

"Can you please explain?" Neophytos asked.

"Look. Every particle within the psychonoetic worlds is capable of complete awareness. Within the psychonoetic worlds we do not only see and hear with our eyes and ears but with every cell and particle of our existence. It is for this reason," Kostas said, "that only with a fully developed psycho-noetic body you can have true exomatosis."

"You mean to say, Kosta," I asked and repeated what he said, "that you cannot have a conscious out-of-body travel unless you have developed the psycho-noetic body?"

"That is exactly what I am saying. It is with a fully developed psycho-noetic body that you will be able to acquire objective awareness of other realities either through the projection of your awareness or through full exomatosis. A lot of people claim that they leave their bodies. In reality, what they do is enter their own subconscious. They come, in other words, to a comparable state of consciousness as those who take drugs. Instead of using drugs they come to the same state through different means. In reality, they enter into the world of their own illusions. They do not penetrate into an objective reality where events unfold."

"Can you please be more specific?" Neophytos asked, his curiosity aroused.

"Someone may claim, for example, that he or she carries out exomatosis and visits, say, London. Unless one has a developed psycho-noetic body in reality what one actually does is to visit the 'London' that he or she had experienced in times past. To visit London and observe events as they unfold at this very moment you must have a fully developed psycho-noetic body. It is that body you must use to acquire objective knowledge of what, for example, happens at this very moment near Trafalgar Square. If you ask that person to visit a spot on this planet that he had never been to he won't be able to carry out his 'exomatosis' because that spot is not recorded within his subconscious."

"I suppose," I volunteered, "this applies also to knowledge about the various planes and subplanes of the psychonoetic dimensions."

"Precisely. Unless you have a fully developed psychonoetic body you basically cannot acquire a true vision of those other realities. You will in fact be entering into the world of your own fantasy.

"I must add, however," Kostas said, "that the capacity to penetrate into your subconscious is a step forward—assuming, of course, that it is accomplished through natural means and not through drugs. Nevertheless, it is not exomatosis that brings you in contact with other realities and other dimensions of existence." Kostas remained silent for a few moments, waiting for the next question as he scanned the room with his piercing glance.

"Does the permanent personality have only positive characteristics?" asked Panos, a physician.

"The permanent personality," Kostas replied, "is a god. It is not something different from the inner self. It *is* the inner self, the Pneuma. It is that part of ourselves that has descended in order to acquire experiences. But it is a god. It descended into the worlds of polarity consciously. As permanent personality it has not entered inside a persona that has overshadowed the All, as is the case with that part of ourselves which we call the present personality."

"Should we assume that whatever shaping of the psycho-noetic body is achieved in a given incarnation gets transferred through the permanent personality into the next incarnation?" Panos asked further.

"Absolutely. Nothing ever gets lost."

"Is there a possibility," asked Glafkos, a professional artist, "that one who has developed his or her psycho-noetic body to a certain degree may, because of certain experiences and conditions in a future life, return to a lower state of psycho-noetic development?"

"Never," Kostas replied categorically. "What you have gained you have gained. You may get stuck in the same state for many incarnations, but you will never fall back to a lower level. Whatever advance a human being has made in reference to self-awareness is never lost."

"Now," Kostas went on, "as Researchers of the Truth your primary task is to shape your psycho-noetic body, because by doing so you attain mastery over your three bodies and therefore you will be in a position to be of service."

"How can we develop our psycho-noetic body?" Maria, a psychologist, asked.

"You develop your psychonoetic body through the meditations you must regularly practice, through the assimilation of knowledge, and through self-analysis. This is how your awareness, your psycho-noetic body in other words, develops." Kostas then revealed that during the night for very brief periods he and Daskalos 'shape' their adepts' psycho-noetic bodies.

"What is the purpose of doing that?" I asked.

"So that you may be able during sleep to assimilate within your subconscious the knowledge and wisdom you are offered during your waking consciousness. In addition, by temporarily having your psycho-noetic body shaped you can be of service in those other dimensions of existence. All that, of course, is done subconsciously.

"Believe me," Kostas continued, "unless your psycho-noetic body is shaped by your masters you are basically useless as helpers within those vibrations. Of course, the primary reason for this intervention on the part of your earthly masters is to assist you in the process of developing your psycho-noetic body. With a shaped psycho-noetic body you may, even temporarily, absorb experiences of these other realities. Once you are back into your gross material body what you have experienced usually gets distorted in your waking consciousness since the natural state of your psycho-noetic body is not fully shaped and fully matured."

"Is our behavior different during the brief period at night when our psycho-noetic bodies are fully shaped by our masters?" someone asked.

"No. Your behavior will be exactly as that of your normal state of awareness. Your level of awareness, your way of thinking and feeling will remain the same. The reason that your master shapes your body temporarily is to allow you to acquire experiences that you would normally not be able to absorb, given the level of development of your psycho-noetic body."

"Kosta," I asked, "how do you personally determine that someone has a fully developed psycho-noetic body from one who does not?"

"On the basis of its shape and radiance, of course. When it is not developed it does not cover the entire body. Someone of low awareness has a psycho-noetic body that looks, as I said, like an amorphous mass near the heart, the center of the psycho-noetic body. This mass gradually gets larger and larger. It spreads out until it acquires the shape and form of the material body."

"So you can literally see the spiritual growth of a person in this natural way?" I asked.

"Most natural!" Kostas exclaimed. "Of course there are also other ways that a master can notice the level of someone's psycho-noetic body, such as its radiance, for example.

"Suppose we visit a plane or subplane of the psychic world. Suppose it is a very low psycho-noetic plane, the fifth, for example. Those who go there with authority— that is, of an advanced awareness, who are masters of those worlds—will see, as I said, people having the shape of an amorphous mass. However, if these masters wish to see these people in the way they themselves perceive themselves and are aware of themselves they will appear to them as fully shaped. They will appear with the exact shape of their last incarnation."

"Are they aware of their real psycho-noetic shape?" Glafkos asked.

"Of course not. They perceive themselves within their own illusions, within their own low levels of consciousness."

"It is similar to the way people perceive themselves within gross matter," Panos added.

"Exactly," replied Kostas. "That is why I have said that before one is capable of real exomatosis it is important that one have a developed psycho-noetic body. It is not as easy as some assume that with artificial means such as drugs and LSD they can leave their bodies and acquire knowledge and experience of other realities. With such means you can enter inside the worlds of your own fantasies. Again, to have true exomatosis within time and space or within any of the dimensions of existence you must have a shaped psycho-noetic body, because it is through that body that human awareness is expressed."

"Is it possible to have a psycho-noetic body that is badly shaped?" Maria asked.

"There is no good or bad psycho-noetic body. It will either be shaped fully or it will be incomplete. Again, let me repeat: The more shaped the psycho-noetic body, the higher the awareness of the person. The shape of our psycho-noetic body expresses the level of maturity of our present personality."

"But how do we exactly work as Researchers of Truth in the direction of shaping our psycho-noetic body?" Neophytos asked again, seeking more clarification on his original question. Kostas replied that every human being that descends upon the earth has as his or her central task the shaping of the psycho-noetic body. This body, he said, is the inheritance that our 'heavenly father' has offered us as Prodigal Sons and Daughters. In addition to the gross material body He has offered the Prodigal Son the capacity for emotion and reason; that is, the psychic and noetic bodies. Every human being from one incarnation to the next tends to shape this psycho-noetic body, the sum total of thoughts and sentiments. This process goes on subconsciously through the law of cause and effect, the law of karma. Inevitably all human beings will present themselves at the threshold of Theosis with a fully formed psycho-noetic body. This *is* the existential project of every human being descending upon the earth. The Researchers of Truth work like good cosmic sculptors in the direction of shaping their psycho-noetic bodies. Through conscious and purposeful action they transcend the law of karma and the endless cycles of incarnations, which is a path of ignorance, pain, and sorrow.

"We work gradually and patiently by placing pebble upon pebble toward that direction. This work is done through the subconscious."

"How is that related to awareness?" Neophytos asked.

265

"Your awareness develops through the knowledge you acquire at this very moment. Don't you in fact work on your awareness whenever the knowledge you gain here becomes assimilated within your consciousness?"

"What I want to know," Neophytos persisted, "is in what way do the meditation exercises help us in that direction?"

"Look! The assimilation of knowledge proceeds simultaneously in two ways, by absorbing the theoretical lessons that are offered here and through meditation exercises. Through meditation we are working on our etheric double. We energize the various properties of etheric vitality so that knowledge may be absorbed and become part of our lives. Knowledge by itself, you see, becomes more often than not an obstruction to our spiritual path because it has a tendency to stimulate our egotism. That is why the meditation exercises and self-analysis are so imperative. Knowledge by itself adds little to the formation and shaping of the psycho-noetic body. In fact, it is possible for a person to be a giant of knowledge but have a completely amorphous psycho-noetic body."

"Therefore," Emily interjected, "the knowledge that we acquire in universities totally ignores this aspect of human consciousness. In the universities we are not concerned with the development of the psycho-noetic body. Therefore the individual remains incomplete."

"Exactly." Kosta nodded. "I should further say that even most mystery schools today are unaware of the reality and nature of the amorphous psycho-noetic body. Only the very advanced Researchers are in a position to differentiate and recognize the reality of the psycho-noetic body."

"You mean it is possible to literally 'see' the psycho-noetic body?" Maria asked incredulously.

"Of course," Kostas replied. "That's what I have been telling you. An advanced Researcher of Truth, by just looking at someone, can identify what level of consciousness that person is at. It is possible to do that by observing the degree to which a person's psycho-noetic body has been shaped, the platform and the center of awareness for the present personality.

"Now"—Kostas smiled—"you have not asked me the following question, which you should have asked. Does the perfect psychonoetic body have an etheric double? And does the amorphous psycho-noetic body also have an etheric double?"

Suddenly noise spread throughout the room as everybody began to talk and offer opinions.

"Both of them do have an etheric double," Kostas answered his own question. "Remember, for anything to exist it must have an etheric double. But for both of these bodies the etheric double is fused into one."

"Why?" I asked.

"Had it not been so, Kyriaco, there would have not been any linkage between the two. The fusion of the one, the amorphous, into that which is already perfect would have been impossible. When we meditate using the perfect body as the model, in reality we energize the etheric vitality of the amorphous body in a way that facilitates its development."

"Kosta, what is the relationship of the amorphous psycho-noetic body to children?" asked Rea, standing in the back of the room. "What did Christ mean when He stated that we should become like children?"

"It is the purity and innocence of children that He had in mind."

"Does that mean," Rea asked further, "that before they become socialized and before they begin to have experiences children express themselves primarily through their perfect psychonoetic body?"

"Not exactly. Children come into the world with an amorphous psycho-noetic body whose development and form is based on experiences from previous incarnations. We have said before that we come into the world with a level of awareness that is the sum total of experiences from previous lives. It is possible, therefore, that a child may come into the world with an already highly developed awareness, meaning a highly developed psycho-noetic body. In other words, we do not come into the world all alike in terms of maturity and level of awareness."

Kostas stressed that the amorphous psycho-noetic body is identical for all human beings only at the first birth into gross matter, the start of the incarnational cycles. Beyond that point every human being develops differently, since no two human beings utilize etheric matter the same way. Every person through thoughts and sentiments constructs a unique psycho-noetic body.

"As we have said many times, we are the architects of our subconscious. The instruments we are offered by the Absolute to complete our project is the capacity to have thoughts and sentiments that we project outward as elementals."

"Kosta," Rea asked, "how could a Researcher of Truth, like we are, become conscious of the fact that our psycho-noetic body is developing and is being shaped? Are there any clues or criteria that can help us in that direction?"

"Yes, of course. It is the continuous alteration and transformation of your consciousness."

"But how do we know that our awareness has changed and developed?"

"For example," Kostas replied, "events that formerly used to generate psychic turmoil and havoc within your consciousness no longer affect you. You discover that you confront problems with tranquility and without great ups and downs in your emotional life."

"I think it is time to have a break," Rea announced before anyone had a chance to ask another question. With the help of Maria she brought forward a couple of trays of pastries and a cup of coffee for Kostas. We stretched, walked around, and chatted with each other. Kostas' bimonthly meetings were also an opportunity for friends to socialize. It was eight-thirty in the evening and Rea turned on the television so that we could watch for a few minutes the news as everybody was intensely interested in politics—particularly the developments of the last few months, following the election of the new government. Rea and many others in the audience were exuberant that their favorite candidate, George Vassiliou, had defeated the incumbent president, Spyros Kyprianou. A few others were deeply distressed. Kostas asked his followers to refrain from political discussions since within his groups all political divisions were represented. He kept his own political views strictly to himself and, in spite of his passionate interest in the outcome of the elections, only his very close friends were aware of how he voted. The circles, he insisted repeatedly, must remain above politics.

Before the newscast was over Rea brought Kostas a photograph of a man suffering from a physical ailment. She asked whether it was possible to offer him help. Kostas closed his eyes and held the picture firmly with his right hand. He breathed deeply several times and after a couple of minutes he opened his eyes. Kostas offered a diagnosis of the man's problem and promised to do whatever was possible to help him. He had explained earlier that it is "very easy" to examine someone's state of health by feeling the photo. On an ordinary photograph the vibrations of a person are imprinted. An advanced healer and Researcher of Truth can then come in contact with such a person by feeling the photograph. In this particular case, as in all others, Kostas said that he constructed an elemental of himself which was to work on the patient and offer assistance.

Kostas and Daskalos have also taught that it is possible through photographs to find out whether someone is dead or alive. Daskalos' skills were fully employed after the Turkish invasion to ascertain the fate of some of the missing of the 1974 war.

When the news was over and Rea turned the television off Kostas, responding to a question, explained how a clairvoyant like himself can determine whether one is dead or alive by simply touching a photograph of a person: "Every form of matter has its own luminosity. When you bring a photograph to an advanced Researcher of Truth and ask him or her whether this person is alive or has departed from his gross material body he can automatically feel what color the luminosity of the person will radiate. If the vibrations of that person generate the blue or white-blue color, it means that that person lives within gross matter—that is, he or she is alive."

"Why is this so?" Neophytos asked.

"Because the vibrations that generate the blue color are the vibrations of the gross material body. And we have said that the center of the gross material body is the chakra at the solar plexus. It is for this reason that when we meditate for the good health of the gross material body we concentrate at the solar plexus and we visualize white-blue luminosity covering that region."

"How do you determine from a photograph whether one no longer lives within a gross material body?" I asked.

"It is very simple," Kostas replied. "If you can feel only white-rose color, the color of the psychic body, it means that that person lives only within the psychic dimension. Believe me, it does not require great spiritual development to master these psychic abilities. I should point out that to determine whether one is dead or alive you need not carry out exomatosis and search for that person within the psychonoetic dimensions. If you know what you are doing, a photograph is a very reliable means to ascertain the state of health of a person and whether that person is dead or alive. When you can detect all three colors, the white-blue of the gross material body, the white-rose of the psychic body, and the white-gold of the noetic body it means that that person exists within all three dimensions of existence."

"Do you ever encounter situations when you are unable to determine whether one exists within gross matter?" Maria asked.

"Yes, of course. It may not be appropriate to reveal a certain truth. Under such circumstances the higher masters may intervene to prevent you from doing so. If it is a serious case they may ask you to stop searching, and you just quit. Or even in cases where you have discovered the truth about a person the higher masters may intervene and ask you not to reveal what you have found out. What usually happens in such circumstances is that you stop before you discover anything yourself."

"What reasons would prompt higher masters to intervene?" Maria asked.

"Sometimes if you reveal the reality surrounding the fate of a person you may alter experience people must receive within a certain environment. Usually, however, you are prevented from revealing the truth whenever such a revelation will cause pain and suffering to the people concerned."

"Any other questions?" Kostas asked as he looked around the room.

"Is self-knowledge or consciousness of the inner self a precondition for mastery over the three bodies?" asked Panos the physician. "Or is it possible for one to master the bodies before the attainment of self-knowledge? Is it possible, for example, for someone to learn how to do healing, how to utilize the various bodies, without advancing on the path of self-awareness?"

"No. Before you are able to penetrate into the sun which we call Christ-consciousness you must have already shaped your amorphous bodies. Let us not entertain any illusions. Unless you are capable to a certain degree of coordinating your consciousness with the Logos you cannot attain mastery over these conditions. And when I say 'to coordinate yourself with the Logos' I mean to attune yourself with the wisdom inside you." Kostas pointed toward his heart.

"What about black sorcerers?" I asked. "Do they carry their evil psychonoetic feats without having developed their bodies?"

"Black sorcerers do not have shaped psycho-noetic bodies. And thank God for it," Kostas replied with a smile.

"How come they have power?" Neophytos asked.

"First of all, their power is limited. They have managed through unorthodox means, through certain psychic techniques, to misuse Mind for selfish purposes. In reality, of course, they are harming themselves. The higher masters have power over the so-called black sorcerers. They are just ignorant fellows who are abusing their divine inheritance of Mind. The reason they are allowed to exist is identical to the reason evil is allowed to exist. It is for the sake of experience and balance within the worlds of separateness. We live within the worlds of polarity within the worlds of cause and effect."

Kostas argued that the presence of evil is "the justification of harmony and balance. It does not exist for the sake of punishment as punishment. And those we call servants of evil, the class of Lucifer, in reality are the masters of polarity and separateness. They are also archangels that oversee these worlds. They are simply servants, our own servants." Kostas characteristically pointed toward his heart.

"I suppose," Maria said, "the existence of evil is perhaps for the purpose of provoking us toward the good."

"Yes. Without the existence of evil we would not be able to know what good is."

"I have a problem with this logic," Maria responded. "You are suggesting that in order for harmony and balance to exist the more good there is the more evil there must be."

"Yes, precisely, this is what we are saying. This principle exists within the totality of creation, within all the universes. There has never been a period when this law has not been in operation. However, for us our aim is to transcend this law of cause and effect. Our aim is to go beyond the worlds of separateness."

"I am still puzzled," Maria persisted. "Let me put things in a rather simplistic way. If the human beings of this planet continuously evolve and become better and come closer and closer to perfection, who is going to do evil? In what shape and form would evil present itself?"

"Just a minute, my dear! Just a minute, my dear Maria," Kostas reacted with slight exasperation and moved his right arm forward. "Are we the only ones within the universes of creation? Are the universes just us, this earth, this grain of sand within the infinity of the Cosmos? Are we, the relatively few entities entrapped on this grain of sand, the only ones in existence?"

"I see what you mean," Maria nodded. "We can assume, then, that there will be a moment when life on this planet will improve qualitatively and that evil will not manifest itself any more?"

"Of course, of course," Kostas replied earnestly. "This is our goal and purpose. Had there not been such a possibility, then why the Research for the Truth? Why did the Logos descend? Why have so many masters been arriving on this planet to show various avenues toward our self-realization and perfection?"

"But how can we live without the barbarians, Kostas?" said Glafkos the artist with a strong dose of humorous irony, alluding to the famous poem by the Alexandrian poet Cavafy, that without the "barbarians" we wouldn't know who we are and what we should do.

"We will reach a point, my dear Glafko, that we will have no need for barbarians, no need for polarity," Kostas answered with a smile.

After everybody had an opportunity to ask questions Kostas proceeded with the usual meditation exercises for relaxation and concentration as well as the one for service.

"I must remind you," Kostas said after we completed the meditation, "that it is very important also to practice the self-observation exercise before you go to sleep. Just spend five to ten minutes right before you sleep and review the day's events. Pick an episode and examine yourself. Examine your feelings, your thoughts, your behavior around that incident, but from the point of view of an outsider. Don't judge yourself in one way or another. Just observe and explore how your ego was entangled in that particular episode."

Kostas and Daskalos taught that such exercises of self-observation will tend in the long run to make us masters of our emotions and thoughts—masters of our psychic and noetic bodies.

11   Visions

The following morning I accompanied Tina, the wife of a foreign ambassador, to see Daskalos. When we knocked at his door he was painting in his studio and listening to the news. Having learned of Daskalos' great love for flowers Tina brought along a sizable blooming white gardenia. After I introduced them Tina, a broad smile on her face, handed Daskalos the flower pot. The old master was delighted. He marveled at the healthy-looking plant, smelled it, sighed with sensuous pleasure, and thanked Tina several times. Then we went on with the business of our visit. Sitting in the living room, Daskalos listened to Tina's tribulations.

For the last thirty years she had suffered with stomach problems and occasional severe headaches. So far the doctors had been unable to help her and it was widely assumed that her difficulties were psychosomatic, resulting from the stresses of her husband's diplomatic profession. She hoped that perhaps Daskalos could identify the source of her problems and prescribe a cure. Tina was open to Daskalos' teachings and worldview; she was already familiar with the work of Rudolf Steiner.

Daskalos looked at Tina for a few moments without saying a word, just listening and nodding. Then he gave his evaluation. "Your problem, madam," he said, "is not psychosomatic. The doctors are wrong. Your troubles all these years are due to germs, nothing else."

Tina looked somber as Daskalos continued. "You have a certain kind of germ that got stuck inside your intestines. Your problem began in Turkey while your husband was stationed there. A certain kind of germ got into you then. Your situation got worse when you moved to Japan. There you got infected with another type of germ that cross-fertilized with the one from Turkey. The result was the creation of a new germ that remained inside you, inside your bowels. No medical tests could have detected this kind of germ. Your headaches are caused by the germs periodically blocking the blood vessels to the head."

"What must I do now?" Tina asked, a certain apprehension in her voice. Daskalos appeared thoughtful for a few seconds and then he prescribed his medicine: "First you must stop taking any pills or any other medications for your headaches and stomach problems. This is a must. Second, I want you to do the following. Mix a spoonful of honey with two spoonfuls of grape vinegar and half a glass of water. Stir the mixure well and drink it. Do that one or two hours after supper, twice a week.

"Third, put two fingers of carob syrup in a cup." Daskalos brought forward two fingers of his right hand to indicate the amount. "Then squeeze a lemon and mix the juice with water and the carob syrup. Drink that as many times as you wish. It will be better and more refreshing than any soft drink you will buy in the market. Also, and most importantly, get about five or so cloves of garlic, squash them and then mix them up with yogurt, some olive oil, and very thin slices of cucumber. You may cut the cucumber into tiny pieces if you wish, but do not peel it. Eat this mixture with your meals. It will clear your bowels and kill all the germs."

"How do you know what medicine to prescribe?" I asked after hearing Daskalos repeatedly suggest herbal prescriptions with predictable successful results. He had a simple answer.

"Each physical problem emanates certain kinds of vibrations. The way to deal with the problem is to identify certain substances that emanate countervibrations. When you bring the two together they annihilate each other. After all, what have we been teaching?" Daskalos proceeded to answer his own question. "That everything is movement, vibration, pulsation."

Daskalos said that his medical prescriptions were based on this principle. In his younger years he roamed the Cypriot countryside and mountains discovering and identifying various herbs the vibrations of which were the opposite of the various diseases he was seeing in his patients. With practice and experience he knew what herbal prescription would work for what kind of disease. Daskalos' explanation made me wonder whether perhaps much of non-Western traditional medicine, such as the type dispensed by shamans, was not invented in the same way—that is, experiential work through 'vibrations.'

"Just a few days ago," Daskalos said as Tina wrote down in a notebook everything Daskalos had told her, "I had a similar case with a boy who was thought to have a problem of epileptic seizures because he would fall down and foam would come out of his mouth. In reality the source of his problem was germs in the bowels that used to reach the brain." Daskalos reported that he had prescribed a similar treatment, and the seizures stopped. Tina's problem was also cured. When I checked with her several weeks later she informed me happily that her thirty-year ordeal was over and she and her husband had made Daskalos' recipes part of their regular diet.

I was not surprised that Tina was cured. I had observed

Daskalos and Kostas so many times making accurate diag-
noses of problems when doctors were totally in the dark
that after a certain point I accepted such feats as routine.
In my experience, only once did Daskalos apparently fail
to provide an accurate evaluation of a patient's situation.
He diagnosed that there was nothing the matter with a
particular patient, yet problems persisted. The patient
went to America for testing at one of the best medical fa-
cilities in the country. The tests showed that in fact the
patient was clean, that there was no cancer. The medical
tests and Daskalos' diagnosis were identical: no cancer.
Yet the man died a month later, from cancer. When I confronted Daskalos with this case he spread his hands and
sighed. "We are just human," he said. "We can also make
mistakes."

After I drove Tina home I returned to continue my conversation with Daskalos. Kostas' lesson the previous night
remained in my mind. The idea that we literally construct
our own awareness like sculptors and that the level of our
understanding of reality has a physical appearance, at
higher levels of vibrations, that can be apprehended by an
advanced master was breathtaking. Of course, for me such
a notion must remain hypothetical awaiting my own personal and experiential verification. Like much of what Daskalos and Kostas teach, such views can be verified only
after we ourselves have reached a certain level of spiritual
awareness that would make verification possible.

Throughout history Western philosophers have struggled
with the epistemological question of what makes knowledge possible. Positivist thinkers and scientists from De-
mocritus to Auguste Comte and Bertrand Russell have
vigorously argued that true knowledge of "reality out
there" can be attained only through mathematical logic,
sense observation, and scientific experimentation. But the
eighteenth-century German philosopher Immanuel Kant
had already demonstrated how illusory that notion had
been. Kant demolished the hope that through hard scien-

tific knowledge we can know the world as it is "in itself." Reality, Kant said, is "out there," all right, but we are doomed never to approach it directly. Everything that passes as knowledge is in reality a construction of the human mind. True knowledge of reality, therefore, is impossible.

Parallel to the endless debate between the positivist and idealist tradition in Western thought there is another hidden or esoteric philosophical tradition. Advocates of this "perennial" or "hermetic" philosophy have proposed that true knowledge of reality is possible, but only through mystical practice. This can lead to the uplifting of human consciousness and awareness to higher and more profound levels of cognition.

I thought that Daskalos' and Kostas' notion of the psycho-noetic body makes concrete this perennial philosophical tradition of the mystics. It does so by postulating that spiritual evolution and higher awareness literally implies the growth and development of the psycho-noetic body; that through incarnational experiences and spiritual practice the psycho-noetic body matures, thus making possible greater levels of awareness and therefore more objective and authentic apprehension of reality. The more developed the psychonoetic body is the higher the capacity of the individual for objective knowledge of reality as "it is in itself."

The theory of the evolving psycho-noetic body has further implications, I thought. The existential project of every human being that comes into the world of the three dimensions is in fact to develop the psycho-noetic body. When we left the "Palace of the loving Father," as Daskalos said many times, we as Prodigal Sons and Daughters were given our inheritance, a gross material body, a noetic and a psychic body through which to express ourselves within time and space. The capacity for thought and feeling—that is, the construction of elementals—is possible because we were offered this psycho-noetic body. And the moment we embark on our incarnational cycles we begin the process of our spiritual evolution by shaping these bodies and making them perfect. The actual accomplishment of every individual as a present personality therefore would be predicated on the degree to which that individual has shaped his or her psycho-noetic body. Daskalos and Kostas have stressed many times that it is not the roles, the worldly positions, the university degrees, or the wealth that one possesses which are important but the degree to which one has managed to shape the psycho-noetic body. This is our sole, overarching purpose in life as human beings. It is our road to self-realization and God-consciousness or Theosis.

I mentioned to Daskalos the discussion of the previous night with Kostas and my thoughts on the subject. He smiled and commented that many practicing mystics through the ages have assumed that the psycho-noetic body has as its center the chakra at the solar plexus. "That was a mistake," Daskalos asserted. "Their error was based on their experiences during prolonged meditations on that sacred center. By concentrating there they were able to get glimpses of the psychonoetic dimensions. However, they were not entering inside those realms as full self-consciousnesses. They were looking into these realities through, let us say, a form of psychonoetic telescope. To penetrate into these other dimensions and live fully there as a self-conscious being you must develop your psycho-noetic body first."

"A basic question that Kostas' students have been asking was how one could accelerate the growth of his or her psycho-noetic body," I said, after further discussion of the subject.

"They can develop it through meditation exercises, of course," Daskalos said. "When we ask you to close your eyes, take deep breaths, and focus inside your entire body you are working toward the shaping of your psychonoetic body. The way is through concentration and systematic practice."

Daskalos pointed out that the safest way to consciously develop the psychonoetic body is in addition to the self-observation exercises, the concentration exercises he and Kostas had been assigning. "Just sit in a comfortable position," he said, "and feel that you are inside your body."

"Is it important that one sit in a special way?" I asked (I had in mind the way Indian yogis practice their meditations).

"No. In our Research we follow different methods. Just sit in any way that is most comfortable to you. The point is to avoid uncomfortable positions that would distract your concentration. The moment you feel comfortable begin to breathe deeply as you focus at various parts of the body. You can begin from the toes of your feet and come up all the way to the head. This is to practice the various properties of etheric vitality. Then you must reach a point when you feel not the entire body but that you are *inside* the material body. Just pay attention to this difference. You will feel that you are in a full consciousness inside your gross material body. Stay in that position not more than ten minutes."

"It is not easy to do that," I said. "All kinds of thoughts get in the way."

"Chase all other thoughts away. Then employ the sensate property of etheric vitality and feel that you are inside your body. When you carry on this exercise consciously, subconsciously your psycho-noetic body begins to form and tends to take the shape of your gross material body. With the imprinting property of etheric vitality you must begin to see and experience that you are inside a radiant body within the gross material body. This is the psycho-noetic body."

"Is this the method that will eventually enable us to leave our bodies at will?" I asked.

"Well, you will need to work hard before you are able to use your developed psycho-noetic body as a vehicle to get experiences within other worlds and other dimensions.

When you are ready things will begin to happen. With hardly any effort you will find yourself outside your gross material body and you will be able to see the latter as something outside yourself because you as self-consciousness will be inside your radiant psycho-noetic body.

"I must remind you that at first you must not stay out for too long. You will discover that your second exomatosis will be incomparably easier than the first, and after a while such a state will become second nature to you. It would be as easy to leave your body as it is to lift your hand. All it would require is to wish it.

"This method that I have just described"—Daskalos leaned back on his armchair—"is the easiest and safest."

"You mean there are other risky methods of exomatosis?" I asked.

Daskalos smiled and said that for a mature, well-balanced individual and for one who knows there are no risks. "There is another way of developing the psycho-noetic body, but it is a much more difficult road to follow."

"I would like to know."

"For this second method," Daskalos said thoughtfully, "you will need more intense effort and exercises on the imprinting property of etheric vitality as well as on the kinetic and sensate."

Daskalos paused before proceeding. "Mystics have known about this method throughout the centuries. They would construct through the imprinting property of etheric vitality an elemental of themselves standing outside their body. Then they would transfer their consciousness into that elemental and use it as a new vehicle of self-expression. Then from that new vantage point they would look upon their gross material body as something external to themselves and consider and feel as their real body the one they had constructed."

"Could we assume that through that method we could construct our psychonoetic body?" I asked.

"Not exactly. What we can do with such a method is by using etheric energy to construct an elemental of ourselves.

However, when we project our consciousness into that elemental we also carry along our psychonoetic body. When we concentrate inside that elemental of ourselves in a similar way, as we concentrate inside our material body in reality we work toward the shaping of our psychonoetic body."

"I suppose that for one to be able to do that one must be quite advanced in meditation practice and concentration."

"Absolutely. It takes time, patience, and peaceful concentration."

"What do you mean by peaceful?"

"It means don't be in a hurry. Don't be impatient. Don't push yourself in an obsessive way. To be impatient is self-defeating. You generate vibrations that dilute the elemental of yourself that you are trying to construct. What one really needs is steadfastness and habitual practice of meditation exercises without stubborness that tends to generate fatigue and disappointment.

"So," Daskalos continued, "we have identified two methods in the conscious construction of our psychonoetic body, which we may eventually use as an independent body to express ourselves as self-consciousness. Once you develop these abilities you will discover experientially that you are neither your gross material body nor even the psycho-noetic body that you have constructed. You will realize that both are just vehicles for the expression of your self-consciousness. This is the first gain that one derives from these exercises. You learn how to disentangle your I-ness as self-consciousness from your bodies. Through the mastery of the properties of etheric vitality you will be able to fully use these bodies.

"But again," Daskalos said gravely, "these exercises are safe for the serious Researchers of Truth. For unbalanced and neurotic personalities such methods may create problems and confusion. What is of crucial importance is to purify our subconscious through self-observation and analysis. We must transcend our egotism first."

Daskalos leaned back in his armchair and sighed, a clear

indication that he was getting tired. During the past week he had been offering day-long courses to a group of Germans and Swiss, followers of Sai Baba. After one of these sessions and as we were coming out of the Stoa I suggested to him that he should slow down, rest, and take some time off to avoid overwork. As soon as I said that he grabbed me firmly by the arm. "Kyriaco," he said, "I am going to leave very soon. I must pass this knowledge on." When I protested he reminded me of his advanced age, that he was over seventy-seven years old. "Thank God," he murmured, "that Kostas is taking over. The Erevna is in good hands." Daskalos repeatedly told me "I and Kostas are one. What I know he knows. What he knows I know. I am him and he is I."

"I had a vision this morning," Daskalos said casually as I was getting ready to leave. I sat down to listen to Daskalos' latest story. It was not a dream, he stressed. He was fully awake and conscious when he underwent the experience.

"I found myself in the house of my father. When I was growing up we had a big house with many rooms. The house was demolished long ago. It is no longer on the gross material level. Of course, it does exist in the psychic and noetic planes. I found my father and mother there. I said to my mother, 'Mother, I will go up to my room and get some rest.' I actually didn't need any rest. I had a large room for myself, twice as big as this one. I had my piano, my books. Everything was there. My mother said 'Oh my son, you have been away for so long and I had given your room to your cousin last night, to Andrew.' 'All right, Mother,' I said. 'Never mind.' Then my father said 'Come with me.' We went to the back side of the house. There I saw something which never existed on the material level. It was a staircase. The steps were wide, made of shining alabaster. 'Let us go, Father,' I said. We started going up. We climbed many steps and my father got tired. 'We must rest here,' he said. 'I cannot go any farther.' 'All right, Father,' I said. 'You sit here and I will go by myself.' Once he stayed behind I began flying up. I didn't need to move the ordinary way of climbing step by step.

"I reached a platform made also of alabaster," Daskalos went on. "There were absolutely beautiful, exotic flowers all around. There, I found myself in front of a palace, again made of shining alabaster. When I stood in front of the door it opened by itself. There was a very big hall filled with many precious objects that I enjoyed having in my younger years, carved chests and things like that. All my past desires, past wishes, and attachments paraded in front of my eyes. They were all there. Right in the middle there was a pool with golden fish and a fountain. A lad of about eighteen dressed in white welcomed me. 'Welcome home,' he said. 'This is your home.' I explored the rooms by expanding my consciousness and seeing them all with one glance. 'Did you say this palace is mine?' I asked. 'Yes,' he said. 'It is made from material that you have been sending us from down on earth.' 'I don't recall sending you any material,' I replied. He proceeded to show me one more palace, a very big one far away in the distance. He said 'That is yours too. Go visit it and use it. You even have more like that.' I started shaking my head, laughing. He said 'Tell me why you are laughing.' I said 'Down on earth we need a house because it rains, it snows, it is windy. Why these palaces for me here? To protect me from what?' He said 'You have sent these materials and we prepared them for you. If you so wish you can have them.' Well, I went further in and examined those beautiful things but without any fascination, without any desire to have them or call them 'mine.' Then an old man came and said 'Welcome home, my son.' I said 'Thank you. But why did you call me? This fellow said that this palace is mine.' 'Of course it is,' said the old man. I said 'I believe I have gone beyond the meanings of mine and yours. Besides,' I said, 'if I so wish I can expand my consciousness over the waves, over the rocks and gardens and feel them all and make them part of myself. I am in no need for a house to live in.' Then we went on to talk about the nature of desire, that by being stuck to desires in reality we indulge in self-punishment.

"Now, what do you suppose that vision was all about?" Daskalos folded his arms. "Was it about a foolish ego, a restless ego?" he asked, laughing, expecting me to play the role of some sort of an analyst of visions.

"It sounds to me," I said with some reluctance in my voice, "as if you carried on a dialogue with your inner self. The angel and the old man were aspects of yourself."

"Precisely!" Daskalos' eyes lit up. "What is the most precious thing in life other than to find yourself? And when you do so you need nothing else. You own things in this life because you need them for your material survival, but don't be fascinated by them. When you find yourself you have everything."

"So that was the lesson of the vision?" I said.

"What else could it be?"

(Daskalos' experience reminded me of a vision Kostas had experienced some time earlier. He described it to me and Petrovna the day after he had it. "I was walking on the road," Kostas said, "when I saw an old bearded man dressed in white carrying a large heavy cross on his back. I went up to him, trying to give him a hand, but he stopped me. 'I have something else for you to carry, my son. Here,' he said and presented me with a large sack. I opened it and what do you think I found there?" "Thousands of little crosses!" Petrovna burst out laughing. "Exactly," Kostas replied.)

"Before you leave, please go into my bedroom and fetch those photographs lying on my bed," Daskalos asked.

It was a huge pile of photographs, sent to him from all over Europe. Daskalos' reputation was spreading and large numbers of people were seeking him out and sending photos for healing from a distance. I remained seated next to him, staying a little longer as I tried to help him sort out the photos, repeating my admonition that he really needed a good rest.

He examined each picture one at a time by feeling the

vibrations of the person. Daskalos instructed me to make three piles as he passed each photo to me. One pile was for the cases he felt he could do nothing about. In one instance, for example, he felt the vibrations of a boy and concluded that it was too late. The boy was already dead. The second pile was for urgent cases that needed immediate attention. And the third and largest pile was for cases he was going to work on gradually, as there was no emergency. After forty-five minutes all photos had been examined. He then asked me to place the urgent cases on the altar and under the Unpointed Sword. I then stood up and walked out the door as another group of foreign visitors entered the house.

Matters were beginning to get out of hand. Daskalos and Kostas were inundated with visitors seeking spiritual guidance or healing, or being just curious. When I originally mentioned to Daskalos that perhaps the time had come for the setting up of some kind of an organization to cope with the logistical problems of the international interest in the teachings and in himself he shrugged it off. He showed no particular interest, content as he was with his casual open-door approach, informal ways, and total accessibility. A group of us, however—including Kostas—began to recognize the inevitability, indeed the necessity, of some form of foundation not only to offer support to Daskalos and Kostas but also to handle the growing interest in the teachings and the demand for taped talks, overseas circles, and so on.

"Why on earth do we need an organization?" Daskalos protested to me once. "Jesus, after all, taught very effectively under the olive trees. At least we have the Stoa and a roof over our heads." I tried to explain to him that the Roman era was over and that for better or for worse we were living in the jet age. After pondering the logic of this argument and faced with the increasing number of spiritual tourists arriving at his doorstep in an ad hoc fashion Daskalos began to have second thoughts about his earlier reluctance. He finally gave his consent for the creation of a nonprofit foundation after he and Kostas had undergone an experience during one of the meetings of the inner circle. Kostas told me that during that meeting Yohannan, speaking through Daskalos, advised them of the wisdom of setting up a spiritual center and of their duty to disseminate the teachings and the spiritual training to wider audiences.

"Yohannan," Kostas said, "emphasized that this center must not be limited only to people who are Christians but to everybody, whether Buddhist, Hindu, Muslim, Jewish, or whoever is capable of expressing his or her love nature. There must be neither dogmatism nor any discrimination against anyone. The only criterion for membership in the organization must be the capacity of a person to express love for humanity."

Daskalos told us that he himself would not be involved with the administration of such a foundation and that whatever structure was created must serve the aims of the Research for the Truth.

At the inaugural meeting of the EREVNA, the legal name that had been chosen to register the new institution, there were close to two hundred members, including some Germans and Americans. Daskalos was sitting next to Kostas as the latter explained to the audience the nature of the foundation and its goals. After the brief formal presentation Kostas asked Daskalos to come to the podium. The old master stood up slowly, betraying obvious signs of emotion on his face. It must have crossed his mind during those few moments that finally his work was becoming recognized not only in Cyprus but also internationally. For decades he had been carrying on a lonely struggle to pass on the teachings in the midst of a society more hostile than sympathetic to his work and activities. At last now, in the twilight of his life, the knowledge that had been pouring out of him—and now also through Kostas—was beginning to attract an increasing and appreciative audience. His original reluctance for setting up the foundation seemed to have all but vanished.

"My heart is filled with great joy," he began in a slightly

broken voice, "that the work is now being systematized. I have no words to thank my brother and most beloved Kostas for the great task that he has undertaken. Because it is he who will actually bear the burden and difficult task of systematizing the teachings."

Daskalos said that, being advanced in age, he would not involve himself in any of the activities related to organizational matters. Besides, he added, he was already overburdened with spiritual and healing responsibilities. He then proceeded to remind his audience that to enter inside the meaning of the Research for the Truth it was imperative to learn how to be of service to fellow human beings.

"As Researchers of the Truth," he concluded, "we must realize that our primary task is to slay the dragon of our egotism and, through the assimilation of our present personality with the inner self, to replace it with the shining brilliance and dignity of our souls."

After the banquet Kostas, at the urging of members of the audience who were either newcomers to the circles or guests for the special inaugural evening, volunteered to give an impromptu introductory lesson.

.   .   .

The summer of 1989 was coming to an end and, as in so many other summers, we were getting ready for the return trip to Maine. Our good friend Yiannis, a member of Kostas' circles organized an excursion up into the Troödos Mountains the last Sunday before our departure to celebrate the inauguration of EREVNA. Yiannis' passionate vision was to see a spiritual retreat set up somewhere on his beloved mountains. A British-trained accountant and environmental activist, Yiannis was a veteran of other spiritual groups before joining the circles.

The gathering was at Platés, a rather inaccessible but majestically beautiful river valley in the Troödos Mountains right below the village of Tris Elies, where Yiannis grew up. He had a particular affinity to Platés not only because he roamed those mountains and valleys when he was young but also because he almost singlehandedly had saved the valley from being turned into a dam. Thanks to his efforts the new government had declared it a nature preserve. Yiannis' long-term plan was to mobilize the various environmental groups to save the entire Troödos mountain region from developers.

After an adventurous journey through dirt roads, around narrow curves, and over bridges we arrived at Platés. We unloaded our cars and spread our blankets on the riverbank near the water and next to an ancient stone bridge built by the Romans during the early years of Christianity. The thick foliage and high altitude combined with the coolness of the flowing water protected us from the August heat.

Kostas and Antonis arrived from Limassol with their families and Petrovna, who was there for the summer. She had already begun circles of her own for the Research of Truth in both London and Belgium.

Emily, our children, and I traveled to Platés with Yiannis and Sophia, who had come to the island three weeks earlier. Our conversation two summers before had apparently had an effect on her. Not only did she meet Daskalos and Kostas repeatedly but she also attended several of their meetings.

Sophia was to stay in Cyprus for her sabbatical year; she planned to carry on research related to the local ethnic strife. She also looked forward to becoming involved with the Center for Women's Studies that Emily, with the support of the United Nations and the encouragement of Daskalos and Kostas, had been instrumental in setting up during her stay on the island. In addition, Sophia was to attend Kostas' Nicosia circle. In the meantime she had read many of the books I had suggested to her two years earlier as a way of introducing herself to esoteric philosophy.

Doros and Stephanos with their families also came along, bringing as their guest Linda, a New York executive who with her valuable experience with research foundations had played a decisive role in the setting up of EREVNA.

Doros was a social instructor of the Research for the Truth and, like Yiannis, a veteran of several other spiritual groups before joining the circles. Social instructors are those Researchers of the Truth who, although not masters themselves, have sufficiently assimilated the teachings of Yohannan, both in theory and practice, that they have assumed circles of their own under the supervision and guidance of Daskalos or Kostas.

After our lunch of vegetables, olives, bread, and the special Cypriot goat cheese called *halloumi*, we discussed, while sitting in a circle, some of the organizational matters of EREVNA. Kostas repeated what he had said many times, that there must not be any personality cult or guru worship and that the organization be set up simply to facilitate the dissemination of the teachings. "The Research for the Truth," he said, "is neither me nor Daskalos nor anybody else."

Sitting on a blanket and leaning back against a tree trunk, Kostas said that the social instructors must always maintain their vigilance and not become uncritical devotees.

"Please clarify what you mean," Petrovna asked.

"Well," Kostas replied, "I have said many times that masters are also human beings with ordinary human weaknesses. As long as you are living within a gross material body you cannot be perfect and you cannot be infallible. To give you a crude example, suppose somebody hits me or Daskalos on the head and there is damage to the brain. That brain can no longer function as an instrument for the dissemination of knowledge. Would you still continue to take us seriously, no matter how illogical we may sound? Remember, the aim of the Research for the Truth is experiential knowledge and the growth of human awareness, the discovery within us the source of wisdom deeply buried within our inner self."

"Kosta," Emily asked, "sometime ago you told us that

you and Daskalos 'supervise' the spiritual development of the members of your circles and of the work of the social instructors. How do you do that? How do you 'monitor' our spiritual development?"

"Through the elementals, of course."

"Elementals that you and Daskalos create?"

"Precisely. That is why sometimes some of you would come and tell me 'I saw you there.' And I guarantee you I was not 'there.' " Kostas chuckled.

"Who was 'there,' then?" Emily asked.

"The elemental of myself, of course. In such cases your consciousness has been coordinated with the elemental I have created and which is always with you. This is part of the work and the responsibility of the master."

"Kosta, does this elemental offer protection?" Antonis, lying sideways on a blanket, asked.

"It protects and admonishes, assuming that the present personality does not act in a naughty way," Kostas said, laughing.

"Why?"

"Because that present personality may act in a way that is outside the guidelines of The Erevna. You see, there is a certain (let us say) programming that goes on in accordance with what has been stored up within the subconscious of the individual as knowledge, guidance, suggestion. From the moment, however, that a present personality steps outside these guidelines, then the elemental cannot offer protection. Otherwise the individuality and freedom of the will of the person is violated. Alas if that had been the case."

After further questions about how these protective elementals work Kostas went on to describe for us an episode as an illustration of how these elementals work.

"About a month ago some people sent us from England a picture of a fellow. It was a very serious case. The doctors have given up on him. They asked for help. The patient doesn't know anything about this. Actually, he is not in a position to know. When I received the photo in my hands I recognized that it was a very advanced case of cancer. Our objective, of course, is to help that person. Fortunately he no longer has any pains. We have been trying for a month now to help him.

"Last week," Kostas went on, "they phoned me from London. It was late at night. The person—speaking English, of course—introduced himself. I am so-and-so and I am the brother of the fellow whose picture we sent you. I want to tell you something. Last night, after several months during which time my brother never spoke a word at all due to his condition, he began to focus on us. He had never done it before all these months. And he said the following that made us very worried. He said 'These people in Cyprus get in the way.' Now this man did not know anything about us or that we were from Cyprus. The English fellow asked me on the phone 'what's happening? It seems that you are obstructing him about something.' 'Of course we are,' I said. 'We prevent him from leaving this life. This is what we are doing to him.' We have created elementals that are helping him remain within the gross material world as much as possible.

"Now, this is to show you how we work with elementals and also to make you understand that this man is now being expressed within the psychonoetic dimensions of existence. Our contact with that person is known to him there. Then he transfers to the gross material level the memory of what went on on the other side. To be honest with you, this man is expressed mostly within these other vibrations by now.

"Let us assume now for the sake of argument that this man becomes completely well; he is freed from his illness, from this experience. Is he going to maintain the memories of our encounters? I tell you no. Do you know the reason why? Because his psycho-noetic body is not so developed as to enable him to maintain the memory of his experiences he underwent within those psychonoetic realms."

"Is it not better to just let him depart?" Sophia asked.

"We have a duty even to the last moments to help him recover. We can never know what karma will decide. In this particular case," Kostas said, "a lot of people expressed interest, both in England and here in Cyprus."

"Is that important?" Stephanos asked.

"No. But the moment a human being expresses concern about another human being and such a case has reached our awareness we must as Researchers of the Truth stand by this expression of love of one human being to another."

"But why not allow this fellow to depart?" Sophia, sitting on the pebbles next to Emily, asked again.

"Look. The longer you help this fellow stay in this life the more you help him pay off his karmic debts. It is not only our duty to preserve life but to also help him disentangle himself from the weight of his karma. So why not pay now instead of remaining tied to negative karma that he will have to carry over into the next life?"

"Since he is dying doesn't it mean that he will be freed of his karma?" asked Linda.

"No, my dear," Kostas said with emphasis. "Had it been so, then suicide would have been a pathway to freedom.

"Look! In such situations as this, human beings express themselves more fully within these other worlds and they become enchanted there. This is a fact. They don't want to return to their bodies. You see, these other worlds are far superior to the gross material world. People like it there and they wish to stay. In other words, they loosen up and stop trying to stay within their bodies. When you go to assist them to remain in their bodies they react, as in this case."

I pointed out: "Many people who have had near-death experiences have reported that they had a strong desire to remain within the reality they found themselves." I noted that some actually reported encounters with Christlike beings who advised them on the necessity of returning to their bodies, as in the case of the "dolphin psychiatrist" John Lilly, who wrote about it in his *The Center of the*

Cyclone. I also mentioned the very impressive work of Dr. Raymond Moody who researched extensively the phenomenon of the NDE (Near Death Experience).

"When a person like this man finally decides to return to his body and remains in this world longer, will he become transformed? Will his awareness be more advanced?" Linda asked.

"Not necessarily. He would simply pay a little more of his karmic debt."

"When you look at this issue from such a point of view, Kosta," I said, "then you must conclude that the pain and suffering that you go through should, on a deeper level, satisfy you because in reality you are paying off karmic debts."

"Precisely so, my dear Kyriaco. Let us be realistic about this. In truth it is through suffering that we ascend and grow in our understanding and awareness. That is how we mature. However, you can transcend suffering by eventually becoming a master of meanings. Because suffering in the final analysis is an idea, a meaning. It is not something real. The very moment you become master of these meanings you disentangle yourself from their power over you."

"Please make this clearer," Yiannis asked as several others of us showed a similar puzzled look.

"You just become master of your three bodies. Then you can no longer be affected by the worlds of pain. Just look around you and you will see this principle operating in your everyday reality even though people are not aware of it," Kostas said. "Different people who find themselves within the same circumstances experience and interpret pain differently. It is happening all the time around us, but we don't pay attention. For example, certain situations that formerly caused us a lot of pain no longer do so, no longer affect us."

"What about bodily pain?" Antonis asked.

"This principle works with physical pain as well," Kostas insisted. "Think about it."

"You know, Kosta," Petrovna said excitedly, "what you

are saying makes a lot of sense to me. I have always felt, for example, that Jesus Christ being who He was could not possibly have suffered on the cross the way we have assumed in our religions. I always felt that."

Kostas smiled but made no comment.

I stood up and stretched after we conducted the meditation exercise for service. I then joined Constantine, Vasia, and Doros' children who searched for crabs at the banks of the flowing stream. I took off my shoes, pulled up my pants and sat on a rock, letting my feet enjoy the coolness of a little lagoon created by the flowing crystal-clear water. I mused on the words of the ancient Greek philosopher Heraclitus, that "you cannot place your feet twice in the same river" and that "everything is in a state of flux; nothing stands still."

When Moses climbed Mount Sinai to receive the Ten Commandments he asked God, appearing to him as a burning bush, "Who are You?" And Moses got the answer "*I AM that I AM.*" When Pontius Pilate asked Jesus the same question he received an identical answer: *"I AM Who I AM."*

The '*I AM I*' Daskalos and Kostas teach is the only reality behind the flow of events and phenomena. The words of polarity, of creation, exist for the sole reason of serving the *I AM I* as It descends into these worlds to acquire experience. Our planet exists for the sake of Spirit-egos, of Pneumata who have been assigned to this planet to develop their Ontopeisis, to attain their uniqueness and individuality within the oneness of Divine Autarchy.

I pulled my feet out of the flowing water and let them dry for a few minutes as I pondered the philosophy of Heraclitus and the teachings of Yohannan. I then put my shoes on and joined the others for a long hike by the river.

Glossary

Absolute Beingness (or **Absolute**).   The unmanifest reality behind all phenomena; the Godhead or God.

Akashik Records.   *See* Universal Memory.

Anamnesis.   Greek word meaning "memory"; that which through experience we store within our subconscious and we can retrieve at will.

Anapodos.   The five-pointed star upside-down. It symbolizes a demonic condition.

Angels.   Projections of archangelic entities; the elementals of the archangels constructed for the purpose of serving creation. Unlike archangels, angels are not eternal entities but benign elementals. Human beings can also project such benign angelic elementals. *See also* Archangels.

Antilepsis.   Greek word for perception, awareness.

Archangels.   Eternal holyspiritual entities that serve creation. Major holyspiritual archangels are, for example, the Michael, master of the element of light and fire; the Ga-

briel, master of the element of water; the Rafael, master of
etheric vitality; and Ouriel, coordinator of the other three.
Archangels perpetually project angelic elementals (angels)
to serve creation. There are also logoic archangels, like Yohannan, who are at higher levels of the spiritual hierarchy.
Human beings are also logoic archangels in the process of
awakening into their godly state. *See also* Angels, Holy
Spirit.

Archetypes. The Laws, Causes, and Ideas that serve as the
molds of concrete phenomenal reality. Archetypes are at
the highest levels of vibrations of Mind. One such archetype is the Human Idea. *See also* Human Idea, Mind, Higher
noetic world.

Astral travel. *See* Exomatosis.

At-onement. State of unity between subject and object;
the overcoming of separateness between the two. You become one with that which you study.

Cayce, Edgar. Famous American psychic and clairvoyant
known by such names as "the sleeping prophet" or "the
prophet of Virginia Beach." Born in 1877, Cayce displayed
extraordinary powers in diagnosing illnesses while in a
state of trance. A foundation was set up at Virginia Beach,
Virginia, in his honor.

Chakras. Psychonoetic centers on the etheric double of
the individual. It is through the chakras that the human
personality absorbs etheric vitality for its maintenance.
Through appropriate practices and meditation exercises the
mystic tries to open his or her chakras for the acquisition
of psychonoetic powers. To a clairvoyant the chakras appear as revolving discs. The most important chakras are
three. One is at the solar plexus and relates to the gross
material body. One is at the heart, the center of the psychic
body as well as of human awareness and consciousness.
The third is at the head and is the center of the noetic body.
The three centers must develop together for the maintenance and growth of a balanced personality. Also known as
sacred discs.

Christ-consciousness. The attunement of the present personality with the Christ Logos within. The opening of the heart chakra. State at the doorsteps of Theosis.

Creative property of ether. The property of etheric vitality that makes life itself and the phenomena of materialization and dematerialization possible. The creative property is directly under the province and control of the Holy Spirit. *See also* Etheric double.

Divine Autarchy. The static and self-sufficient condition within the Absolute prior to all manifestation. The Absolute has everything within Itself and lacks nothing. The state of Being. *See also* Absolute Beingness.

Divine Self. *See* Pneuma.

Elementals. Thought forms. Any feeling or any thought that an individual projects is an elemental. They have shape and a life of their own independent of the one who projected them.

EREVNA. The nonprofit foundation set up in Cyprus to serve the goals of The Erevna.

Etheric double. The energy field that keeps the three bodies (the gross material, psychic, and noetic) alive and linked to one another. Each particle of the body has its corresponding etheric double. It is etheric vitality that makes healing possible. The universe is filled with etheric energy. It can be transferred from one individual to another and is absorbed through the chakras. *See also* Creative property of ether, Imprinting property of ether, Kinetic property of ether, Sensate property of ether.

Exomatosis. The ability willfully to abandon one's body, live fully conscious within the psychonoetic dimensions, and then return back to the body. It implies remembering whatever one experiences in the out-of-the-body state.

Fifth dimension. *See* Psychic world.

Fourth dimension. *See* Noetic world.

Green Line. The boundary drawn by the United Nations forces (UNFICYP) in Cyprus to keep the peace between the Greek and Turkish Cypriots after Turkey invaded the island in 1974, capturing 40 percent of its territory.

Gross material body. One of the three bodies that make

up the present self-conscious personality; the material body. That part of one's personality that lives within the gross material world, the three-dimensional world. The lowest expression of self. The center of the gross material body is the chakra of the solar plexus.

Hermes Trismegistus.   Any human being who reaches the state of superconscious self-awareness. Anyone who has mastered his or her three bodies (the gross material, the psychic, and the noetic).

Higher noetic world.   The world of ideas, of the archetypes. The world of causes and laws that provide the foundations of all phenomenal reality. *See also* Archetypes.

Holy Monads.   The component parts of the Absolute. Each Holy Monad emanates myriads of rays that pass through different archetypes and acquire shape and phenomenal existence. When one such irradiation, a Pneuma, passes through the Human Idea, a soul is created. Human beings who belong to the same Holy Monad have a particular affinity for one another. *See also* Pneuma, Human Idea, Soul.

Holy Spirit.   The impersonal superconsciousness that expresses the power of the Absolute, making the creation of the universes possible. The dynamic part of the Absolute. *See also* Archangels, Angels.

Holyspiritual.   That which pertains only to the Holy Spirit. Animals live within a holyspiritual state. They lack the logoic expression of the Absolute; that is, they lack self-consciousness. Human beings are both logoic and holyspiritual. *See also* Logos, Holy Spirit.

Human Idea.   The human archetype, an eternal archetype within the Absolute. Once a Pneuma or Spirit-ego passes through the Human Idea, human existence begins. *See also* Archetypes, Holy Monads, Pneuma.

Imprinting property of ether.   The property of etheric vitality that makes the construction of thought forms and noetic images possible. *See also* Etheric double.

Incarnation.   According to the teachings of the Erevna a person as an ego-soul undergoes many lives as a present personality for the purpose of acquiring experience of the lower worlds of polarity. Every incarnation is a step higher on the scale of spiritual evolution.

Inner circle. The small group of initiates, advanced Researchers of the Truth, and members of The Erevna who were offered the white robe. Ideally they will be masters of their three bodies and capable of conscious exomatosis, healing, and service as invisible helpers. *See also* Exomatosis, Invisible helpers, White robe.

Invisible helpers. Masters who live on the psychic and noetic dimensions and are invisible to material eyes, such as Father Dominico, one of Kostas' spiritual guides. Also masters who, like Daskalos and Kostas, live within the gross material dimension but who carry out exomatosis and assist humans living within the gross as well as the other dimensions.

Kamaloka. Hindu concept equivalent to the Catholic Purgatory. A psychonoetic space for the convalescence of troubled personalities and for the assimilation of lessons received from the life just lived.

Karma. The law of cause and effect. The sum total of a person's actions, thoughts, and feelings that determine his or her successive states of existence. Human beings are fully responsible for the creation of their karma, their destiny. The attainment of Theosis, God-realization, implies transcending one's karma.

Kinetic property of ether. The property of etheric vitality that makes movement and vibration possible. *See also* Etheric double.

Kundalini. Hindu concept referring to the claim that at the base of the spine there lies dormant "sacred fire," a form of psychic power in the shape of a serpent. When the Kundalini is awakened this energy rushes up through the spine endowing the individual with extraordinary psychonoetic abilities. A premature and unguided awakening of the Kundalini may lead to insanity. Archangel Michael's fiery sword symbolizes the Kundalini within the Eastern Orthodox tradition.

Law of cause and effect. *See* Karma.

Logos. The part of the Absolute that makes possible the existence of self-consciousness and free will. As eternal entities human beings are both logoic and holyspiritual. Animals are only holyspiritual. Jesus as the Christ Logos represents the most complete expression of the logoic nature of the Absolute. The more spiritually advanced human beings are, the more the logoic part in them is dominant. *See also* Holy Spirit.

Maya. Hindu concept meaning "illusion." The world of existence is the world of eternal flux, of ultimate un-reality. Reality as Brahman, or Godhead, is beyond the world of Maya.

Metanoia. The Greek concept of repentance; the purification of the present personality from the burdens of sin and guilt.

Mind. The means by which the unmanifest Absolute expresses Itself. Mind is the supersubstance by which all the universes, all the dimensions of existence, are constructed. Everything is Mind.

Noetic body. One of the three bodies that make up the present self-conscious personality; the body of thoughts. The noetic body exists within the noetic world, the fifth dimension. Its image is identical with the other two bodies. The center of the noetic body is the chakra of the head. *See also* Noetic world.

Noetic world. The fifth dimension. Within the noetic world, space as well as time are transcended. A human being living within the noetic world can travel momentarily, not only over vast distances but also across time. *See also* Noetic body.

Ontopeisis. The process by which the Pneuma or Spirit-ego attains its individuality and uniqueness once the cycles of incarnations come to an end after the karma of the lower self has been exhausted. *See also* Pneuma, Karma, Soul.

Psycho-noetic body. The amorphous mass of energy appearing around the chakra of the heart at the first incarnation. Through repeated incarnations that mass of energy, made up of thoughts and emotions, tends to acquire the shape of the gross material body. As it evolves in that direction it becomes increasingly radiant. This is the psycho-noetic body that every individual must form and shape. The degree to which it is so formed exemplifies the degree to which the individual is spiritually advanced. The psycho-noetic body under construction is distinct from the psychonoetic body that is already constructed, radiant, and perfected. The latter psychonoetic body is under the province of the Holy Spirit. It functions as the mold that the humanly constructed psycho-noetic body will tend to fill until the two become one.

Permanent personality. That part of the soul upon which the incarnational experiences are recorded and are transferred from one life to the next. Part of the inner self.

Pneuma. The ultimate and most real self. The Spirit-ego within; that part of ourselves which is qualitatively identical with the Absolute. The Pneuma is our divine essence, unchangeable and eternal. It has never been created and it will never die. It is the Pneuma that has descended into the worlds of polarity for the acquisition of experience of the lower worlds. It has done so in order to develop its individuality and uniqueness within the oneness of the Absolute. *See also* Ontopeisis.

Present personality. What is commonly known as the personality of the individual; made up of the noetic, psychic, and gross material bodies. The present personality is the lowest expression of ourselves; constantly evolving, it tends to become one with the permanent personality. *See also* Gross material body, Psychic body, Noetic body.

Psychic body. One of the three bodies that constitute the present self-conscious personality. The body of feelings and sentiments having as its center the chakra of the heart. The psychic body lives within the psychic world, the fourth dimension. Its image is identical with the other two bodies, the gross material and the noetic. *See also* Psychic world, Present personality, Chakras.

Psychic world. The fourth dimension. Within the psychic world space is transcended. An individual living within the psychic world can travel instantly over vast distances.

Sacred discs. *See* Chakras.

Sai Baba. Indian guru of reputed extraordinary miraculous powers, so much so that his thousands of devotees consider him an avatar, "the living God-Man of India." Sai Baba was born in 1926 and his ashram is at Puttaparti, India.

Sensate property of ether. The property of etheric vitality that makes feelings, sentiments, and sense experience possible. *See also* Etheric double.

Seven Promises. Promises an initiate makes to himself or herself during initiation into the circles for the Research of Truth. It includes the promise to love and be of service to fellow human beings irrespective of their behavior toward us.

Social instructor. Member of The Erevna who, although not a master, has reached a certain level of maturity and esoteric knowledge that can head a circle for the Research of Truth. *See* The Erevna.

Soul. That part of ourselves which is pure and uncolored by earthly experience. The soul is created at the point a Pneuma or Spirit-ego passes through the Human Idea. The soul is the state of Adam and Eve before they descend into the worlds of time and space. Every person has been an 'Adam' and 'Eve'. Human beings do not *have* a soul: They *are* souls having bodies. *See also* Pneuma, Human Idea.

Spirit-ego. *See* Pneuma.

Steiner, Rudolf. German scholar and Christian mystic of the early part of the twentieth century. Founded Anthroposophy, an offshoot of the Theosophy movement. Steiner, a reputed clairvoyant, teacher of esoteric knowledge, and seer insisted that we can develop spiritual science, a "science of the higher worlds." There are Steiner schools in all the major cities of America and Western Europe, founded on the teachings of this extraordinary master.

Stoa. Room or building where gatherings and instructions about the Research for the Truth take place. The room in Daskalos' backyard used for that purpose.

Superconscious self-awareness. State in the spiritual development of the mystic at the doorsteps of Theosis. Mastery of the three bodies. Conscious and authentic exomatosis. Developed psychic abilities paralleling the development of spiritual awareness. *See also* Theosis, Exomatosis.

Synantilepsis. Co-perception. To perceive exactly the same way as another.

The Erevna. The system of teachings and self-exploration as offered by Father Yohannan; the Research for the Truth; the methodical and conscious effort for self-discovery.

The Most Merciful One. Greek Orthodox expression referring to "God the Father."

The Path. Synonym of The Way.

The Way. The path of the ego-soul to self discovery and final Theosis.

Theosis. The final stage in the evolution of the self after it has undergone the experience of gross matter through successive incarnations. Reunification with the Godhead.

Tree of Life. Symbolic design on the structure of creation from the macrocosm to the microcosm as given by "Father Yohannan." Similar but with major differences with the design found in Cabalistic texts. Designates with various symbols the stages of the descent of the Pneuma into the worlds of polarity and its ascent back to the Godhead. Designates also the location of the chakras on the body.

Universal Memory. Every particle of matter of all the dimensions encloses the entire knowledge of creation. Any motion or movement, be it thought, feeling, or action, is recorded within Universal Memory. In the esoteric literature it is often referred to as the Akashik Records.

Unpointed Sword. A symbolic sword without a point used during brief initiation ceremonies. The origin of the unpointed sword is traced to the alleged action of one of the three Magi who visited the newborn Jesus in Bethlehem. He broke his sword in two and placed it in front of Jesus with the words "At thy immaculate feet, O Lord, all authority rests."

White robe. The white robe that initiates wear during gatherings of the inner circle. It symbolizes purity of purpose and of the heart. One is offered the White robe upon being initiated into the inner circle.

World of ideas. *See* Higher noetic world.

Yogananda, Paramahansa. Famous Indian yogi (1893–1952) and venerated saint, author of the classic *Autobiography of a Yogi.*

Yohannan. The Hebrew name of John the Evangelist; Saint John, author of the Gospel that bears his name. Daskalos and Kostas claim they are conduits of Yohannan, that archangelic superintelligence which oversees the spiritual evolution of human beings on planet earth. The Erevna as a system of spiritual practice is grounded on the teachings of Father Yohannan, Jesus' beloved disciple.